Jerry H. Robinson
nov. 1991

R **CORIN REDGRAVE**, 70. Actor in dozens of plays, television shows and movies including "A Man for all Seasons" and "Four Weddings and a Funeral." Brother of Vanessa and Lynn Redgrave. April 6. 2010

2010   MIKE SIEGEL / THE SEATTLE TIMES

LYNN REDGRAVE, 67. British actress who became a 1960s sensation as the free-thinking title character in "Georgy Girl." May 2. Breast cancer.

LIFE AMONG THE REDGRAVES

The closure of the Motion Picture & Television Fund occasioned a storm of coverage from blogs TheWrap and Deadline Hollywood Daily.

BUT OF RIGHT & WRONG

aron wax-
ous web-
uary.
l, deserve
erable
ne chest-
ournos can

tiveness
e dynamics
se with the
Fund.

cy to spark a
ashing their
their
newsies

Feig. Shortly before 10 p.m. that night,
her update featured Feig claiming to
have been misquoted by Goldstein, at

The competitive fervor between
Finke and Waxman may have hit a peak
(or nadir) over the travails of the Motion
Picture & Television Fund.

The org said Jan. 14 it was closing its
acute-care facility and nursing home to
sustain its other caregiving facilities, such
as the assisted-living home that is the
best-known aspect of MPTF's operation.

Officials said the endowment would
be drained in five years at the current
rate of loss if the two facilities were not
closed. But TheWrap posted a series of
stories that probed MPTF's finances and

Thesp part of acting dynasty

2009

After sustaining brain damage in a freak ski accident, actress Natasha Richardson died March 18 at Lenox Hill Hospital in New York. She was 45.

A member of the Redgrave acting dynasty — and a Tony winner for "Cabaret" in 1996 — Richardson was skiing at Mont-Tremblant near Montreal when she fell; she died two days later of bleeding in the skull.

She was married to actor Liam Neeson, with whom she had two sons.

Her entire family was theatrical. Richardson was the daughter of actress Vanessa Redgrave and the late helmer Tony Richardson. Her grandparents were thesps Rachel Kempson and Michael Redgrave. She was the niece of actors Lynn Redgrave and Corin Redgrave. Her first marriage was to British theatrical producer Robert Fox.

She was born in London and made her film debut at age 4 in "The Charge of the Light Brigade," directed by her father. She trained at London's Central School of Speech and Drama and gained experience doing repertory theater in Leeds and Shakespeare at London's Old Vic. She made her West End debut as Nina in Charles Sturridge's 1986 production of Chekhov's "The Seagull," opposite her mother and Jonathan Pryce. Also in London, she starred as Tracy Lord in a stage musical adapted from the film "High Society" and directed by Richard Eyre.

Her biggest triumphs continued to be on the stage, particularly in New York, though she had a successful career on TV and in films. One of her most prominent earlier roles was as the lead in "Patty Hearst," the 1988 biopic by Paul Schrader.

Natasha Richardson won a Tony Award for her performance in musical "Cabaret."

tensive screen work, it was stage that was the most successful venue for the statuesque beauty with the sonorous voice ("Natasha's voice compels you to listen, which is a great gift," her mother wrote in her autobio).

Richardson made her New York debut in 1992 in Roundabout Theater Company's Broadway transfer of Eugene O'Neill's "Anna Christie," originally staged in London by David Leveaux. She earned her first Tony nomination for the title role, playing opposite future husband Neeson and Rip Torn.

She won the Tony as Sally Bowles in Sam Mendes' revival of "Cabaret," also for Roundabout. In 1999 she starred with Anna Friel, Rupert Graves and Ciaran Hinds in Patrick Marber's Rialto production of his play "Closer." And in 2005 she continued her association with Roundabout in director Edward Hall's revival of "A Streetcar Named Desire," playing Blanche DuBois opposite John C. Reilly's Stanley Kowalski.

Among her survivors are her husband; her mother; her sister, actress Joely Richardson; and two sons.

— *David Rooney*

Other notable film roles included Ken Russell's "Gothic," "A Month in the Country," "The Handmaid's Tale," "Nell," "The Comfort of Strangers," "Widows' Peak," "The Parent Trap" remake, "Maid in Manhattan," "The White Countess" and last year's "Evening."

She also worked occasionally in television, notably opposite Maggie Smith in a 1993 remake of Tennessee Williams' "Suddenly, Last Summer," directed by Eyre. But despite her ex-

LIFE AMONG
THE REDGRAVES

Rachel Kempson, Lady Redgrave

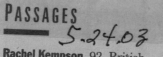

PASSAGES

5.24.03

Rachel Kempson, 92, British actress and matriarch of the

Redgrave acting dynasty, died Saturday in Millbrook, N.Y., at the home of her granddaughter, actress Natasha Richardson. She was the widow of actor Michael Redgrave and mother of actresses Vanessa and Lynn Redgrave.

Lynn Redgrave, actress and playwright

5.2.10

LYNN REDGRAVE, 67, a member of the distinguished British acting family who became an overnight sensation playing the title character in the 1966 film "Georgy Girl," and later achieved acclaim on stage as both an actress and a writer, died of cancer last Sunday in Kent, Conn.

A William Abrahams Book

E. P. DUTTON   NEW YORK

Corin Redgrave, 70, an actor and activist who was a member of the legendary British family of performers that includes his sisters Vanessa and Lynn, died Tuesday in London. 4-6-10

First published in the United States in 1988 by E. P. Dutton,
a division of NAL Penguin Inc.,
2 Park Avenue, New York, N.Y. 10016.

Originally published in Great Britain under
the title A Family and Its Fortunes.

Library of Congress Cataloging-in-Publication Data

Kempson, Rachel.
[Family & its fortunes]
Life among the Redgraves / Rachel Kempson, Lady Redgrave.
p.   cm.
Originally published as: A family & its fortunes. 1986.
"A William Abrahams book."
Includes index.
ISBN 0-525-24629-0
1. Kempson, Rachel. 2. Redgrave family. 3. Actors—Great
Britain—Biography. I. Title.
PN2598.K56A3 1988
792'.028'0924—dc19
[B]   88-2648
CIP

1 3 5 7 9 10 8 6 4 2

First American Edition

Contents

Twenty-four pages of photographs follow page 118.

For my family
and the memory of Michael

I would like to thank Deirdre Redgrave without whom this book would never have been written: also Joan Hirst, Jean Hagberg, Jennifer Beatty, Maureen Cheesman, and my publisher.

R.K.

Oscar-winning director Tony Richardson

Associated Press

11-14-91

LOS ANGELES — Tony Richardson, the Oscar-winning director of the film classic "Tom Jones," died yesterday from AIDS complications, a spokeswoman said. He was 63.

Mr. Richardson died at St. Vincent's Medical Center, said his publicist, Melanie Hodal.

His 23 film credits include "A Taste of Honey," and also directed 30 theater productions.

He was the father of actress Natasha Richardson and ex-husband of actress Vanessa Redgrave. He and "The Loneliness of the Long Distance Runner." He Redgrave were divorced in 1967.

Mr. Richardson made his feature-film debut adapting "Look Back in Anger." His first major critical and commercial hit came in 1961 with "A Taste of Honey."

"Tom Jones," adapted from Henry Fielding's novel about a young man's life in 18th-century England, won four Oscars: best picture, best director and best screenwriter for John Osborne, and best score for John Addison.

Most recently, he directed "Blue Skies," starring Jessica Lange and Tommy Lee Jones. It is scheduled for release next year.

Chapter One

As told to me

Eric William Kempson, my father, was born on October 22nd, 1878, the fifth child and second son of Frederick Robertson Kempson and Madeleine, née Jay. My grandfather's profession was ecclesiastical architecture, his hobby small land-owning. Shortly after his marriage to Madeleine Jay, when she was eighteen, they went to live at Birchyfield near Bromyard in Herefordshire, an estate of five farms originally bought by my great-grandfather. The result was a happy childhood for the children but near ruin to himself and the family by the time my father was eighteen.

Grandfather's architect's office was in Hereford, twelve miles from Birchyfield. In those days twelve miles was too far away from home, by dog-cart or carriage, to commute successfully, and so he neglected both his work and his farms. My grandmother lived in ignorance of their financial situation, so that although she was not an extravagant woman she lived beyond their dwindling means.

There were six children – Claude, Winifred, Muriel, Madeleine (Molly), Eric (my father) and Joan. There was a nurse, and eventually a governess for the girls, probably four maidservants, a gardener and boy under-gardener, a groom and stable boy. Life was quiet and leisurely: hunting and shooting in winter, tennis in summer and visits to friends by carriage or dog-cart. The two boys went to boarding-school. The four girls were educated at home by a governess, who eventually married my Uncle Claude. The girls were sheltered. Claude and my father lived pretty harsh lives at school, which they accepted without protest. In his school holidays Father spent long days roaming about the farms – tickling trout in the streams in summer, sometimes staying out all day. In autumn he would come home after dark with pains in his stomach from eating too many cider apples. His chief companions were Molly and the stable boy who continually played truant from work. During his childhood he absorbed a love and knowledge of the country that he kept throughout his life.

My grandmother was a dutiful, but in spite of a sequence of

miscarriages, a gay and happy woman. Father said his mother spent fourteen years of her life either child-bearing or with her feet up trying to save a pregnancy. She was very strict with the girls. Once they grew up they were never allowed to be alone with any of the young men who visited Birchyfield. Aunt Molly told me many years later that she remembered being called indoors and reprimanded for sitting on the grass beside a young man after tennis. She grew up with a fear of men and recalled that when 'sitting out' with her partner at a dance she accidentally touched his arm with her fan and felt so ashamed that she got up and left the room. At eighteen she decided to become a nun, and much against my grandfather's wishes entered the novitiate of an Anglican convent in Sussex. Perhaps my other aunts suffered some of the same fears; at any rate, they never married.

In her late middle age my Aunt Molly was elected Mother Superior of her convent. She found it in a very bad way and almost despaired of its recovery, but with untiring energy she rooted out the unhappiness and outdated rules and ways, and when she died, exhausted by her work, she left it a happier and better place than it was during my own wretched schooldays there before she took over. (I shall write of my time there in later chapters.)

Grandfather Kempson's financial crash came about 1897 through the collapse of a coalmine in which he had shares. Birchyfield was let. The family moved to a small house in Cardiff. Winifred took a job as a governess, Muriel and Joan became hospital nurses and Claude, already an honours graduate in medicine at Cambridge, married their former governess and became a doctor. He was religious, as indeed were all the family. For a few months during a hot summer – my father told me – he wore a hair-shirt. Uncle Claude finally abandoned medicine for the Church. He studied, was ordained, and obtained a living in Cornwall. His hobbies were sailing, and writing. He wrote three books; two were about sailing and one for children was called *Erica's Blackamoor* and became quite successful. It was amusingly illustrated by himself.

When the crash came my father was taken away from Shrewsbury School and went to work as a clerk in a bank, all his hopes shattered. He had wanted to farm Birchyfield himself. Three years later, when finances improved, he went to Trinity College, Cambridge, where he got a science degree and subsequently went into the instructor branch of the Royal Navy with the rank of Lieutenant. He served for two years in HMS *Albion* on the 'China Station' and then joined the Royal Naval College at Dartmouth. He told me that his mother never complained of their reduced circumstances or the loss of Birchyfield, nor did my aunts. They all set to work and made the best of a bad job. Granny loved my grandfather – 'Fred', as she called him – 'for better, for worse'. She died aged 69; he outlived her by more than ten years. Not only did they not complain but, so far as I know, the girls never broke away from their strict Victorian principles, or ever rebelled in any way.

*

My mother, Beatrice Hamilton Ashwell, was born on December 30th, 1884, the third daughter of Laurence Thomas Ashwell and his wife Henrietta, about whose childhood there is little told except that she had three brothers who were 'bad lots' and therefore never talked about and a French mother from whom it was hinted they inherited their bad qualities. Henrietta (Granny) had a lovely singing voice and played the piano. She was loyal, loving and indulgent to her difficult husband and their three daughters May, Maudie and Beatrice (my mother, the youngest by eight years.)

I have wondered in the light of modern knowledge whether Grandfather Ashwell was bisexual. Mother once said: 'Father loved young men. Our house was always filled with young men.' I can't help doubting whether the young men were particularly interested in Granny or Mother, Maudie or May. One or two may have been, but Mother never talked of any attraction between Grandfather's 'young men' friends and herself, May or Maudie. Of course it doesn't matter, but it may explain his curious temper and drinking. The drinking, as I say shortly, he put down to needing to dream for his painting.

He was by profession a homeopathic chemist and founded the firm of Keene and Ashwell (later Nelson's) in Duke Street. His hobby was landscape painting. He was a passionate disciple of Corot, whose painting he tried to follow. He was not entirely unsuccessful, very occasionally exhibiting his pictures. As he grew older he drank a bottle of whisky every night, partly, he said, to drown his feelings of frustration over his painting and partly because he said it was only when drunk that he had what he called his 'dreams' when he thought he was inspired to paint.

He had a violent temper and my mother was terrified of his rages. He would beat her for some minor offence, afterwards caressing and petting her and trying to make it up to her. She became nervy and delicate, which worried him, so he kept her from joining in games with other children for fear of taxing her strength.

The education of the children started at a 'dame school' and finished at Caterham High School where Mother says she neither understood nor learned anything. She admired her father as a painter and longed to be a painter herself. In this he encouraged her up to a point, but he refused to allow her to go to an art school. Maudie longed to be an actress and she got as far as going to London to see a Miss Latiere who gave instruction in elocution to aspiring actresses. Miss Latiere told Maudie that she would have to tour, possibly in pantomime. When Grandfather heard this he made her give up the idea of the stage as a career. The eldest daughter, May, had no wish for a career.

The tenor of their lives would surely not have surprised Jane Austen. Marriage was the only means of escape. They had a fairly large social circle at Warlingham, where they lived, at that time in the country. They had very little money but managed to keep two maidservants whose wages were about £12 a year. Mother says that when they were grown up they were given small dress allowances and used to make their own evening dresses for a few shillings, so as not to appear too often in the same dress at the various country hops given in friends' houses. They had many friends. The Ashwells kept 'open house', as it was called.

Grandfather Ashwell died when my mother was eighteen. He had developed diabetes which was hastened by drinking. Insulin was unknown at that time. He lived long enough to see Maudie married to Alexander Percy McMullen, the youngest son of a wealthy Hertfordshire brewer, whose home was Hertford Castle. 'Mac's' only sister Norah married Andrew Mellon, the American millionaire, when she was eighteen. She was the mother of Paul Mellon who has accumulated one of the great collections of English paintings and given it to galleries in the United States. Beloved Aunt Norah had plans for a liaison between Paul and myself, but he didn't like me, nor I him, although he is a most delightful man. We renewed our acquaintance in later years with him and his wife Bunny. Mac was a schoolmaster and taught science at the Royal Naval College at Osborne. After Grandfather Ashwell's death Mac and Maudie had moved on to Dartmouth, the Senior College in Devon. Granny, May and Beatrice went to live at Paignton to be near them.

Maudie and Mac were quite well off and lived comfortably, entertaining a great deal at their house called The Keep. It was there that my mother met my father, still an instructor attached to the Naval College. He fell in love with her pale slender beauty almost at first sight. She had red gold hair, her eyes were cornflower blue. She told me she hero-worshipped Maudie, and Maudie and Mac's way of life became her criterion. She was romantic and, like most young women of the day, entirely ignorant of the facts of life. She read novels – Stanley Weyman, Dickens, Jane Austen and possibly Thackeray. She was flattered by the attentions of my father and led him on as

Maudie, an outrageous flirt, had taught her to do. This sounds unpleasant, but apparently it was in some circles accepted behaviour. At twenty-four she had not been in love, although often attracted, and felt it was time she married.

My father courted her with great respect, many luncheon parties and roses. When he first proposed, she refused; the second time she said she would think it over. Shortly after, he arranged a luncheon party with the request that she should come to it and, if she would marry him, wear a red rose from a bunch he would send her. She went to his little party wearing a red rose.

In the photograph of their wedding, which took place at Dartmouth in June 1908, the married pair sit in the centre, my father's head slightly turned to look at my mother. She, upright, a little tight-lipped, faces the camera, her hair piled high under its wreath and white veil. Her dress is white and has long sleeves. In her hands she holds a stiff bouquet of white flowers: orange blossom, lilies of the valley, and smilax, with a strand of smilax carefully arranged to trail across her dress and fall to the ground. On either side of Mother and Father sit Granny and Gramp (Father's parents). Granny is in some darkish dress. Her grey hair is piled high but rather less than the fashion of the time.

Chapter Two

Rugby & the War

My earliest memories, at Rugby, are fleeting and full of gaps. Lying in my pram, looking at light clouds in a blue sky, making shade alternately with sunlight on the white lining of the hood above me: picking up buttercups with my adored Nanny Woodford in the fields in May on the day before my birthday – my third, perhaps? The fields looked golden and I felt as light as the fragile cow-parsley or lady's lace in the hedge bordering the field. I enjoyed the anticipation of the anniversary even more than the day itself which, like most days much looked forward to, was often an anti-climax.

On my fourth birthday I wore a brown serge pleated skirt, a tussore blouse and brown tie, and felt as if a new era had dawned where I had crossed some threshold ahead of which lay a better, newer life. I stood on the hearth rug by the study fire before lunch. On my birthday I lunched in the dining-room instead of in the nursery as usual. Aunt Maudie was staying with us. I loved her because she smelled of violets, but today she spoiled everything. She looked at me and said, 'Darling, you're rather a little bud for a blouse and tie.'

Eight days earlier, on May 20th, my father had come into the nursery after breakfast saying, 'You've got a little brother. Would you like to come and see him?'

My nightly prayer, 'Please God give me a baby brother', was answered. How satisfactory. I jumped up, with my arms around his neck. He smelled of fresh shaving soap. He always used a stick of 'Vinolia' soap and a cut-throat razor to shave. I loved to watch him and touch his smooth clean-smelling face when he sponged it with warm water to remove the last traces of white foaming soap. Today, as usual, he was smoking his first pipe which I thought smelled like lavender.

'Would you like a pickaback?' he asked and bent down, while I climbed on his shoulders and rode up to mother's bedroom.

She was lying in bed with a red, crumpled-looking object in her arms: my brother Nicholas.

It was a great surprise. In spite of my nightly prayer I'd expected to have a baby brother *one* day, but somehow I hadn't imagined he would be so very small and crumpled, and it was strange that he was suddenly in bed with my mother. If I had thought about his arrival at all I suppose I had thought he would be brought in the morning and perhaps placed in the nursery at breakfast time.

*

My Nanny Woodford left because she said she was not strong enough to take on the new baby. With her departure my security was lost with a new 'old' Nanny who only cared for 'the baby'. I became terribly shy. My greatest fears were the large children's parties given in Rugby. The grandest of all being at Dr David's, the Headmaster of the school. Dressed in stiff white muslin I felt sick before we arrived. On arrival, having taken off my out-of-door clothes, Mother took me into the drawing-room where everyone assembled to say how-do-you-do to Mrs David, the Headmaster's wife.

When tea was announced the children had to go to the dining-room and the mothers stayed together in the drawing-room. I clung to Mother, who pushed me away; then someone took my hand and led me to the dining-room with the others. I felt desperate but was seated at a long table, among masses of strange shouting children. I ate nothing – the sight of the plates of rich cakes made my throat close up. Nurses of the various households in their starched caps and aprons looked on me with pity. I tried to stick it out, but eventually cried and couldn't stop.

At last some nurse grabbed me by the hand saying, 'You are a strange little girl', and took me to my mother. Mother was ashamed of me but I wouldn't go back. Years later she told me that my shyness had been a great trial to her.

For some years I had a recurring nightmare. I would find myself at the end of a breakwater, far out in the sea, surrounded by a thick white mist. I could not see to go back and knew that if I went forward I would step off into the sea and be drowned. So I stood still on the end of the breakwater enveloped in the silent mist unable to move until I woke feeling fearful and shaken. Another recurring dream was that someone held a large spoonful of red juice towards my mouth but just as I was about to taste it the spoon was drawn away. Insecurity? Frustration?

In 1914, when the Great War started, I used to rush out into the front garden to see the platoons of soldiers going by with the band playing. I wished I had been a boy and would grow into a man and march away to war to the sound of the band. Once, striding up and down keeping time with the music, thinking I looked rather attractive, a passer-by looked at me and I stopped, suddenly embarrassed.

*

In 1915 Father joined the 220th Company of the Royal Engineers and was given a commission with the rank of Captain. He trained his own company – volunteers – on the school playing fields. Mother sometimes took me to watch them drilling. It seemed very fine to me, for I hadn't realised that this was going to mean three years' separation from the person I loved most in the world. He and the Company left for Palestine at the beginning of 1916.

My brother Nicholas grew very fat – far too fat, Mother said. She didn't take much notice of him, which hurt our old Nanny who adored him. Consequently she fattened him up, which was her idea of making him attractive. Mother used to look disapprovingly as he waddled towards her when he first learnt to walk.

There was enormous sewing activity in the house for the troops. The nursery table was covered in khaki – scarves, neck shields to cover the back of the neck from the Palestine sun, cuffs for warmth in the winter. In the evenings my only moderately happy time was with old Nanny, who taught me 'Keep the Home Fires Burning' by Ivor Novello and 'Pack Up Your Troubles'. Even at the age of four I wondered if there would be many 'boys' left alive to come home.

I have no recollection of the day Father left, but I remember the awful blankness when he had gone and the daily ache which made me cry at night when I went to bed. I once found a letter I'd sent him which he kept. It said: 'Darling Daddy, I cried for you one night. With Love from Rachel.' That was all, because as yet I could only just write in printing, but it told him my feelings. I think from my earliest age we were able to communicate deeply with each other.

Chapter Three

Devon

I was often sent to stay at Dartmouth with Aunt Maudie and my cousins Alexander, called Zander, and John Anthony, called Tony. My silent Uncle Mac, still officially on the staff of the Royal Naval College, had been called up into the Navy and had joined HMS *Agincourt*. It was a women's household, as were most during the First World War: even more so afterwards, when almost a generation of young and early-middle-aged men had been wiped out.

*

My first visit to The Keep at Dartmouth was in late May 1915, just before my fifth birthday. I went alone in charge of the guard, and have no recollection of being met. Kingswear is the station and terminus of the railway line on the opposite side of the Dart from Dartmouth. From there you crossed the estuary in a ferry boat called the *Mew*. There was a covered gangway from the station, and the reflection of the green sunlit water glinted and moved in changing flowing patterns of liquid light on the walls and roof of the gangway.

The *Mew* sidled up, bumped clumsily with much churning of water against the pontoon, and a very old sailor with a purple face in a navy-blue sweater and greasy peaked cap threw a looped rope over a bollard. He always missed the first time as if on purpose, but the second shot secured the boat. The rail was drawn back, the gangplank flopped with a bang on to the pontoon and we were allowed on board. Crossing to Dartmouth took about ten minutes. White gulls screamed and swooped and circled round the boat and the whole procedure of sidling, churning, rope-throwing, banging and securing took place on the identical pontoon, with the same liquid light reflections flowing on the ceiling of the other gangway.

All the passengers walked up to the street, where there were a number of horse-drawn cabs waiting to take those who wished for them to their destinations. There was a short wait while the heavy trolleys of luggage were trundled up and sorted out and then I stepped into a cab. It was dark inside and smelled musty, which I liked.

The town of Dartmouth huddled at the foot of a precipitous hillside and straggled up the steep slopes, thinning out into the country at the top. The Keep was about half-way up the hill and after the first half mile the horse was obliged to walk all the way. I sat well forward on the faded navy-blue, buttoned, seat cushion, listening to the crunch of the carriage wheels, sniffing in the mixture of the fresh air and mustiness. It seemed terribly hard for the horse and I wondered if he would manage the climb.

The Keep – a pretty Victorian Gothic house in imitation of the keep of a castle – was reached by a narrow green lane branching to the left off the winding main road. When we reached the wide heavy gate through which you could see the studded front door and castellated portico, the driver climbed down from the box and opened the gate, led the horse and carriage across the pebbly sweep and rang the doorbell for me. A maid in a starched cap and apron opened the door, and then Aunt Maudie appeared. She put her arms round me, and I smelled violets.

My cousin Tony, who was a few months younger than me, came sliding down the curved banisters. He had black hair and dark-brown eyes. A snake-buckled belt fastened his grey shorts and he wore an open-necked shirt. I was fascinated by him. Aunt Maudie made a point of telling me that girls must not bother boys who wished to be left alone. She maintained this throughout my childhood. As I grew up this gave me an attitude of hers: fear of males, only dispelled at last in my early middle-age.

Tony and I had tea in the upstairs nursery with the governess, called Miss Cameron. There was red linoleum on the floor, a round table in the middle of the room, a big rocking-horse with flaring nostrils, a high fireguard with a brass rail round the fireplace which, being a warm day, was empty. There were two windows almost from ceiling to floor, looking onto the sloping lawn and shrubberies beyond; far below lay the harbour and estuary, from which came the continual crying of seagulls, the chug-chugging of little motor boats and the occasional hooter of an incoming or outgoing ship.

We had bread and butter with Devonshire cream and strawberry jam, and drank milk out of large mugs with pictures on. Miss Cameron was very hospitable. The same could not be said of Tony, who seemed to be entirely wrapped up in himself and in his own doings. He gulped his milk, snatched bread and butter, and got down from the table without asking. Miss Cameron kept correcting him and finally made him sit in his chair again and say grace.

He clasped his hands high at his head and gabbled, 'Thank-God-for-my-good-breakfast-dinner-tea-please-can-I-get-down?', and did.

I followed; I was quite unworried by his lack of welcome. It was enough to be here where the air seemed fresher, the rooms bigger and the days finer than at home.

I loved the quiet, ordered nursery life at The Keep. There was a deep feeling of security here. Another of the pleasures was Aunt Maudie's 'acting box' full of clothes in which I dressed, imagining myself a variety of characters. Aunt Maudie had taken part in many amateur theatricals, as they were called, until the war when so many of the men were called up.

At The Keep my dramatic longings were fed and exercised to the full. Aunt Maudie was my dream of all that elegance and loveliness should be, and she indulged me in my wish to escape into the world of make-believe. She it was who sowed the seed of 'theatre' in my ready mind.

*

This visit seemed very long as I look back. I think the various visits that followed have now merged into one in my memory: picking bunches of primroses in the woods in spring, and buttercups and vetch in the fields, which must have been in the summer; sitting by the fire in the drawing-room after tea in the winter. We played in the garden and sometimes walked round the walled kitchen garden with its box edging; it was enclosed, warm and secret there.

Every morning Miss Cameron took us for a long walk from which we returned with aching legs and hot hands full of wilting wild flowers. Sometimes we went into the grounds of the Royal Naval College and played with the children of officers and masters.

Tony loved everything to do with railways; he had a model one which he never let me touch. I had to sit on the floor and watch, and used to itch all over with frustration. On our walks in the college grounds Tony took two walking-sticks. He held one end of each in either hand and made me go behind him and hold the other ends. Then he would run forward working the sticks like the piston rods of a steam engine and saying 'chuff-chuff'. Now and then he would call out, 'You're all behind, like the cow's tail.' This was a sort of insult, which I thought very unfair since it was he who made me run behind.

Uncle Mac went to sea that summer, but Aunt Maudie didn't seem unhappy; she had lots of friends, many of them men, who were on the college staff and took us picnicking to the coves and beaches round the coast.

*

When I went home after one of my holidays at Dartmouth in August 1916, about eight months after Father had left for Palestine, Granny Ashwell – who lived half the year with us and half with Aunt Maudie – told me I was going to have another baby brother; this was again surprising and thrilling.

There was a thunderstorm. So Nicholas, aged two, and I, now six, played in the nursery, which was on the ground floor. Granny hovered in and out and eventually told us to be very good and quiet and not to disturb the doctor who had come to bring the new baby.

He stood, bag in hand, in the conservatory outside the nursery. I couldn't think why he just stood there and wondered what he had done with the baby. I supposed that having delivered my brother he was just waiting for the storm to pass.

At last it died down and Granny came and said we could go up to Mother's bedroom. Once again she was in bed with another crumpled object. This one, Robin, became rather a nuisance to me as time went on because the new Nanny ('old Nanny' left to be succeeded by many) made me rock Robin's cradle when he cried, which he seemed to do a great deal.

I now found life without my father only a half life. The various very indifferent nannies (they were hard to get with so many women in munition factories) never seemed to like me much. I longed for the happier days with my old Nanny Woodford. I was six and ought to have been at school or having some sort of teaching but wasn't. I was terribly bored except when visiting and playing with my few Rugby friends. I lived in a world of imagination and longings for 'life'. Life seemed attractive to me at Aunt Maudie's with Tony and Miss Cameron. Our house in Rugby with its small back garden, my two baby-brothers with whom I couldn't play – I could only tease poor Nicky to try to goad him into some kind of action which, since he was only two, made him cry – was terribly restricted and so I was utterly bored.

*

When Robin was about seven months old and Mother decided to leave Rugby and take a furnished house in Devonshire so that we could be near Aunt Maudie, I was very excited. It would be a change at least.

I don't remember the packing up of our house in Rugby, but I know that all our own furniture and most of our books and toys went into store.

In April 1917 we moved to a furnished house in a suburb of

Paignton called Preston. I was very excited by the move, but anticipation was short-lived. The house was small and lit by gas. There was a little bare garden; a tiny glass porch covered the entrance. In this we kept our sand-shoes (canvas shoes with rubber soles) and always hung up a long piece of seaweed to 'see what the weather was going to be'. I felt it two or three times a day on wet days, hoping that suddenly the seaweed would have dried and the weather become sunny.

As the summer advanced, Nicholas, Robin in his push-chair and I went down the dusty lane to the beach every day with our new nursemaid. The lane was fenced on either side; wild convolvulus grew over it. Nicky and Robin wore 'paddlers', yellow oiled silk pants with bibs, to keep them dry. Our nursemaid, whose name I have forgotten, was very amiable, wore glasses and was a Christian Scientist.

Robin, Mother's favourite, slept in a cot in her room. I had a small bedroom to myself and Nicky slept on a horsehair sofa in a tiny dim back room we called the nursery. I suppose our nice nursemaid slept in some other small room, but I don't remember ever seeing it.

*

That autumn we spent desolate evenings in the wretched so-called nursery. There was only one gaslight, with a flaming mantle which was always breaking. There was practically nothing to do except read *Rainbow* over and over again, or try to knit scarves that ended in nothing because I either dropped so many stitches or gathered so many that it soon became hopeless and I gave it up. Our nurse wasn't very enlivening because she was often in pain and, being a Christian Scientist, refused to see a doctor. Eventually she had to leave because she became too ill to look after us.

Mother used to go to the nearby church a good deal – for comfort, or something to do? I tried to keep Nicky out of her way as much as possible, because he was very fretful and always annoyed her. At night he took to sleep-walking. I worried terribly about this. I hated the coldness of the slippery horsehair settee on which he slept with a pillow and some blankets. Mother didn't appear to worry about it: she was engrossed with Robin. Her only disappointment was that he was not a girl. She told me she would have called him Charmian. He was wonderfully attractive and always cheerful. He had Mother's colouring – red gold curling hair and pale freckled skin – except that his cheeks were rosy. His cornflower-blue eyes were like hers. In spite of Mother's favouritism Nicky never appeared to resent Robin; he was devoted to him, and their friendship continued until Robin's early death at the age of twenty-five in the Second World War.

Mother dressed Robin in green or blue as a rule: cotton in summer and little jerseys in winter. He had her radiant look. Nicky was pale and freckled and rather plump and shy, and retired into himself more and more. Mother realised there was something wrong, but it was already too late to win him. I remember her occasionally asking him to come and play with us or go for a walk, and the answer was nearly always: 'I'm going to do it by my-self.' So would I, if I had been him. I worried about him and even resorted to teasing him in the hope of getting her to take his part. She fell for this once and angrily told me to 'shut up and leave him alone'. The relationship didn't improve until he was in his teens and at Shrewsbury School, when they grew to be very fond of each other. His generosity and integrity won her.

The summer passed in a monotony of days empty of lessons or toys, trudging down the convolvulus-bordered lane to the sands of fine days, sitting trying to keep Nicky from fretting on wet days. When autumn came I gazed longingly at the bright dahlias in the front gardens of the hideous red-brick villas that bordered the road. There wasn't a flower in our windswept patch. My thoughts were continually with Father, whose letters told of his work in Palestine, of his horse who swam by his side in the sea at the end of a hot day. They were wonderful letters. I could imagine the interminable sands and the sea and him striding into the waves and swimming out with one hand on the withers of his horse. The longing to see him was a continual pain. There was little to occupy my mind in our bare little house with its hissing gas mantles and the dusty, villa-lined road. Food was very scarce. We had almost no meat; grey boiled potatoes and cabbage, followed by milk puddings made of maize and hominy. Mother's boredom must have been unbearable. We certainly saw her very little. Having shopped for the meagre ration, she often went over to Dartmouth to see Maudie. At the end of six months, about the beginning of November, Mother had to find another furnished house, as the lease of the Preston one was up. She only took it for six months because, like everyone else, she thought the war must end soon.

The next house was in Paignton. It, also, was in a row of villas, but I liked it much better than the first. It was much less bare. There were masses of china ornaments. The curtains and chair covers were a riot of flowers. However, after the excitement of the move the days became duller than ever. It was a cold winter; food was scarcer than ever. Our walks were taken along the promenade, the sea was grey, and the angry waves broke and threw their spray across the road. We children wore yellow oilskins and sou'westers. Once Mother took me to the cinema. There we saw the troops marching through the mud in France, and Pavlova dancing 'The Dying Swan'.

*

In May 1918 our six months were up at Paignton. Mother decided that it would be happier to be in the country. Maudie found us a small house at Stoke Fleming, a pretty village overlooking the sea about five miles from Dartmouth. The house belonged to Mrs Tozer, a widow, and one of the daughters of a farmer called Pook. Mrs Tozer needed money to help educate her daughter Louise. She rented her house furnished and went to live with her parents at the farm on the other side of the lane.

On the first night at Mrs Tozer's, as we called it, I *knew* I was going to be happy. When I went to bed I lay listening to the quiet, which was only disturbed by the sound of sheep baaing in the distance. You could see the sea from the house. It lay hundreds of feet below the cliffs. The farm and its barns with lichen-covered roofs huddled in the field across the road. Beyond the garden were the little church and churchyard, reached by a field path. Mother found a young woman called Alice Edgecombe to look after us. Alice lived with her mother in the village, but when she came to us she agreed to 'sleep in'.

Alice was the dearest servant I have ever known, cosy and good and loyal. We were quite a large household (Robin now twenty-one months, Nicky three and a half and myself, seven, Granny, Mother and Alice). But whereas at Preston and Paignton life had been terribly dull, here at Stoke Fleming it was always full and interesting. Feelings of insecurity, fear and boredom, the still recurring dream of the 'dense white mist', disappeared. The weather was fine day after day. I ran about bare-legged, hung about the farm kitchen or the cow-sheds, rode the horses bare-backed and climbed the enormous horse chestnut tree in our garden, from whose branches I got a view of the farm-house garden and barns, and could terrify Mrs Tozer, who would look up when I called out to her and, seeing me, rush indoors waving her hands over her head calling out, 'You'll be the death of me, Miss Rachel.'

I became extremely attached to Louie who was about fourteen years old. She was brown and rosy. Often we would go down the hill to the beach at the foot of the cliffs, Blackpool Sands. It was deeply curved and shingly and lay at the end of a valley called The Vale. A lane ran through The Vale in which was a water-mill called Burgoyne's Mill. All the year round the stream rushed and gurgled. In spring the steep sides of the valley were covered with primroses.

There were little pink cottages at intervals along the lane. Sour milk cheeses hung in the porches. Everything was permanently wet, mossy and luscious.

Pink valerian, mimosa and palm trees grew on the cliff sides, and a little knot of pine-trees surrounded the entrance to the beach so that one's footsteps were muffled by the thick carpet of dead pine-needles that covered the track to the beach. At the far end of the beach were rocks where pools remained at low tide full of sea anemones and limpets. One afternoon Louie and I climbed across the rocks, and suddenly she fell full-length face-down in a pool. I ran back towards the beach calling for help. A man and a woman picnicking hurried across and climbed over the ledges and pools and picked Louie up. She had fainted after a heavy lunch. By the time she recovered the tide had risen, so our rescuers carried us on their backs. In a very short time a crowd of villagers from Stoke Fleming had collected, preceded by Mrs Tozer, white and breathless. She had been told that Louie had fallen down the cliffs and was dead. Country gossip exaggerates at high speed. I couldn't eat any tea and couldn't stop shivering for about an hour.

*

In July 1918 Father came home for his first and only leave. I went to Dartmouth with Mother to meet him. I was speechless with excitement. The sight of his large and suddenly strange figure standing on *The Mew*, as it sidled up, took words away. As we hugged each other I smelled the much-missed wonderful male smell of him. We hugged and hugged. I couldn't say a word.

The next morning I woke very early, got up and went into Mother's bedroom where she and Father were still asleep side by side in a large double-bed. In Rugby before the war they had always had two beds and, young as I had been when he went away, I knew very well they often quarrelled. To see them happy together was my greatest wish, as it must be of all children, although if they are lucky enough to have loving happy parents no doubt they take it for granted. In my home I had been accustomed to a feeling of discord, and so this morning looking at their sleeping bodies and peaceful faces side by side was a double happiness. I sat on a chair by the bed on Father's side to wait for him to wake. I watched his sleeping face, taking in every detail of its shape and lines; his broad forehead; the two deep furrows above his nose between the eyes; his strong mouth with its protruding lower lip, the corners turned downwards a little in sleep, giving him a tired, sad look. I was prepared to wait without speaking. I didn't wake him because I knew he needed to sleep his fill. After what seemed hours he stirred and opened his eyes. We smiled at each other. He stretched out his hand and I put mine into his.

The three weeks went by in a flash. Mother and Father spent a few days in London, leaving us behind. As I remember it, the whole time was fine and sunny. We walked down the hill to Blackpool Sands every day, trudging across the loose shingle that got into our shoes, settling down for the afternoon by the rocks at the far end under the steep cliffs. Father always made a fire and boiled a kettle for tea, and we bathed and climbed over the rocks, paddling in the pools left by the high tide. The days were too soon over and he had to return. Years later he told me what an agony it had been to him to go back to Palestine. For myself I was desolate. I visited the fireplace of blackened stones where he had boiled the picnic kettle, and cried. By now everyone had given up hope of an early end to the war. We none of us knew that the following November would see the armistice.

The rest of that summer I continued in freedom, climbing trees, sitting in the kitchen of the farm with its thick scrubbed wooden table, watching Mrs Tozer shell the peas while I sat stroking one of the many cats and asking endless questions. Most days I watched Ernest, the cowman, milking. He had the filthiest hands I had ever seen, but the milk looked lovely as it hissed into the pails, white and foamy on top. It obviously worried no one that the milk was procured by those dirty fingers working the equally dirty udders of the cows.

Chapter Four

Armistice

In September 1918 Aunt Maudie moved to London, leaving The Keep tenanted by Aunt May and her husband, Uncle Charles, who had not been called up (he also was on the staff of the Royal Naval College), and their only child my cousin Violet.

Mother wrote to Aunt Joan, now a ward sister at St George's Hospital in London, asking her to find us a furnished house in the suburbs of London because, although Father was now a major, we could not afford central London rents. Aunt Joan found a house at Kew. Once more I was full of the highest hopes. Kew Gardens were beautiful, I had heard, and London … London spoke for itself. It was Mecca in my eyes, the capital where the King and Queen lived, in Buckingham Palace, which I believed would look as if it were made of gold; theatres, where actresses spoken of by Aunt Maudie lived and made a world out of one's dreams. Then there would be gleaming, glittering shops – Barkers, Gooches, Harrods – whose catalogues I had seen and whose names were talked about by my mother and Aunt Maudie. They would be full of warmth and light, lovely clothes and beautiful toys. Mother asked Alice to go with us. She agreed to come until the war ended, when she intended marrying her fiancé, George, who was with the army in France.

I do not remember our departure from Stoke Fleming, which is strange because we left Granny to live with Aunt May at The Keep. She had been a loving protector and a cosy friend, with her head full of fairy-tales which she never tired of telling. I wonder if she was sad to say good-bye. I never saw her again. I suppose I must have been sorry to say good-bye to the Pooks, Mrs Tozer and Louie and Ernest the cowman, but I thought only of London.

*

The train steamed slowly into Paddington Station. I had never seen anything so large and murky as Paddington.

It was a great disappointment. Our grandfather 'Gramp' and Aunt

Winifred had come to meet us. They had hired a large car which smelled of petrol fumes. We all crushed in – Mother, Alice, Robin, me and Nicholas who had the worst place, a small let-down seat near the partition and on top of the fumes.

Mother said very scornfully when he didn't turn a hair on the drive to Kew, 'Isn't he extraordinary? Quite insensitive even to that awful smell!'

I knew he was being nice and patient, not saying anything. The house, a small Victorian villa in a row, was another disappointment; but still, even if it was not *in* London, it was very close, and we would be able to visit Aunt Maudie in her flat at Victoria.

This we very soon did. We went by the rattling District Railway from Kew Gardens Station or, alternatively, by bus, usually sitting on the top, open deck, with the waterproof cover buttoned over our knees if it was raining. I enjoyed the top of the bus most because of the pleasure of riding in the open high above the streets. It took quite a time and I used to read the advertisements if we went by train; my favourites were the ones for Bravington Rings and Nestlé's milk. On one visit Nicky amused the entire carriage and Mother, for once in a way, by showing his newly acquired 'reading'. He read slowly and loudly, 'Mothers, *nurse* your babies if you *can't* get Nestlé's'.

Aunt Maudie's flat was at No.32 Evelyn Mansions. I was almost, if not more, enchanted by it than The Keep. A porter took us up to the top floor in a lift. There was a very nice housekeeper called Jessie who hissed her S's in what I considered a most refined manner. She would say, 'Good afternoon, Madam' to my mother and, to me, 'Good afternoon Missss Rachel – yess, Mrsssss McMullen issss in.'

'The Flat', as it came to be called, looked out on to the Vauxhall Bridge Road. Being on the top floor it was above the noise of the traffic, which one heard as a low accompaniment to the steady roar of London. There was a Schweppes sign and a Bovril sign that lit up and went on spelling out each letter separately, to start again at the beginning. If you leaned out of the drawing-room window the facade of the Victoria Palace was in sight. As soon as it was dark I spent a lot of time at the window looking at the lights and listening to the roar of the traffic.

Inside it was all very pretty and elegant: the pale grey drawing-room with its rose-patterned chintz, Maudie's writing desk made out of a spinet case, my grandfather's rather sad paintings of Essex marshes on the walls. Silhouettes of Tony and Alexander hung by the fireplace in miniature frames. There was a lot of pretty china about and a small grand piano on which stood a tiny bust of Beethoven. Then there was the dining-room with its round mahogany table and Chippendale chairs. On the sideboard silver branched candlesticks gleamed almost white. Jessie kept everything perfectly. Meals were little banquets of elegance, eaten rather daintily – even Tony and Zander didn't gobble the food as I sometimes did at home. Maudie's bedroom was chiefly filled by her double four-poster, the prettiest bed I had ever seen. When they went to the country some years later it was in the spare room, and I spent many a happy night in its comfort.

Aunt Maudie and Uncle Mac shared this bed for many years, but I always thought she must have very disturbed nights because of his smoker's cough. We all dreaded his cough more than his silence. I always thought he was going to choke to death when the paroxysms started, but everyone else took no notice in a rather pointed fashion. I think that to elegant Maudie 'taking no notice' was her only way of dealing with it. I did hear many years later that the one thing in which he had his own way was over sharing her room, cough or no cough, and in old age when she insisted on having her room to herself he resented it deeply. He was in love with her all their lives.

She did her duty by him most faithfully until her death when he was staying with his sister, Mrs Mellon, in the USA. He flew home and saw her just before she died. He was far from well and heartbroken. The sight of him at her funeral, his face ashen, no tears falling, told all his grief, which he bore, as he bore his old age, stoically.

*

On November 11th, 1918 I was sitting in a class with about twelve other children of varying ages doing lessons. Mother had arranged for me to join this class, run by a Miss Gregory. We worked in a room in a house in Burlington Avenue, Kew. Our ages ranged from five to eight years. I was eight. There were about four boys and eight girls. The youngest were copying letters. The older ones drew from life late autumn leaves arranged in a vase standing on the table. One or two of us had reached the painting stage and dipped and sucked our brushes. Miss Gregory sat at the head of the table, getting up now and then to look at the work, praise her favourite or hit a pathetic ugly little girl called Doris over the knuckles with a ruler. I managed to avoid notice. I wasn't much good at any of the work because of my neglected education. I had learned to read and write, add and subtract.

Miss Gregory was short and thick and her chest looked as if she had stuffed a huge cushion inside her jumper. I always thought of her kind of figure as a 'grown-up's' figure – most grown-up women had it. Not Mother, of course, who was slim and almost straight up and down like a boy which, besides keeping her very young-looking (she was only thirty-four), was becoming very fashionable. Miss Gregory's hair was mouse-coloured, scraped into a bun at the back of her head. She wore steel-rimmed spectacles and was always bad-tempered.

Boom – boom – boom. Guns! We all looked up. Miss Gregory looked at her watch. It was eleven o'clock, time for break. She dismissed us. We jumped up, grabbed mugs of milk from a tin tray, gulped it down and tumbled out on to the pavement outside the house. It was foggy, but all down the street people were hanging out flags of various shapes and sizes: Union Jacks, red white and blue ensigns, even squares of red rag or bright-coloured handkerchiefs.

Someone said, 'The war is over.'

We started to jump up and down, shouting 'The war is over, the war is over.'

'Please, Miss Gregory, can we stop school today because the war is over?' asked one. 'Oh, yes, please, Miss Gregory.'

'Certainly not,' Miss Gregory replied. 'You will get on with your work.'

So back we went and settled quietly down while all London went mad filling the streets and squares and almost storming Buckingham Palace because an Armistice was signed at last. My heart and my head were light and I couldn't concentrate on work. Father would come home now and perhaps my parents would start a new life together. I loved them both in entirely different ways – Mother for her beauty, her pale face, her red-gold hair and her blue eyes that were often sad, sometimes angry and occasionally joyful. She smelled sweet when she let you hug her. Her hands were cool and freckled. I *adored* Father, not for any physical attribute, although he was tall and broad, his hands were big and he could make and handle things with care and precision, but because I was like a branch of his tree. He was my life in my childhood, we loved each other and were entirely happy in each other's company. Now he would be back and we would start a new life and be happy for ever and ever. Once more my optimism went ahead of possible reality.

My father was demobilised and arrived at Kew just before Christmas. With him came Alice's George, who stayed the night, before going back to Devon. My father writes, in his private autobiography, that Christmas dinner 1918 was 'stewed rabbit, followed by prunes and custard'. This I don't remember. I do remember that my mother and father quarrelled continually and that in January he went back to Rugby where his post as senior science master had been kept open. Mother refused to go with him because, she said, she could never bear to live in Rugby again. When Father realised that nothing would persuade Mother to go back to Rugby, he resigned from the school and got a job as an inspector of schools for the Board of Education. His district was Essex and he worked from Kew.

*

Granny Ashwell died in the spring. Alice left to marry George and was replaced by another Devon woman called Lena Tribbel. Lena was very goodlooking, with black hair and dark eyes. She was always kind to us and we liked her. Every day during the school holidays she took my brothers and me to Kew Gardens. There, in the hottest greenhouse where the Victoria Regia is kept (a huge waterlily with giant plate-like leaves, large enough for a person to sit on), she fell in love with one of the gardeners. After that each day she went straight to the Victoria Regia, usually leaving us outside to amuse ourselves, while she talked and flirted with her young man. We never told Mother, who would have been furious. Lena turned out to be a bit dishonest. She took Mother's only evening dress and had herself photographed in it. Stupidly she stood the photograph out on her dressing-table. Mother soon discovered the loss of her dress, got it back and sacked Lena.

Father returned for the spring vacation and then started visits to Gramp and Aunt Winifred at No. 16 Trafalgar Square, Chelsea, on the site of the present Chelsea Square. They had very small incomes: Gramp's annuity and Aunt Winifred's salary as head of 'the women's side' of Chelsea Polytechnic, the 'Poly', as she called it. Aunt Winifred was devoted to us all. The chief aggravation of these visits was Gramp with his beard and wheezing chronic bronchitis. I really didn't like kissing him, especially as there was so little space on his cheek not covered by beard. Then he had ghastly spasms of coughing which I found disgusting.

One day before going to '16', as it was called by Father, we went to the Natural History Museum at South Kensington. This was very exciting, chiefly because Father said there was a whale called a 'grampus'. Nicholas and Robin were equally excited. We dared not put the question into words: Would the whale resemble our 'grampus'? At least, I thought, it won't wheeze and splutter. On the whole I thought it would be preferable.

Nicky and Robin tore down the corridor, giggling and shouting, 'To the whales, to the whales!'

I, fearing that Father would detect the reason for our interest and be hurt, walked with him. Of course when we saw the whale it was so enormous that all ideas of likeness to our grandfather vanished.

Nicholas said meaningfully as we came out, 'I thought the whales would have been more amusing.'

I knew what he meant. We went to tea at '16' and took care not to mention the whales to Gramp.

'16' compared very badly with 'the flat'. I think it wouldn't have been at such a disadvantage without Gramp, and yet after he died and we visited Aunt Winifred alone there was something sad and puritan about the atmosphere. Aunt Winifred was loving and we would toast crumpets and sit close to the fire, but then she would pat us with her dry hands in a certain rhythmic way which annoyed me terribly. Her hair was always so untidy, her poor eyes gazed disturbingly at us through those thick lenses. Also she would never just let us alone on visits; there was always what she called 'a plan'. She'd say, 'The plan will be, etc. etc.' If only the plans had ever included a theatre! I was becoming obsessed with the idea of the theatre although so far I had only seen a touring company in *Peter Pan* at the King's Theatre, Hammersmith. She always wanted to walk along the Embankment and go to Battersea Park. The truth was she had very little money. However, we could have gone in the gallery for a shilling each.

When Father left Rugby after the summer term he had bought a house in Burlington Avenue, Kew – No. 41, within a few doors of the house where I did lessons with Miss Gregory. It only cost £650 and I helped him to paint and distemper it. I didn't look on this move with the excitement of the others; my optimism was calmer. However, this time we got our own furniture out of store and the toys and books so missed throughout the war appeared again, although they seemed to have diminished in size and number from my memory of over two years back.

My especial hope was that Mother and Father would get on better. I dreaded those slamming doors and her asking me to go to him. I would go and try to say something and see the tired look on his face. As a rule he would suggest we went for a walk to Kew Gardens or, in the summer, for a row on the river. He taught us all to row as soon as possible. We used to hire a boat from a boathouse at the back of Kew Green. Later he took us to Richmond and we learned to punt between Richmond and Twickenham, where we spent some lovely days picnicking. Father eventually had a special small pole made for Robin who at six years old took to punting like a duck to water.

What I couldn't know and he couldn't tell me, even if he and Mother realised it, which I doubt, was that they were in an impasse of sexual frustration. I think it was during this period that the dread of anger and quarrelling became an obsession. To this day I have a deep fear of angry words. I swore to myself that, when I grew up and married, whatever my husband did I would never nag him. I didn't understand what my parents' quarrels were about, but it seemed to me that Mother was always getting at him about something whenever he was in the house. He would react angrily and go out, slamming the front door.

Chapter Five

Boarding School

In the summer of 1919 when I was nine father and mother decided to send me to boarding school. I think they both realised that their relationship was becoming a strain and felt it would be better if I were away from home during the school terms. They chose an Anglo-Catholic convent in Sussex for three reasons: first because Aunt Molly was a nun of the order, although at present she was Sister Superior of one of the houses in South Africa; secondly it was in the country; thirdly the fees were not high – ninety-two pounds a year. Buying my school outfit was a great pleasure to me. It was only slightly marred by my mother's refusing to buy me the regulation scarlet beret: she insisted on getting me a crimson one because she said scarlet didn't suit me.

The clothes were ugly but I liked them because they were new. For years I had had clothes passed on from somebody's daughter older than me – badly hand-knitted jumpers, as they were called, or badly made garments from some sewing-lady Mother found.

For school we had to have navy-blue serge skirts, blue and white striped flannel blouses, black stockings and shoes: another disappointment here – the regulation shoes were the Phat Pheet brand made by Daniel Neal but these were too expensive and so I had to have an ordinary strap shoe from Schollbreds who supplied the regulation coat, skirt and blouses. My underclothes – wool combination, liberty bodices, navy bloomers and black wool stockings – were all bought at Gorringes, chiefly I suspect because it was near Aunt Maudie's flat and meant we could drop in after shopping.

Very occasionally we went to tea with Aunt Joan in her room off a men's surgical ward in St George's Hospital. I thought the hospital a thrilling place and hoped I would become ill enough to spend some time there. The romance of hospital was entirely dispelled later by *having* to be there while my appendix was removed: I remember the shock of the anaesthetic with the masked nurses and surgeons standing round and holding one's hands to stop one fighting when the awful stifling in the first stages started; then the whirling off into an abyss lit by roaring Catherine wheels and the waking, as it seemed, days later in great pain and feeling and being very sick; the wretched days that began at 5.30 a.m. with washing, the continual bed and leg straightening because I used to curl up my legs and fix them against the bolster that was placed under my knees. I could only sleep curled up, but this was not allowed, and so I was continually wakened.

Finally on the evening before I went home I had a fever but ate a large cooked dinner of roast beef and potatoes for fear that if I refused it they would think I was too ill to go home. A bad night followed this, in which the nightmares of anaesthesia returned and I crouched on my heels and screamed. Next day they let me go; the noise I made had unnerved the night nurses and kept the ward awake. I returned to Kew with a temperature of 103 but recovered gradually in the security of my own bed.

*

Mother took me to school for the first time at the end of September 1919. I was rather plain and small for my age. I had reddish hair cut in a bob with a fringe, a pale freckly face and light eyelashes. It was a warm day, so on arrival at the station we took a cab. The yellow sandstone convent buildings stood in their own grounds. The approach was down a long straight drive between green fields fenced with iron railings. Then came a lodge with its twin apartments joined by an arch. The senior chaplain lived here. Opposite the archway was the main door of the convent where we got out of the cab. Mother rang the iron bell-pull which clanged somewhere in the distance and after a few minutes the door was opened by a nun. She told us we must go round to the school door and showed us the way, saying she would have my trunk taken over later. So, as I carried my one-night attaché case, we walked down an asphalt path past the chapel and lawns and flower-beds filled with scarlet salvias, which I thought very beautiful.

Again Mother pulled an iron bell-pull. This time the door was opened by an 'industrial' as the maids were called. She was dressed very strangely in a long, full, blue cotton gown with a large apron which had an embroidered bib. On her head was a hideous mob-cap. Her hair was scraped tightly from her neck into a little bun on top of her head under the cap which had an opening at the back. She preceded us down a highly polished slippery red-tiled passage to the room of the sister in charge. Sister A. was tall. Her face was like grey parchment, her grey eyes small and like a snake's. I was very nervous when I shook hands and felt those cool, dry, thin fingers take my hand in hers. She smiled, however, and suddenly looked less forbidding.

'I have put Rachel in the nursery this term as we have no vacancy in the big school until the term after Christmas. I think she'll like the nursery,' she said.

Mother had to leave to catch her train back to London after a very few minutes. I had a little ache in my throat and nearly cried as we hugged farewell. Her pretty face and radiant smile always made it hard to say good-bye. However, once parted I felt all right – indeed my spirits began to rise with the excitement of my new status as a boarding-school girl. Sister A. took my hand and said she would show me up to the nursery. The staircase to the nursery was in the old building, or 'old side', as it was called. Sister A.'s room was in the 'new side', as was the school hall, a music-room and the fifth and sixth forms. Up a polished wooden staircase were the medicine room, sickroom and two dormitories.

The staircase to the 'old side' was stone with iron banisters. There were gas jets shaped like fish-tails at intervals for lighting after dark. The walls were painted in a high gloss paint, deep cream above a black dado and dark green below. We went up the first flight and along a highly polished corridor, smelling strongly of beeswax, past the open door of a dormitory. At the door beyond this dormitory we stopped. A great deal of noise was coming from the room. Sister A. knocked and went in. I followed.

There was an immediate hush; five girls stopped what they were doing and stood to attention. We went over to the nun who had risen from her chair where she had been sitting sewing. Her face was gentle and smiling. I was introduced and Sister A. left immediately. As soon as she had gone the noise broke out again and the serene-faced nun sat down and continued with her work.

Two children rushed forward and seized my hands. 'Come on the rocking-horse,' they said. The rocking-horse was large. You could get six children on at a time – two in the saddle, one on the bar at each end of the rockers and two underneath, although that was a poor position since it was the base and place of least movement. Being a newcomer, I was put in the saddle behind someone else. The two who seized my hands, Mary Nell and Betty Ore, were cousins; Mary had a little sister called Jo who was six and the baby of the nursery. I later discovered that these three stayed at school all through the holidays because their parents lived in India. I quickly felt at home and was soon talking, even shouting, with the rest.

Someone said that Cissie would be here soon to take us down to tea. Cissie was the sister in charge of the nursery. I don't think we ever knew her real name, she had been called Cissie for so many years. One or two now in the nursery were the daughters of girls she had had in her care in their childhood. Her nickname held expectations of someone gentle and cosy, so I had a shock when she waddled in ten minutes later. She seemed very old, short and plump, with a pale face, steel-rimmed glasses and an enormous double-chin held in by her wimple. Once more everyone stood to attention in silence. She looked around and beckoned me over to ask my name. I replied in a voice just above a whisper. She asked a few questions of the others who said 'Yes, Cissie', or 'No, Cissie.' Then she told us to get into pairs according to height. As I was the tallest she put me in front with Mary Nell. The gentle nun went away and Nurse in cap and apron joined us.

Nurse gave me a blue cotton pinafore to put on over my blouse and skirt. These were issued and kept at school and were worn during work and play to keep our blouses and skirts clean.

It was time for tea. Cissie and Nurse went to the back of the crocodile. Cissie took Jo's hand. 'Come, my chicabiddy,' she said. There was a little whispering and shuffling as we formed the double line. Then Cissie said: 'Silence!' You could have heard a pin drop. Then, 'Lead on.' Her voice was like a threat. Each pair joined hands and at the pace set by Mary, the leader, we marched off like a platoon of soldiers, back along the passage, down the stone staircase, along another very long passage flanked by doors with glass at the top. These were the form rooms, one to four. There was a big studded door at the end which divided the school from the convent – the refectories were all in the convent. Mary opened the door with its large black iron latch and we went into the cloisters which surrounded a courtyard with roses and neatly cut lawn. The smell of incense and old hassocks filtered through the open chapel door in the south corner.

The nursery refectory was small with two trestle tables; the walls were covered with holy pictures and faded photographs of past nursery children. Cissie sat at the head of one table, Nurse at the other, Jo next to Cissie and the rest according to age – the younger at Cissie's table, the older at Nurse's. There were plates of thick bread thinly spread with margarine on the tables and a mug of milk by each plate; also dishes of gooseberry jam, which I noticed was slightly fizzy. The jam was fermented, but at the time I thought it rather interesting. I hadn't tasted fermented jam before. We seemed a very small group, but Cissie told us that the rest of the girls would arrive at six o'clock.

After tea we went back through the cloisters and up the stairs to the top floor where the night-nursery was. I could hear a tremendous noise of chatter as we mounted the second flight of stairs. Cissie having departed into chapel for vespers, there was no one to quell the noise of greetings between the early and late arrivals and so I met the girls in whose company I was to spend my first term.

The night-nursery was a long room with a large window at each end and a high raftered ceiling. White-curtained beds stood in a row down the walls on each side. A small fire burned in the grate, round which was a high nursery fireguard. Victorian nursery pictures and a cuckoo-clock hung on the walls. The mantelpiece was covered with ornaments, little dolls and china animals. On the landing outside the nursery was a large bookcase called The Library. This was filled with Cissie's childhood books, the Andrew Lang *Fairy Tales* – 'Yellow', 'Grey', 'Blue', 'Lilac', 'Crimson', etc. – *Grimm's* and *Hans Andersen, Mrs Molesworth*, volumes of *Little Folks* and many others. We were allowed to take a book out twice a week provided we took care of it. During that first term I read many of the loveliest stories written for children.

At about 6.30 we undressed, folding our clothes neatly and laying them on a stool at the end of the bed. Putting on our dressing-gowns, we knelt in two rows on the big hearthrug in front of the fireplace. Until Cissie came in there was a good deal of chatter and shoving; arguments were whispered, each one trying to get in a last word before Cissie arrived, when there was silence.

She stood in front of us with her back to the fire and in her wispy voice started the gabbling prayer. The prayer was not written down, and through the years had become a sing-song of indistinguishable words. Newcomers joined in as best they could. I only discovered one coherent sentence, which was: 'The changes and chances of this mortal life.' The rest might have been a foreign language. Eventually we reached the 'Amen', crossed ourselves and dispersed quietly, taking mugs of milk, which I noticed was sour, from a tray, and a grey-looking bun that they'd nicknamed 'pooh' because it was so musty to smell and taste that someone once said 'pooh' before trying to eat it, and subsequently hide it or get rid of it down the lavatory pan.

After supper we could read or play with dolls quietly. Cissie moved about the room, now and then singling someone out to sit on her knee. This was alarming, but there was a reward for the ordeal, signifying a little favour. The chosen child was lent one of Cissie's own dolls with strict instructions to take great care of it. This honour was bestowed on me about half-way through the term.

During the five embarrassing minutes on Cissie's knee she told me she liked me and wished I could stay in the nursery and be head girl next term. I wished it too, but knew I would have to move downstairs since my nursery term was in any case a temporary measure.

It was about this time that I first sensed strongly a feeling of never quite belonging to any circle; indeed of being 'all behind, like the cow's tail' as my cousin Tony had said in earlier days; of trying to catch up and be 'like other people'; this has followed me through life. I never quite fit into any of the social categories or 'sets'. It is as if I always just missed the boat. Here, in the oasis of the nursery, I did not belong because I was only a temporary passenger. I think this feeling partly stems from Mother's non-acceptance of the circumstances imposed on us all by lack of money. She was forever hankering after Maudie's circumstances or the life lived by Father as a boy at Birchyfield. She hated the suburban people among whom we lived and always tried to prevent us playing with the children of those who lived in our street and tried to explain that they were not our class. However, income precluded us from knowing those she considered *our* class and so we never seemed to have a coterie.

On the first night, when I lay down and pulled the curtains around me I did not think beyond the moment. Snuggled under the bedclothes, I slept soundly.

*

The next morning we were wakened by Nurse at seven o'clock. We all dressed quickly and knelt on the hearth-rug again for prayers. Breakfast in the refectory consisted of grey-looking porridge and bread and margarine. After breakfast, as no one told me which class I should go to, I kept with the younger ones and went into the kindergarten, which was held in the playroom. The mistress took no notice of me and the class began cutting out coloured paper. School so far was proving very easy. However, this feeling was soon dispelled. A girl from downstairs came in and asked if Rachel Kempson was there. I looked up. So did the others, and when I answered to my name she said I was to come down to the Second Form.

I got up and followed her out and down the stone staircase, along the passage the way we had marched to the refectory the day before, but this time we stopped at a door near the end, and went into the Second Form room. Here it was all very different. The form was entirely composed of 'downstairs' girls and a geometry lesson was in progress. I hadn't learned geometry and couldn't understand a word of that or any other class that day. At the end of the afternoon I was called up to the form mistress, who told me she thought it would be better for me to start in Form One.

I found the work a bit more comprehensible here and after a few days settled down fairly well. I know I was lazy about work but I can't help thinking that many subjects, especially history, geography and French were badly and boringly taught. History seemed to consist chiefly in learning strings of dates and endless facts about characters and events which failed to take on any but the driest significance. Geography was mostly lists of rivers and towns, which could have become fascinating had they been given life or reality. French was impossible since we treated our poor French mistresses as figures of fun to be teased unmercifully in their hopeless efforts to keep order.

I found Form One difficult enough as I had had almost no education during the war. The only things I was good at were reading aloud, script-writing and sewing. I was handy with my fingers, and plain sewing was beautifully taught and has been very useful to me. The term passed by in walks and lessons and playtimes in the nursery. We did lessons from nine till eleven and then had a short break. During break we tore about screaming and playing 'Touch' (in the nursery we could make a noise without being punished). Lessons again from 11.15 to 12.45, up to the nursery to wash and brush our hair for lunch, a walk in the afternoon with Nurse.

On misty days we had to wear the red berets instead of our navy-blue school hats and walk in a crocodile so as never to get out of sight, but on fine days we only started in a crocodile and were soon allowed to break and walk in twos and threes, talking and teasing each other, picking nuts and berries and anything we could see to bring back and put in vases in nursery and form room. An hour's lessons before tea, and after tea up to the night-nursery to read or play till bedtime.

At Mass on Sunday we wore blue serge dresses and on our heads blue velvet skullcaps. Mass always made me feel sick because of the incense. If you didn't behave perfectly, Cissie would stretch her hand out to any fidget and give her a hard slap. The entire community was at Mass – nuns, industrials and orphans, 'downstairs' and nursery girls. The orphans sat on the left of the chapel in front, the nursery on the right in front, and the upper school behind them.

We were insatiably curious about the orphans and stared at them as they came scuffling up the aisle dressed in rough blue serge frocks with white pinafores, their faces scrubbed and shiny, smelling of yellow kitchen soap. There were some tiny ones, in fact all ages from two to seventeen or eighteen, when they graduated to being industrials and eventually went into domestic service. The babies had embroidered white bonnets, the middle-sized girls enormous, hideous, shoulder-length, white, heavily starched sun-bonnets. The seniors wore mob-caps. In winter they all had chilblains on their fingers. We wondered about their daily life and I used to hope, but doubt, that their food wasn't worse than ours.

Mass over, we went back to the nursery to read holy books. Then lunch, followed by a long walk in crocodile; tea, and more holy books;

milk and bed. Sunday was always the most unpleasant day in the week: we had cold lunch and were not allowed to play or make a noise – no rocking-horse, no game of Touch.

*

On the whole it was a happy term and although I was thrilled to go home for the Christmas holidays, I was sorry to be leaving the nursery.

On the last morning of term all the other girls put on their home clothes. I was the only one in uniform because Mother hadn't known you travelled in your home clothes. Those going to Victoria were taken to the station and accompanied to London by a mistress; we talked hard all the way and got wildly excited when we came to the suburbs, and then the train steamed into Victoria. We all jostled each other and tumbled out on to the platform.

Suddenly I saw Mother. I rushed at her, leaping up with my arms around her neck and never stopped talking all the way home in the District railway to Kew, and so the first term ended.

Chapter Six

Peter Pan

My second term was like starting again, because I was to go into the downstairs part of the school, in the charge of Sister A., but at least I was familiar with the look of the place. Mother took me to Victoria to join the school party; we found the group on the station, most of whom I knew only by sight. There was one new girl. She was very pretty with long, soft, brown, curly hair, big almond-shaped eyes with long, thick lashes and a pale oval face. She was wearing a pink tweed coat. I was sure I would like her. She was crying and her face looked just as pretty; the tears welled out of her eyes and ran down her cheeks and she sobbed occasionally, but she didn't seem to dab and blow her nose and become red and blotchy as I always did. Although I was plain I was not unduly worried, but I was drawn to pretty and attractive people.

When it was time for the train to leave and we said good-bye, the carriage door was closed, the guard blew his whistle and we were off. On the journey Betty calmed down a little and seeing me trying to put my coat on the rack offered to help me. I asked her age and volunteered mine and we found we had only a month between us, my birthday being on May 28th and hers on April 29th. She wasn't shy, but not too on-coming, and I entirely approved of her. I liked her because I slightly envied her, both for her looks and her good clothes. Everything that Betty had was right.

On reaching school Betty and I found we were both in St Agnes dormitory; the junior dormitory of downstairs. It was next door to the playroom of the nursery and only divided from it by a partition. The floor was polished boards, the beds black iron, with red blankets and white spreads during the day; by the bed a thin rush-mat and a locker, on which stood a jug and basin, mug and soap dish, with a piece of yellow household soap, non-existent now. It came in long bars and was cut off into chunks.

You were allowed to keep a Bible and prayer-book in the dormitory. No other reading was allowed at bedtime, but most of us smuggled Angela Brazil stories upstairs tucked into our navy bloomers and hoped not to be caught. We were caught very often because the nun or mistress on the 'charge' as it was called seemed to feel bound to try to catch you out, and for no reason would say, 'Has anyone got a book in the dormitory?' You were on your honour to own up if you had. If you didn't own up when you had a book it was acting a lie, and acting a lie was mortal sin; and if you died in mortal sin you went to Hell, as Sister A. constantly taught us in Bible class. As we were also told that the world might end at any moment of any hour of any day, which came to the same thing as dying, we were in great fear of dying in mortal sin. However, most of us thought Angela Brazil worth the risk.

There were many periods in the day when we had to be in silence; dressing in the morning, before breakfast lined up in the hall to wait for Sister A. to march us to the Refectory. You could be put in silence and made to stand up to eat your meal if you laughed very loudly or spoke too loudly in the refectory; if during playtime in the big hall you laughed very loudly or shouted you were put in silence. You were in silence half the time when undressing for bed and always at tea on Sundays. The awful thing was that occasionally one made some explanation of annoyance to oneself during a silent period, especially if when undressing for bed you tore a button off or perhaps laddered a stocking and if when asked if you were speaking you said, 'I spoke to myself', and on being given the silence mark tried to explain, as often as not you would end with about ten bad marks. The bad marks were various: silence marks, half-conduct marks and conduct marks. A conduct mark meant one hour's detention, and was given for breaking a strict rule. You were allowed three bad marks free of punishment, but every one after three counted for detention.

On Saturday morning the prefects collected our slang-lists. You had to write down on paper every word of slang you had uttered during the week. You were fined a penny for 'ass', 'fool', etc., 2d for 'dash', 6d for 'damn' plus a conduct mark and a day in bed on bread and water if Sister chose. Saying 'damn' was the greatest crime you could commit at the convent and so, really, the 6d fine was not heavy. However, bed with bread and water all day was like prison to us.

As far as I can remember I spent nearly every Saturday afternoon of my four years doing lines in detention, the detention list was read out after lunch on Saturday and those with their names on the list went miserably into the classroom and sat down to write lines for the number of hours' detention earned. Sometimes it was impossible to work it off and so it was taken off any treat one might have during the term. We never became cowed by punishment, only rebellious to an exaggerated degree. We would do anything to break rules, invent mischief – any ridiculous stupidity we could think of.

*

Betty was sleeping next to me in the dormitory. We had to draw the curtains of our cubicles when we undressed and keep them drawn until we were dressed again next morning. It was forbidden to look into another's cubicle and the penalty for doing so was a conduct mark, one hour's detention with lines to write. We did constantly look into the cubicle next to us, going to elaborate trouble to draw the curtains, dividing each ring separately, an inch at a time. The slightest sound brought the question, 'Is anyone looking into anyone else's cubicle?' and you owned up because of the fear of mortal sin.

The first night of term things were less rigid because girls often felt homesick and cried and we always comforted each other with smuggled sweets. Betty was terribly homesick on her first night. She sat up in bed crying, wearing a pretty pink nightdress of rather fine woollen material; it had been made by her mother. I got the feeling that things would be especially hard for Betty who had obviously been used to comfort at home.

Next morning breakfast consisted of a slice of ham, bread and margarine and rather mauve-looking tea. Ham was always called *je suis* for obvious reasons. It was cured by a gardener in a stinking shed which we always passed going to the games field. We could smell it from quite a distance and we used to look in, fascinated to see the ham he had cured. I can't think what he did with it, but the result was that the fat of the ham was always yellow and purple with dark blotches and tasted disgusting. However, we just laughed at it and called it *je suis*. We had in rotation, *je suis*, 'donkey', porridge, a rasher of fried bacon (never more than one rasher) or one square of 'donkey' or a small bowl of porridge, followed by bread and margarine. 'Donkey' was really a kind of potted meat, so named because it was grey in colour.

Betty had a letter from her mother her first morning. She read it to me. It worried me rather because one sentence read, 'We shall be wondering what you are having for breakfast', and I felt embarrassed and almost responsible. Betty settled down very well, however, far better than I ever did; she wasn't upset by the food as I and a few others were. Her mother always provided her with eggs and jam for tea, which, combined with her prettiness, helped to make her popular. We were allowed to have these extras for tea if our parents provided them. If you had an egg for tea, you were obliged to give the top of it to a friend – to be given one was a sign of being liked. Egg tops were rarely given to me. I was not popular because I was plain. Plain girls were terribly bullied. I suppose it was because in such an austere regime everyone loved prettiness. My life became brighter when I had eggs for tea and could give away the tops. Only white bread and margarine and the mauve tea were provided. Mother sent jam as well, as soon as she realised the situation.

Our mid-day lunches were tolerable – stews and vegetables, lots of suet puddings and treacle tarts, very watery milk puddings, occasionally prunes and dried apricots. I never remember having fresh fruit, but in those days the value of salads and uncooked fruit was unknown in schools. We had names for most of the dishes. The ones I remember were 'Father Hutton and Mr Marsh' and 'Treacle or Currant Tammy'. The first was a large sort of half Christmas pudding with a little one beside it. Father Hutton was our large, fat head chaplain and Mr Marsh the dwarf-life organist, hence the names given to the large and small puddings. 'Treacle or Currant Tammy' were so called because they were round covered tarts filled with treacle or currants and were the shape of a Tam o' Shanter.

Before going to bed we had a mug of watery cocoa and a 'pooh', those same awful-looking grey buns we had in the nursery, with caraway seeds added. We threw them behind the piano of the First Form room where we had supper. The result was that the room usually smelled of mouldy 'poohs' as well as dead mice. *We* thought the mice died of the 'poohs'. Dead mice were often found under the radiator gratings and made a horrible smell. Although the building had antiquated central heating it was pretty inefficient, so as the weather grew cold we felt the lack of warmth.

*

Although there were services throughout every day for the nuns, we were only obliged to go to Mass on Sunday mornings and Evensong on Sunday evening. Early Mass daily was voluntary. Sunday Choral Mass was turgid with incense, which made me feel sick, and vestments and much pomp and parading.

The nuns in their stalls flanking the Chapel very nearly covered themselves in their black veils. These devout figures with ashen faces, except for one or two, seemed bent on destroying any pleasures we had. I used to wonder if their private thoughts did not occasionally break out into some terrible longing for free bodies that could move and run and dance. Does God really intend that human beings should mortify themselves so terribly in His name? We only knew the nuns attached to the school: Sister A., the Sister in charge, Sister C., the nursing sister, Sister H., gay and happy-looking as a novice; but even she began to show signs of strain and bad temper once she had taken her final vows. How beautiful she was with her big, dark eyes, flawless complexion and large generous mouth. Sister F. who taught us sewing was like a rather sad old tortoise. Cissie in the nursery lived in her childhood for the most part. Only one, beloved Sister Eva, of all our school nuns, seemed to belong to God.

During Mass I used to watch Father Hutton waddling to and fro, and the servers in their red cassocks and lace-trimmed surplices. I was most intrigued by the little boy server, who followed his father, swinging the censer and probably loving every minute of it all since he had plenty to do. He was a handsome little boy and I used to think with some envy that at least he went home after the service, probably to a lovely hot lunch of roast beef and Yorkshire pudding and not our miserable meal of corned beef and pickled red cabbage, followed by the wobbling blotchy *blanc-mange*. I realise now that Sunday lunch had to be cold so that the aged crone-like cook, Sister Feckler, who was bent with rheumatism, could go to Choral Mass. I usually got through Mass without feeling too sick, and if I filled my thoughts with other things it passed, and we filed out and joined Sister Eva for Bible class.

This dear woman would gather us round her in the First Form room, tuck our cold hands under her scapula and read us the most delightfuly holy fairy tales – *The House Built on Sand, The Grumpy Saint*, etc. The all too short hour spent with her brought us within imagination of God and a possible acceptance of Him through her. She smoothed away our feuds and dislikes; even the plain stupid ones becoming attractive through the warmth of her loving kindness. For that hour enemies became friends and we experienced peace.

*

Lunch was silent on Sundays for some inexplicable reason. After lunch we returned to the school buildings and dressed for the walk in crocodile down the main London road. A mistress was usually in charge of the walk and seemed to dislike it as much as we did.

Colder than ever, we returned to the big hall, where we sat in pairs at table desks for letter-writing home, and sweets. The sweets were your own, given out from a cupboard by a prefect. They consisted of provisions from home and anything you had been able to afford to commission from the shopping team on Saturday. My parents thought, quite rightly, that an excess of sweets was bad for you, so I had very few. You had to engage yourself for sweets, and naturally if you hadn't many you could only engage yourself to one as poor as yourself. I was left week after week with the same greasy-haired, spotty girl with protruding teeth held in by a gold band. The rest sat munching at their laden desks until teatime, when we went to the refectory for bread and margarine and the mauve tea. Most of the girls couldn't look at the tea after the sweet orgy, but I was hungry and would have welcomed something more appetising than the bread and margarine.

*

Summer terms at the convent were not unhappy. The grounds were beautiful and with warm weather the nuns seemed to relax a little of their rigidity. As soon as possible we went into cotton blouses although we still wore the heavy serge skirts. We wore lisle stockings and if there was a heat wave we were allowed to leave off stockings altogether.

Punishments became less because with the greater freedom of running about in the open air our natural high spirits were given an outlet, and if we shouted loudly in the garden the sound was dispersed on the air and did not offend. Occasionally we had a lesson in the garden. We did not have to go for walks but amused ourselves on the see-saw under the horse chestnut trees in the grass playground, or played Red Indians among the trees that surrounded it. There was cricket which bored me, but at least it was in the open air, and sports practice which I adored. On Sunday we stayed in the grounds for the sweets and letter-writing periods and did not have a set walk. Much of our frustration was temporarily eased.

*

The highlight of the school year was, for me, the form play which took place in the autumn term. I lived for it and in it; all emotional desires seemed satisfied.

In Form One, in which I spent four terms, our form mistress wrote the play. My second autumn term I was cast as the prince who had to go through numerous adventures to find his princess. The princess was played by a Scots girl called Marjorie Gordon Brown, chiefly because she had long pale yellow hair. It reached her waist. Marjorie Gordon Brown had been a butt for teasing because she was stolid and pale and her nose bled constantly and she was always talking about the shaggy cows in Scotland. However, taking the part of the princess in the play put her up in my estimation quite a bit. The play had a great many songs in it. One of mine began:

My own good sword is keen and bright
And strong in battle for the fight
The fiercest foes I'll put to flight
To win my bride.

Then the chorus of fairies came in with: 'His own good sword ...' etc.

There was another song which I sang lying on the ground. It told how the dragon had carried off the princess and one line was: 'It very nearly broke my manly heart.' To my astonishment the audience roared with laughter at this. I could see nothing funny in it; I was ten years old and I believed myself to be a young man during the performance.

There was another song which began 'Crystal of vanity, fairies of gold'. I stood in the centre of the stage holding three silvery balls in my hand, the kind used for decorating Christmas trees. On either side of me was a pathway of fairies, the good on the right in pastel colours and the bad on the left in reds and golds. I had to choose which path to take. At the end of the song I was supposed to decide on the good path and to throw down the crystal of vanity.

At the performance I threw it down and it did not break. I had hoped this would happen so that I could keep the silver baubles which looked very beautiful to me. In my fear that they would be trodden on I leaned down quickly and grabbed them, but unfortunately the curtain hadn't quite fallen and the audience laughed. Miss Reynolds was very cross indeed and said I spoilt the whole scene. I was slightly ashamed, but having got the silver balls intact made up for it. At the first dress parade wearing a green tunic with a belt and long brown stockings, and a circlet of cardboard painted gold on my head, Miss Reynolds had said, 'I could fall in love with the little prince myself.' This was the first time I became conscious of the possibility of being attractive.

There always had to be a final dress parade in front of Sister A. to make sure that all the costumes were decent, as it was called. Too short a tunic was considered indecent; it had to be nearly to your knees.

*

Sometimes we had a fancy-dress dance in the Christmas term, which was the most enormous excitement. For one of these Mother had a Peter Pan outfit made for me. I was so excited and thrilled when it arrived I felt I had never been so happy. The box contained a very short red tunic with a white scalloped collar, a pair of red bloomer knickers, also short, and long brown stockings and shoes. I thought of nothing else for days. I was going to *be* Peter Pan at the dance.

Since seeing a company playing *Peter Pan* at the King's Theatre, Hammersmith, I had constantly identified myself with him. I had always wished I'd been a boy and I didn't at that time want to grow up. I made myself quite unhappy sometimes with a longing to become Peter Pan. I used to stand at a window about sunset and believe that if I could only be free of everything and everyone and school in particular, if I could have complete freedom at sunset and could get to the bluey-purple line of the horizon made by the setting sun, then I would indeed find the never-never-land. Looking back, I think it was partly a longing for woods and country and the freedom of long days in the open and time to dream – so far all my life, except for the Devon holidays, had been spent in urban places and although the convent was in the country we were given little freedom: even walks were mostly along roads sometimes verging on to lanes but seldom going into woods or fields.

The evening of the dance arrived and I put on my suit. The tunic was very short, only just below my waist, with the short knickers beneath it. I was in a state of euphoria as I dressed in my cubicle in St Agnes dormitory.

We all went down to parade in front of Sister A. before the dance started. It came to my turn.

Sister A. looked at me. Her face seemed to go greyer than usual. She pulled at my tunic. 'My dear child, you can't appear in this, it's indecent.' She called a mistress and told her to get a piece of material out of the acting box to drape round me.

I was scarlet in the face and nearly crying. It wasn't only that she was going to spoil the Peter Pan suit, but also that what she said was a criticism against my mother. My mother had thought the suit all right. I had wanted to write and say how lovely it was. Now I would have to pretend. And who would want to dance with me in my ruined costume? I'd felt I was an attractive boy when I'd first dressed. I had a very slender body, with long legs and my lack of feminine prettiness seemed to be right as I looked at myself in the little mirror above the wash-stand. Even the feeling of not belonging had disappeared. I belonged to my Peter Pan fantasy world and could be happy in it for an hour or two.

I don't remember anything about the evening. As far as I was concerned it was completely washed out. I only longed to creep into my bed and forget. I think I did go up to the dormitory fairly early and knelt on the window ledge where I could hear the music, 'Destiny Waltz' etc., and see the brightly coloured whirling throng of girls dancing together. They looked happy. They belonged. The nun had cast me out because I wore a short tunic.

Chapter Seven

Mother & Father

One summer holiday Father took a house on the Wye in Herefordshire, Wilton Bridge House, with a garden going down to the river. His sister, our Aunt Muriel, and her friend Scottie, came with us to share expenses.

The Wye was almost unfrequented except by people who owned the salmon fishing. The only boating in those days was extremely limited because there are no locks and at that time only two people we ever heard of could negotiate the rapids. One was a boatman at Symonds Yat called Jack Gardiner and the other my father, whom Jack had taught to punt up rapids when Father was a young man.

We had some lovely picnics, taking the boat quietly down the stream and stopping for lunch and to swim at one of the wide reaches. In places where the water was very dark and deep, there were long green weeds like green hair; we called it mermaid's hair. I made believe that it was indeed the hair of mermaids buried under the river bed.

I learned to punt some of the easier rapids between Ross and Goodrich. This was rather exciting and depended on accuracy of steering. Instead of the long punting stroke you had to take short stabbing strokes in order to be able to correct the movement of the bows against the swift shallow stream. Once the bows started to swing you were beaten and the boat would swing round and a new start had to be made. As well as the knack of the short stroke, with constant readjustment of the steering, you had to know the course of the deepest water, which is very narrow in a rapid. As one approaches, the stream becomes shallower and faster; then the course can be seen in a smooth gusset bordered by rippled water. The nose of the boat must be kept up the centre. At the top there is always a twist of the current to right or left according to the curve of the banks, and then a ledge of water like a miniature waterfall. This is where it becomes really hard going and in the bigger rapids the boat must be practically lifted over the ledge. The passengers walk and the punter stands in the stern so that the bows are slightly raised. Father directed me from the bank; I used to fail many times at first, but finally I learnt to do it.

*

We always spent the winter and spring holidays at home in Burlington Avenue. We had to make our own amusements. Except for the treats of going to Aunt Maudie's flat or to a play in the winter holidays there was little outlet. On walks with Nicky and Robin in Kew Gardens I usually made for the wild lake or the woods around Queen Victoria's cottage, and some days we walked along the towpath of the river opposite Syon House. Both gave a semblance of country, and looking across the river to the water meadows of Syon you could actually see country although it was private. On wet days we read or played cards, *Bezique* mostly.

Robin read perfectly at four years old and by the time he was five read translations of the *Iliad* and the *Odyssey* to himself. Nicholas, who had been delicate as a baby and small boy, had a slower mind although he was like Father to look at, especially like the photographs of Father as a boy.

Nicholas was often sent away to stay with our numerous aunts and cousins, who found him adorable, and I know from things he said when he returned from these visits that they did everything to make up for his lack of happiness at home. He had a very deliberate way of talking. My father's cousin Lucy told me that once when he spent his holiday with her he turned to her elderly housemaid as he was leaving and said very gravely, 'Should I tip you, Holmes?' Holmes said equally gravely, 'Oh, no thank you, Master Nicholas, it's been a pleasure to look after you.'

One year after Christmas Mother was taking Robin to see *Treasure Island*. She loved to take him to plays with her alone. It must have been enjoyable, he was very intelligent and such a good companion. During lunch Father suggested that they should go by a certain bus which would take them via Westminster, past the Cenotaph and Horse Guards Parade, and in this way Robin would see some interesting sights. Robin's face became very red and finally he said, 'I don't want to see all that muck – I want to get to the play.'

*

I came home at the end of one summer term to find that Mother had left some weeks before and was in the country. We were to join her there. In her will Granny had left my mother, Aunt Maud and Aunt

May about £300 a year each. Mother had saved up and bought a workman's cottage in Herefordshire. It was called Yew Tree Cottage and was on Coppet Hill, above the Wye valley.

Mother made it very pretty for about £50. It consisted of two rooms on the ground floor with a lean-to kitchen, and three little bedrooms upstairs leading out of each other. There was a privy outside. A shed in the garden was converted into a bedroom for Father and Nicholas when we joined Mother. This shed had a concrete floor and a corrugated iron roof. Mother gave Robin and me a bedroom each in the cottage. Father was very good at carpentry and painting, so when he got there he made cupboards out of packing cases which he painted blue. One day he beeswaxed the deal table in the living room to give it a polished surface and a swarm of bees came and settled on it. It was quite alarming.

Mother made friends with a farmer and his sister, Joey and Norah Stock. She spent a lot of time helping Joey with the harvest. She always wore a sun-bonnet. For the first time in my memory she worked from morning till night without saying she was tired and as far as I know slept well and certainly ate well.

I came to realise she was in love with Joey. As Father didn't appear to mind I thought very little of it. We were perfectly happy because Mother didn't nag Father, or bother about what we did. We were bare-legged and dirty, bathed in the river every day, picnicked in the cornfields, made friends with Norah and did a great deal with Father. During this holiday he and Mother didn't quarrel, so we were all at peace.

Years later Mother told me about the two months she spent on Coppet Hill before we joined her. She had become exhausted and dispirited to the verge of a breakdown over her life at Kew. She and Father were at a deadlock and in consequence she mentally tore him to pieces. Having bought Yew Tree Cottage she told Father she must go away for a time. After she had been settled there for a few weeks she met Joey Stock, who worked his small farm in the valley, and they had fallen in love. At first the knowledge of being in love and his being in love with her was a refreshment in itself and so she started helping with the work in the fields. At the end of the day they used to wander along the hedgerows and sit and talk and presumably make love up to a point. Mother felt terrified of giving herself outside marriage: not only fearful, but she felt it would be a sin. Discussions went on and on and at last he asked her to leave my father and marry him. During this idyllic courtship she had become well and strong. She said she used to come back to the cottage late in the evening and eat great hunks of thick bread and butter. She was in love and found it hard to see clearly whether or not she was really fitted to be a working farmer's wife, but she seriously considered it.

When we got back to Kew with Father she wrote to tell him how she felt. Bitterly hurt in his pride he wrote to her that she could go if she liked but that she should never set eyes on the children again. He told me about this after I was grown up. He said he realised what a cruel mistake he had made; however, that was what he said at the time. She broke with Joey, sold the cottage and came home because, she said, she couldn't live without being able to be with us, part of the time at any rate. Also she had doubts whether marriage on the farm with its totally different background and the hard work of a farmer's wife would not have ended the whole affair in disaster. I think she was right but it was a sad situation.

If only married partners would generously allow each other a little latitude how much more easily marriages could stay together. A person *may* only ever love one man or woman in the world; that is fortunate. But it is an extraordinary rule that once married no man or woman should ever have some of the love that men or women have in them to give. For a man never to experience any other woman after his wife, or for a woman never to experience love with another man can be a kind of imprisonment. People become frustrated and guilt-ridden and finally cannot love each other any more: whereas it seems to me that if a husband and wife can be generous and understanding to each other in this respect they can love each other even more deeply.

Father had been generous and clearly not unhappy during that summer holiday, but no doubt he didn't realise that Mother was in love. I think it would never have entered his head that a woman as fastidious and sweet-smelling as Mother could fall in love with a rough, sweaty, working farmer, and so the shock was all the greater. He probably felt a fool for not having noticed what was happening, and yet nothing was happening except in her mind and Joey's, who no doubt did not want to look ahead or face reality while Father and we children were around.

Lovers often want to keep those early stages of love almost unrecognised. Love is so precious and delicate. It is hard to keep and easy to break and Mother must have so longed to keep it and yet not change her life entirely. The great difficulty for Mother and Father was incompatibility — yet they stayed together until he died. When he was dying they came together in understanding. Indeed he said to me when I was visiting him at the hospital two days before his death, 'We have got through to each other at last.' It gave him peace and great pleasure.

Chapter Eight

Wickham Bishops

During the holidays I suffered from colitis. I didn't return to school in January but convalesced at home. As I got stronger Mother started taking me to the theatre. We couldn't afford good seats but to me this was no hardship. I found the greatest joy in the time spent anticipating the play in the gallery queue.

Mother loved it too, I am sure. The theatre was an escape from *her* unhappiness. She was a lovely companion at this time. She gave herself to nursing me back to health and shared to the full my pleasure: the thrilling moment when the doors opened and the queue moved forward, putting down a shilling each at the little box-office in return for a metal disc, and racing up the steep flight of stone stairs to the gallery in order to get the best possible places.

I recovered steadily during the next five months. Mother was at her very best, as always when it was really important. I think nursing me probably helped her to heal her love affair. She put herself aside completely. Father did too. I expect their mutual anxiety drew them together for the first time at any rate. They hid their troubles in their common interest.

We saw a great many plays, among them a revival of J.M. Barrie's *Mary Rose* with Fay Compton, and *The Little Minister* with Fay Compton and Owen Nares, a thrilling production of Shakespeare's *Henry VIII* with Sybil Thorndike as Katherine of Aragon, Norman V. Norman as the King, Lyle Sweet as Wolsey and Angela Baddeley as Anne Boleyn. The sets were by Charles Ricketts. I was swept off my feet and my growing longing for the theatre took shape into determination to go into it myself. It was Sybil Thorndike's performance of Katherine of Aragon that crystalised my feelings. I can hear her voice in my ears to this very moment. 'My Lord, I am a poor woman born out of your country' and 'Good Griffith, lay me lower'. Griffith was beautifully played by Lewis Casson.

Back in the sitting-room at 41 Burlington Avenue I got out my Shakespeare, a school prize from Form One, and read and reread the play and said aloud the part of Katherine. I even recited it to Mother, who was a little impressed although she maintained then as always that the theatre was not for me.

*

Another school had to be found and Father was recommended to a PNEU school at Buckhurst Hill in Essex where, he was told, the food was very good, the atmosphere was homely and the headmistress Miss Gardner had an understanding of colitis and the necessary treatment, as she had lately had it herself.

I went there in the summer term of 1924. The recurring fear of insecurity made me feel rather wretched on the day I had to join the school, but I quickly settled down.

There is not much to be said about Oaklea except that it lived up to its reputation – it was delightfully comfortable. The food was excellent and the atmosphere homely. Miss Gardner was a kindly little woman with very little personality, but the easier life there made me grow strong. I put on pounds of weight and did the minimum amount of work. I loved the gym classes most of all and fell madly in love with the gym mistress, a young, rather prim but pretty Scots girl. I worked so well at gym that I got put into her 'star' gym class. The great joy was the vaulting. At the end of the class each girl could choose what vault she would like to do. I always chose the 'short fly' because it meant springing off the board into a flying position with one's hands on Miss MacArthur's shoulders while with her hands she supported your thighs as she walked backwards with you flying above her head until you landed neatly on the large coconut-mat in front of her. At night in bed I conjured up ideas of going with her on a night train to Scotland. Needless to say she had no idea of the love in my heart and my dreams were very innocent.

I had only one theatrical venture, as acting and plays were not a part of the school life. I wrote and put on a fairy tale play in which, of course, I played a prince. I have no recollection of the story. I am certain it was an absurd effort but Miss Gardner let me get up the little production which we acted in the gym on a small platform, on which the staff always stood for prayers before school in the morning.

I stayed at Oaklea for four terms, during which time Father and Mother decided to move to the country and bought a house in Essex not too far from Aunt Maudie and Uncle Mac. It was no longer financially possible to keep me at boarding school now that both Nicholas and Robin were away at school; also since I was now strong and well, Father felt he must try to get me educated even at this late stage. I was now fifteen and had not taken School Certificate. He chose the Colchester County High School. It had an excellent reputation and a very good headmistress. From Wickham Bishops in

Essex, where the new house was situated, I could travel to school and back each day by train. Father could also work conveniently from Wickham Bishops, Essex being his district for inspecting.

*

The Elms at Wickham Bishops in Essex was a small late-Victorian house standing back from the road inside high hedges and in about a quarter-acre of garden giving onto fields.

In our spring holidays we all took part in setting up the house and making the garden out of the rather derelict ground that surrounded it. Father dug a vegetable garden and we made some very poor grass into a tennis court which Nicholas, Robin and I cut and rolled and finally marked out with enormous enthusiasm. There was a small stable at the side of the house and Father said that he would try and find me a pony. I had learned to ride one holiday while staying with an elderly friend of the family. Riding had temporarily taken over from the theatre in my mind.

As soon as we were living in the country I longed for a pony of my own. Father, an excellent rider himself, wanted me to become a good horsewoman, chiefly for the pleasure you can get from riding about the countryside.

One day we read an advertisement in the local paper of a pony for sale, price £15. We answered it and drove over to see the pony which belonged to some people at Hatfield Peverel, a village on the Chelmsford to Colchester road. Sally, as she was called, was about fifteen years old but quiet and a pretty dun colour. Father decided she would do well, wrote a cheque, and I rode her home.

I soon got to know a girl of my own age, the daughter of neighbours. Elizabeth Walker was a lovely creature with long golden curly hair, rosy cheeks and blue eyes. She was also a superb rider. She and I with other children she introduced me to had some of the happiest times of my childhood. In summer after school we went hacking through the lanes or practised jumping in a field belonging to friends, in autumn cub-hunting. In winter on Saturdays we followed the East Essex hounds, hacking miles to meets and getting back late, tired and dirty, but relaxed and happy.

I have come to think fox-hunting a cruel sport, but as a child it wasn't the killing of the fox that interested me but riding over country otherwise forbidden, the sight of the scarlet coats, the fine horses and their smartly turned out riders, the pack of hounds streaming over a field on a sparkling winter's day, the curious communion of the field – or again at some check, the sudden stillness, with the sound of the hunting-horn on the frosty air and the crack of the whip by a scarlet-coated whipper-in sitting quietly on his horse by the edge of a wood.

A neighbour, Lord Champion de Crespigny, hearing that we were keen on riding and that Father had no horse, offered to lend him an aged one-eyed mare, so that he could join me for the cubbing in late August and early September. It was a kind gesture in a way; but I was hurt for Father, who in his youth at Birchyfield had ridden Grandfather's hunters and followed the hunt of which Grandfather was a member and wore the hunting pink. I resented Father being treated like a poor relation. I hated anyone treating him as though *anything* would do for him.

Father, however, showed no sign of being in any way slighted. We went to fetch the poor old mare on a hot late August afternoon, the day before the first cubbing meeting of the season. We called at the stables and a groom brought her out. She was rough and ugly with her blind eye. However, when Father mounted her she seemed to sense a good rider. He handled her so well, with a gentle but firm rein, and very soon she held up her head and picked up her feet and we walked her home at quite a respectable pace.

Father and I cleaned our saddles and bridles that night, brushed our breeches and jackets ready for a very early start. He called me at 5 a.m. next morning in a cold but rosy dawn. We boiled eggs and drank coffee in the kitchen. At 5.30 we crept quietly to the stables, saddled and bridled our horses and set off for the twelve-mile hack to the meet. We talked in low voices at first, in the silent misty dawn. The sun coming up sent shafts of light across the flat Essex fields and lit the dew on the cobwebs that draped the hedges covered in wild clematis. The air smelled of approaching autumn.

Father talked of meets and rides when he was young and advised going very gently since although cubbing is leisurely we might well have an even longer ride back. It was our first mounted meet so we kept well in the background.

When we arrived a few people said 'Good-morning'. Father raised his hat to the master as he passed us. The whippers-in rode close to the hounds, called them by name, keeping them together. It began to get quite hot although it was only 7.30 and by eight o'clock it was very hot indeed. The hounds streamed off to the first cover, the field following. We kept well back, being newcomers.

Father knew all the etiquette of hunting and I wanted to do the right thing for his sake. I remembered how upset he had been two years earlier when we were staying in Essex for the summer holidays and the boys and I had tumbled out of bed, flung on our clothes and gone bare-legged on foot to join a cub-hunt as it came to a nearby wood. We chattered loudly and generally got in the way. My legs were scratched, as we stamped in and out of brambles, and were streaming with blood. Father, coming out later, found us and was terribly upset. No young person nowadays could understand this attitude, but as a man brought up in the traditions and little ceremonies of the country and hunting, it hurt him to see his children behaving and looking like hooligans. With all his tolerance and big-hearted gaiety Father liked disciplined, orderly behaviour in the right place at the right time. He loved custom and ceremony, as Yeats says in 'Prayer for my Daughter'.

We had a very quiet morning. An earth was dug out and the cubs were killed. I didn't watch. The killing was the part I never got used to and in maturer years turned me against fox-hunting. By mid-morning it was sweltering and Father's mare was lame, so we decided to return home. Father insisted on dismounting and walking beside her so as not to tire her more. It was twelve miles to get back. We stopped at a pub about halfway. Father had beer and I lemonade and we ate hunks of bread and cheese. We arrived home very hot and exhausted at about teatime. Father rubbed down his sweating mare and eventually, when she was cool, let her drink. We gave them a good feed of oats and chaff, and when they were comfortable Father let me change and changed himself.

Riding with Father with all his good instruction had been one of the great pleasures of my life and one I have tried to make possible for my children. Lynn, our youngest child, was given a fine chestnut pony when she was thirteen and became an excellent rider. I loved to see her setting off in the early mornings for hunting in Hampshire where we had a cottage and to recapture that part of my childhood in retrospect through her.

*

I joined the Colchester County High School in the autumn term 1925. The standard of education was excellent, but at sixteen I was so far behind others of my age that I found it impossible to keep up, especially in maths and Latin. Through bad grounding I had lost interest in school education and found myself at a complete disadvantage with the other girls. All I could think of was getting back to my pony and making up for lost time over country things, of which I felt starved.

*

Our first winter at Wickham Bishops Mother started a drama club for the Women's Institute. I joined in the holidays. There was a certain amount of frustration because Mother's ideas of acting inclined to be sentimental. I was instinctively anti-sentimental but having neither experience nor knowledge I couldn't put anything constructive in its place. She called me 'a stick' and said I would never be an actress. However, we had some amusing times, especially in the winter holidays when Aunt Maudie asked us to get up some sketches for an evening at her village hall at Tolleshunt D'Arcy, about eight miles away.

Mother, Father, Nicky, Robin and I in our ramshackle car, with its canvas hood and talc side-screens, buried under costumes, drove in freezing cold and fog to Tolleshunt D'Arcy. Heaters, in small cars at any rate, were unknown in the 1920s. The evening seemed successful, we adored our own part of it: *The King's Breakfast* by A.A. Milne, partly mimed. Father was the cow and made a brightly painted cardboard stall and a cow's head for himself. Nicky was the king. A young girl – the daughter of a neighbour – was the queen, and I was the dairymaid. Mother produced. She and I fought over the way I should say my lines. She wanted me to say:

> Excuse me your Majes*tee*,
> for taking of the liber*tee*.

I didn't want to say it like this. I felt instinctively it was wrong. What neither of us realised was that perhaps I should have spoken with a slight burry accent. Anyway, it was a great success.

The elderly handsome vicar, a lifelong friend of the family, fell for me and tried to put his arms round me and kiss me. Maudie and Mother were furious. I thought it was rather exciting. He was a very debonair character who when young had gone into the Church because the parents of the girl he wanted to marry said she should only have a substantial dowry if she married a parson. So he took orders and preached hell-fire in Tolleshunt D'Arcy church where he had a living from the time soon after he was ordained until his death at 85. In his young days he was reputed to be the father of a number of children in the village, due to his wife's frigidity, Mother said. Anyway no one seemed any the worse for him. He and his wife both took part in all the village entertainments and one way and another provided enormous fun with their open house, delicious food and drink. They had a very old cook, a Mrs Poundsbury, whom a friend called 'Mrs P.' and with whom he had frightful quarrels, shouting at her from the hall while she shouted back.

'You keep in your kitchen, Mrs. P.,' he would bellow.

'I will,' she'd reply, 'and you keep out of it.' They both enjoyed their rows.

One thing that always surprised me was that Mother, who was so beautiful, always played rather ugly Cockney character parts in one-act sketches. We did one called 'The Family Group' and another she played with Father called 'That Brute Simmons'. I enjoyed 'The Family Group' in which I played a ghastly snivelling child called Ede. Perhaps her lack of confidence in herself made her want to hide behind an ugly character. I like hiding behind a character far from myself. When I act a part close to myself I feel somehow naked. In fact no part is 'oneself' unless one makes it so, and I never want to do that.

On the whole family life was much happier at Wickham Bishops. Father found his work of school inspection easier from the country than from Kew. Mother became more contented now that her theatrical talents and interests were used. She was also fond of playing tennis in the summer. Tennis parties were still the fashion and although no one played very well we all enjoyed it.

We constantly visited Aunt Maudie. The McMullens moved into a small Queen Anne House called Follyfaunts in the village of Goldhanger near Tolleshunt D'Arcy, where once again to poor Mother's envy they lived in some style with three servants and a gardener.

We also made great friends with the owners of a most lovely water-mill house at the foot of Wickham Bishops hill. There I fell madly in love with a cousin of Owen Nares, Innes Nares, who lived in a cottage and managed their small estate of cricket bat willows. He was my first love. It made me feel terribly ill, especially since I dared not divulge the fact to anyone. I was sixteen and feared to be ridiculed. However, I spent a lot of time bathing in the mill-stream in summer, playing tennis and watching my beloved from a distance.

Chapter Nine

Brittany

We only stayed two years at Wickham Bishops because while we were there the headmastership of the Royal Naval College at Dartmouth became vacant. Father applied, and to his and our great pride, was appointed. We children were a bit sad to leave Wickham Bishops because it had been the happiest home we remembered, but of course Dartmouth held promise of an even better life. Before the move, however, Father and Mother decided to take me away from school, where I was doing no good, and send me for six months to live with a family in France so that I could learn to speak French fluently.

*

Aunt Winifred was consulted and helped in finding a suitable family. Madame Mativet and her divorcée daughter called Young Madame had an apartment in Paris, but for the summer had taken a villa at Pont Aven in Brittany where they could have four girls as paying guests to help pay for the villa.

Mother accompanied by Maudie escorted me to Brittany early in June. We crossed the channel from Newhaven to Dieppe. It took three hours. Maudie was a bad sailor but her fastidiousness prevented her from being actually sick. She sat quite still on a seat, her face grey-green, her mouth tightly closed. She wore a little navy-blue cloche hat with a scarlet ribbon, a pale grey suit with a crisp white blouse and smelled as always deliciously of violets.

'Just don't speak to me,' she said, at the start of the crossing.

I stood solicitously near her most of the time. Mother, a splendid sailor, looked eagerly about her and strode gaily up and down the deck.

Eventually the French coast came into sight and we entered the harbour. Blue-overalled French porters, with their leather luggage straps instead of trolleys, swarmed on board as soon as the boat was secured to the quay. Maudie, still feeling pretty green, was (as always) perfectly in command of herself. With almost no French between the

three of us we secured a porter, who escorted us to the train for Paris.
Once the train started I sat looking out of the window at what seemed
to me the most interminably dreary countryside I had ever seen. This was
as big an anti-climax as our arrival in London had been in September
1918 nine years earlier. The country seemed to *rush* by as a flat grim
greyish land dotted with ugly little grey houses with windows that
opened the wrong way. However, we were speeding towards Paris where
we had to change trains. Mother and I had dinner on the train. Aunt
Maudie couldn't eat and stayed in the carriage.

After four hours we steamed slowly into the Gare du Nord. It was
far darker and blacker than any London station. If only we had had
time even to peer beyond its grimness and glimpse the enchanted city –
but there wasn't time and we all had the gravest distrust of French
timetables. 'Foreigners never kept to time' – we had heard that often
and we believed it, so that even if we had had time we would never
have dared to leave the station just in case the train for Brittany
should leave before the scheduled hour. So, with another blue-bloused
porter who seemed by his gruff manner to dislike us, we changed
platforms to wait for the night train for Quimper where in the early
morning we would have to change again to the local train for Pont
Aven.

We didn't have sleepers but fortunately got a carriage to ourselves.
Maudie and I shared one side. Mother had the other, where she lay
down and slept peacefully through the night. Maudie, still feeling
nauseated from the crossing, didn't sleep at all and neither did I for
lack of space. We arrived at Quimper about six in the misty morning
and woke Mother who said, 'Oh for some coffee.'

Maudie said, 'Oh, Beanie dear, don't mention coffee. The very
thought makes me feel sick.' 'Why, haven't you slept? I slept like a top.'

This made Maudie and me laugh, as she said to me, 'Trust Beanie,
with a side to herself, she's as bright as a button.'

We got our luggage out and went into the station café. Mother
drank hot coffee. I sipped some. Maudie again couldn't manage a
mouthful but insisted she'd soon be all right. 'Once we get there,' she
said.

The Concarneau train was in a side-bay. It stopped at all stations,
Pont Aven being two or three before Concarneau. We got in among
chattering Breton peasants in their working-day costumes, black
dresses, white coifs and wooden sabots for the women, black smocks
and breeches and sabots for the men. At each stop some would clump
out and others get in, always laden with large bundles or market
baskets.

*

We arrived at Pont Aven at about 7.30. The sun was shining and the day was already quite hot. A few people were about. Women were doing their washing in the rushing streams that interlaced the little town. There was no one to meet us. We took a taxi: the driver couldn't find the villa at first, but eventually, after enquiries, dropped us at a little gate at the foot of a pine-covered steeply sloping garden with a narrow pathway leading to a small villa still tightly shuttered.

My stomach tightened with the old fear of strangers, and the same sick feeling I used to have at early morning Mass at the convent. We trailed up to the house and knocked. A sleepy maid opened the door and very soon woke Young Madame, who came down in her dressing-gown. She talked volubly in French which we did not understand. However, she realised who we were and soon directed the maid to take Mother and Maudie to the cottage where they were going to lodge for a week before returning to England. They went off, and I was taken to my room by young Madame.

Later I went down to the cottage where Maudie and Mother were staying. It was in the lane at the foot of the garden. I found them quite recovered and in the best of spirits. I cried from exhaustion and strangeness and Mother was terribly cross with me.

'Just like you,' she said. 'For goodness sake stop crying.'

Maudie was kind and said, 'Oh darling, it's just tiredness. You'll feel better later.'

And by the evening I did. I met old Madame Mativet and the other girls at lunch to which Mother and Maudie were invited. There were two *bonnes* – one to cook and one to do housework and serve the meals. All was orderly and *comme il faut* and by the afternoon we were all getting on splendidly.

Mother and Maudie loved their week. The cottage where they had bed and breakfast was simple but spotlessly clean. The Breton widow who owned it impressed them with her daily airing of all the bed-clothes and feather mattresses in the sun and her continual washing in the stream of her household linen. During the week Mother and Maudie went everywhere with us, to cafés and to the sea at the mouth of the river by the local *vedette*.

Mother had not been out of England since her honeymoon, and enjoyed every moment of it. All her life she could enjoy herself tremendously if she had something to enjoy. I know that her life was sexually frustrated due mainly to her puritanical Victorian upbringing. This must have been so for millions of women of her period and some women in any period. Sexual frustration nips the spirit like a frost. To me the extraordinary women are those who, like two of my aunts, Muriel and Joan, and their cousin and mine, Lucy, found work and companionship of friends a substitute and were not apparently harmed at all. My Aunt Winifred's whole life was frosted and hurt although she would have scorned to admit it – indeed been ashamed. Another cousin, Jessie Wedgwood Kempson, Lucy's oldest sister, was completely soured and inclined to be sadistic. I suffered from her treatment.

Pont Aven was a lovely place in those days, still very unspoilt, although more built up than its reputation of *quatre maisons, quatorze moulins*. It is on a river fed by many small streams which used to work the mills, and is only a few kilometres from the sea. We spent whole days on the wide sandy beaches sun-bathing and swimming. Sometimes we would go to Concarneau, the sardine-fishing port. The harbour was crammed with boats and the nets hung like blue veils from every mast and spar.

Our household consisted of the two Madames Mativet and four girls, including myself. I, just seventeen, was the youngest. The oldest, Jo, was nineteen. In between were Audrey and Frances, an American girl. We all got on very well together. After the first month Audrey and Frances left, their time being up.

Then came the excitement of the summer in the person of Le Baron de Montreuil who was Young Madame's lover. He was very tall, rather heavy and wore a black patch over one blind eye. He'd lost his eye in the 1914 war. Young Madame, who had tended to be moody, now became gay and happy, her eyes shining with pride and pleasure. She and Le Baron, '*très distingué*', she said, spent a good deal of time alone together, but were very nice indeed to Jo and me and included us in little drinks at cafés, motor-boat trips and once an expedition to stay the night at an island called Belle Isle. Before Audrey left she had told us about the Baron. She said that he was married and lived in Paris, where he hardly ever saw Young Madame, but always took his summer holiday alone and at a place where he knew she'd be, so that they could have two months in each other's company. Young Madame was far from well off, but with a great deal of care, making and renovating clothes herself, looked extremely chic whenever she went out with the Baron. We got to know various people around, including an English couple called Charnley and some French people called Sablé.

*

During this hot summer time passed quickly. The Baron returned to Paris and only Jo and I were left with the Mativets. I remember one evening just before we left Pont Aven for Paris, Monsieur and Madame Sablé, our neighbours, had visited the villa and Jo and I escorted them back to their house in the dusk. As we walked Monsieur Sablé put his arm through mine and lightly caressed my bare forearm with his fingers. I shivered with pleasure and felt slightly ashamed.

I told Jo later, who laughed pityingly. Jo at nineteen had a young man whose mistress she'd been for a year. I envied her and her marvellous freedom and knowledge. It was one thing to talk about lovers and mistresses as I had learned to do, but to *have* a lover and the knowledge and joy that clearly went with it would be so infinitely wonderful. But how, oh, how was I even to get a husband with my fears and ignorance and my parents' strictness? I knew that Mother was extremely anxious for me to get a husband when *she* considered me old enough, but of course it must all be very correct. Lovers were unmentionable at home. I became quite obsessed with a longing at least to know what it would be like. I wished in my heart that I could go back to Dartmouth with its teeming numbers of cadets and officers with an 'experience' behind me. But how? How? And indeed, if I had, what decent man would ever marry me? According to Mother if a girl were so cheap as to give herself to a man before marriage that was the end of her.

It certainly didn't seem like the end for Jo, who appeared fairly confident that her lover would marry her eventually and I daresay he did. She was very attractive, like the young Jessie Matthews, with short brown hair cut in a fringe. She was very *chic*. Any of Madame's men friends who met Jo were attracted by her at once. The only one who'd taken any notice of me was middle-aged, fat, short Monsieur Sablé, and my longings were so great that the touch of his hand on my arm had made me shiver with pleasure.

*

Jo and I travelled back to Paris together, as the Mativets had gone ahead to prepare the apartment. Jo dressed and made up very carefully because her lover was to meet her. They were going to spend the weekend in Paris together and then go home to England. I would be the only paying guest left, as Madame had only room for one at the apartment in Passy.

Jo's young man was at the Gare de Lyon. I tried not to watch their meeting, but what I saw looked very correct, just like a married couple. I had to get to the apartment, so after a hurried good-bye to Jo

I got a taxi, gave the address and sat on the edge of the seat so as to see everything we passed. Not a moment must be lost. The streets looked a bit dark at first, but suddenly we drove through the Place de la Concorde and into the Champs Elysées, with the Arc de Triomphe at the top. I had never seen anything so lovely as the long wide street gradually rising to the great arch at the far end, all those gleaming cafés and restaurants with their foreground of pavement filled with little tables. As we reached the Place de l'Etoile I could see the naked flame burning on the tomb of France's Unknown Soldier.

Young Madame was very welcoming when I arrived. I was delighted by the little flat. The *salon* was formally arranged and divided from the *salle à manger* by double doors. I had a small but cosy bedroom and looked forward to the three months ahead.

During my first week Young Madame escorted me to museums and picture galleries, starting with the Louvre and the Carnavalet. After that I went about a great deal on my own. I learned my way about by métro and bus. I had a small allowance but managed quite well. I didn't want to take taxis. I thought it far cleverer to go by the public transport. I loved every moment; I walked and rode miles.

I met the Mativets' friends, and about once a fortnight Young Madame took me to the theatre or the opera. I saw *Faust, La Bohème, Carmen, L'Arlésienne, Le Bourgeois Gentilhomme, Phèdre*, and many more. I visited Versailles many times and was dazzled by the beauty of the great palace and its superb gardens and park, and Le Petit Trianon. I went to Fontainebleau in the autumn when the great beech trees of the forest were almost afire with colour. The time passed all too quickly.

Mother came over to fetch me at the end of November and stayed at the Mativets for a week. I loved showing her round and took her to the opera wearing my *robe de style*. It was brilliant blue taffeta, sleeveless, with a silver band round its ballet length hem, and had the 'new' waist in the right place instead of round the behind as had been the fashion during the early twenties. Young Madame had chosen the material and it was made by a good dressmaker. It was one of the simplest but loveliest dresses I have ever had. I think it cost the equivalent of £20, which in those days was a great deal of money. I can remember that to my great pleasure a few people stared at me, as Mother and I walked in the foyer during the intervals.

Chapter Ten

Royal Naval College & RADA

We returned to Dartmouth I had so loved as a child at the beginning of October 1927. I was seventeen and a half years old and felt very sophisticated with my French attitude towards lovers and mistresses which had shocked Mother, and yet I was still entirely ignorant of the facts of life.

The Royal Naval College stands on a hill in view of the estuary and harbour of the river Dart. The main building to be seen from Kingswear and the river is long and three-storeyed with a clock tower in the centre. This clock strikes bells as in a ship instead of the hours. In front of the main building is a parade ground with a figurehead of Britannia, from the last cadet training ship of that name. She, whose binnacle had been used as the font for my christening, stood, trident in hand, gazing towards the sea. Behind the huge figurehead was a flagstaff on which the White Ensign is raised at sunrise and lowered at sundown to the mournful sounds of a bugle. The big hall is called the quarter-deck and the officers' rooms cabins. There is a wardroom for officers and gun-rooms (living-rooms) for the cadets. The rooms they sleep in were still called dormitories. The Royal Naval College is run like a ship, and ship's terms are used. The Blue-jackets attached to the College are called the ships' crew and have HMS *Britannia* on their cap-ribbons.

Mother and I arrived at Kingswear by the Torbay Express from London at about four o'clock. Father had arranged with the Captain to have the Captain's barge (motor-boat) and coxswain to meet us at the Pontoon and take us direct to the College's own landing steps at Sanquay a little way up the river. The coxswain saluted smartly as we boarded the barge from Kingswear Pontoon and glided quietly and quickly away while the ordinary passengers went by the old *Mew* as I had done as a child. At Sanquay there was a car and driver to meet the luggage but we decided to do the steep climb up the steps on foot. They were the same steps down which Miss Cameron had so often taken Tony and me to pick primroses in what are called The Captain's

Woods. The steps and path at the top led to the front door of the Headmaster's house.

When we got there we were met by a very smart little parlour-maid and the housekeeper, a Jersey woman called Miss Le Lacheur. She was a dear, loving woman, rather pale and thin with yellowing white hair, but her eyes smiled through her thick spectacles. I liked her at once. The house which I had never seen, even in the days when I used to stay at The Keep, is low and square and very comfortable. A beautiful warmth from excellent central heating met you as you went into the square hall from the porch by the front door.

Before going upstairs Father said, 'I have a surprise for you. Would you like to come out and see before you go up to your room?' Of course when he said 'come out' I realised what it was, so went across to a small stable a little way from the house, and there was a lovely cream-coloured pony with his head over the loose-box whinnying as we approached. 'Biscuit' we called him. I felt almost choked with excitement of this new life. It was so entirely different from anything we had ever known. Four servants and a man for Father's clothes, a stable man to help me with the pony – marvellous comfort in every way. I was so overwhelmed that evening that I could hardly eat the dinner at the long dining-table where the parlour-maid waited in the room.

Our life had always been lived in the simplest way. One help and sometimes none was the most we had ever had, and although all this grandeur was very thrilling it was so terribly unfamiliar that at first I felt as if I was a visitor and had no home any more. Naturally in time one adapted oneself, but the comforts and service and complete change of the way of life were a great shock. However, I soon settled down. Luxury is very pleasant, especially if you have rarely experienced it.

*

The College ran a pack of beagles traditionally hunted by the commander on horseback. Those cadets who liked beagling followed on foot. There were about four cadet whips who wore shorts, blazers with special buttons, and velvet caps. The commander wore full hunting outfit, but his coat was navy-blue with a black velvet collar. The coat had brass buttons with B.B. engraved on them. A master, Mr Bashford, whom I had met as a child staying at The Keep, was hunt secretary. He rode and wore the uniform outfit. He looked exactly the same as he had done thirteen years before, with his pale face, light brown hair and pointed beard.

Anyone who had a horse followed on horseback and so I started going out twice a week. The horseback followers were few, usually the farmer over whose land we happened to be hunting, an officer or two, a few local girls and me.

The commander when I first went to Dartmouth was called Philip Neville. He was extremely good-looking and I fell in love at first sight. As time went on I seemed to develop a sort of mental nymphomania which I suppose was not surprising since one was surrounded by a few hundred cadets and officers apart from masters, but it was the officers that stirred *my* heart in their beautiful uniforms. On Sundays at mid-morning service I had a perfect view of this, to me, exquisite male congregation from my place between Father and Mother in the choir stalls, and I am afraid I paid very little attention to the service.

There was a custom at RNC that cadets should dance for about an hour every night on the quarter-deck. Masters' wives and daughters were allowed to join the dance on Saturdays, but as Headmaster's daughter, and if there had been a Captain's daughter, one could go every night. It seemed that I went to the heads of the senior term (November 1927), the Rodneys, in a big way, for they claimed me as their own special property and one evening a big row took place because one of the cadets from the term junior to the Rodneys had asked me to dance and I had accepted. On the night of the row I wasn't there. The Rodneys joined hands, spread out in a line across the quarter-deck and forcibly drove every other cadet from the floor. There must have been quite an uproar because Mr Bashford, working late in his classroom in the gallery, hearing the noise, went out and demanded to know what was going on. When he was told he apparently said it was to stop at once.

'You are treating her like a lounge-lizard,' he said.

This was reported to me by my particular beau, cadet captain Rodney Manners. I was enchanted. I expect today they would have had a 'sit-in', except that the situation could not arise today.

*

During our second winter Mother, who had done a certain amount of riding when she had had the opportunity, decided to buy a horse and come out beagling with me. She got an enormously heavy mare called Peaceful and became an indefatigable follower, looking quite beautiful in her neatly fitting side-saddle habit and bowler hat. I know that this riding period was almost the happiest time of her whole life. She adored it and seemed to blossom not only in looks but in attitude of mind. For the second time in her marriage she had got an interest outside domesticity and family. Instead of always feeling tired she became full of energy and life. She also took to coming dancing on the quarter-deck and young officers swarmed round her. She flirted outrageously, but what fun she was, and what fun she had.

She had some lovely clothes made for her, especially evening-dresses. It was a rule at RNC that anyone entering the building from dinner-time onwards should be 'dressed'. Father wore a dinner-jacket every night except Sundays, and even if Mother and I weren't going to dance on the quarter-deck we changed for dinner. I remember especially two of her evening frocks: one leaf-green velvet with tightly fitting bodice and swirling, dipping skirt – she looked like a flower in it; the other, rather the same shape but black satin with a flame-coloured feather flower at the waist, in which she looked almost sophisticated.

Her nickname as a girl, which was always used by Aunt Maudie and Aunt May and my cousins, was 'Beanie'. Alexander and Tony McMullen and Violet, May's daughter, called her Auntie Beanie and one gay evening she suggested to one young officer that he should call her Auntie Beanie. Others soon followed suit, and that she remained during the few happy heyday years before the slump and the Second World War. The end-of-term dance became called by some 'Auntie Beanie's night out'. I fear it was much frowned on by the professional staff, and their wives especially. Mother didn't care for her own sex very much and made it fairly clear that she thought the masters' wives for the most part pretty frumpish.

It is curious that, with her success with the opposite sex, she fussed me so terribly over what she called my lack of 'the art of leading men on'. I could never bear any kind of tricks. Tricks were an accomplishment in women of her generation, but not in mine. She started to try to educate me in flirting and I hated it. I really cannot think why she thought it necessary. I had plenty of young men around me. I think that perhaps the frustrations of her life made her take a vicarious interest in that side of my nature. She would question me endlessly, minutely, about every budding romance at the close of which she saw marriage. She quickly divined anything irregular and got into a fearful state. 'Is he honourable? Does he treat you properly?' etc. etc. Hours of questioning. And as I was, as I have already said, almost a mental nymphomaniac she must have had quite an interesting time up to a point. I wonder what she would have said if one day I had answered, 'Well, Mother, I went to bed with Lieutenant X last night.' Would she have fainted or shut up? Would she have turned me out of the house? Or would she have said I must of course never do it again but 'You must tell me exactly what happened.' I fear this is a rather cruel speculation but our relationship was at that period a very unhealthy one.

Father knew of it and one day he asked me to try and become less subservient to her and refuse to talk in this way. I was very weak where she was concerned for indeed I hated it too. Anyway I never did go to bed with any one of my romances. I and they instinctively felt it would be impossible. Nowadays, with the pill, young men and girls would think one must be mad, but I was totally ignorant of any form of contraception. I think the modern ways are happier, although the present 'free love' attitude possibly has its own difficulties and causes its own unhappiness of a different kind.

*

Through these four years my two brothers Nicholas and Robin were both at school but returning for the holidays. Nicholas was thirteen when we went to Dartmouth and at Shrewsbury School. He wanted to go into the navy as his career but Father thought it better he should enter by public-school entry rather than be under the eye of his own father at RNC. Robin was eleven and at prep school at Malvern. We three were still very close to each other even though I was now grown up and they were still children. When we were together we always seemed to find a level of our own.

Father bought them a rough Dartmoor pony called Dandy. He'd have been better named Devil, for that he was. Robin, never very keen on riding, became terribly nervous and gradually gave it up. Nicholas, a good rider, somehow managed Dandy's wild and bad temper. The first great difficulty used to be catching him. We would lure him with apples which he would snatch and then blowing, snorting and kicking, tear round the field with the apple in his mouth. If you got hold of his headstall and managed to slip a rope through the ring he would fight, rearing, pawing the air, lunging to and fro until he was exhausted when, trembling and sweating, he would at last let you lead him to the stable to be saddled and bridled. The next business was to mount him. This had to be done very quickly and, once on, Nicholas and I could control him. After he'd had a certain amount of exercise his excesses of temperament calmed down. We always thought he must have been very cruelly broken in or perhaps never completely broken at all. I think the former is the most likely. We bought another horse in 1929, a funny-looking dun mare with her head held too high but a tremendous goer. I loved her, and let Robin ride my quiet Biscuit which he really quite enjoyed.

Beautiful Robin. Looking back I realise what a maternal love I had for him. It had always fallen to me to look after him if he was unwell. It was to me he came in 1941, after he had been wounded in the trawler *Turquoise* and suffered shellshock. I know that he recovered his shattered nerves while staying quietly with Cousin Lucy, me and the children, Vanessa and Corin, who has grown a little like him. To look at, Robin still resembled Mother. He still had curly red-gold hair, her brilliant blue eyes, the difference being his thick dusty-miller's eyelashes, as we called them, and his same brilliant rosy complexion. It was a tragedy for us that he was killed in the war at twenty-five.

Nicholas and Robin and I spent a tremendous amount of time together in all their holidays. In spring and summer, as well as riding there were the boats. I had bought a small sailing dinghy and we were allowed to use the college cutters and rowing boats and occasionally motor-boats. With my brothers I was entirely happy and became like a child again, freed, during college leaves when most of the officers were away, from their torturing proximity. One spring-leave a lieutenant-commander, Edward Sim, who adored riding and owned a horse, asked me to stay at his house in Wiltshire, chaperoned by Nicky. It was the greatest fun, but after we got home he wrote asking me to marry him and as I wasn't in love with him I had to write that it wasn't possible, much as I liked him. We didn't see him again. He married later and was killed in the war. He was a delightful man, a sort of sailor-country squire, with great simplicity of character and a gentle sense of humour. He had a very deep voice and laugh which used to sound rather like 'haw-haw'. We nicknamed him 'Simmy' and we all liked him enormously. If he was ever duty-officer during the leaves he rode with us or went on picnics up the Dart which Father loved.

We would borrow one of the motor-boats and with baskets loaded with sausages, eggs and bacon, a kettle, coffee, etc., go up the river, landing at supper time on some stony beach. Father always made a fire and we cooked sausages and eggs and bacon over it.

Guy Grantham, a lieutenant-commander, and his mother and sister when they came to stay, joined us sometimes. Guy was skilled at sailing and sailed the college yacht *Amaryllis* on many trips, sometimes inviting me to join the cadet party. I dared not say no as I thought one ought to like sailing, but often if it was rough the cadets and I lay green in the scuppers all the afternoon. However, on fine calm days of light breezes I would enjoy it as much as anyone and would climb out on the bowsprit, dangling my feet in the water.

Guy was quite unlike the officers who feared being seen with a girl. He always invited me out in a completely unselfconscious way and I am sure no one ever dared tease him. He went to the top of his career, one of the navy's finest officers, and eventually became Governor of Malta.

*

I began to long for one of the officers to be in love with me whom I could be in love with in return, but the trouble was I was in love with all of them. Officers at the Royal Naval College if married weren't allowed to have their wives at the college, and bachelor officers taking up with girls were very frowned upon. What would the modern psychologists have said to that, I wonder? It was very difficult to get to know them because they were terrified of being teased if they took one out, and on the whole, except for a few, avoided it. However, they used to come to dinner and there was beagling for the riders among them, and so one way and another I did get to know one or two quite well.

The whole situation was pretty frustrating on both sides, so that I and one or two of them began to have exaggerated romantic ideas about each other, and in the summer term one warm evening after dining at our house an officer whom I barely knew asked me to marry him. I accepted at once and was very soon horrified at what I had done, especially as all the time I was in love with another one, but the one was bold and the other shy, so I accepted the bold one. The whole situation was completely unbalanced and quite abnormal and Mother was, as I have said, somewhat to blame, but equally so was the naval attitude of the RNC. These young men, the bachelor ones, at any rate, denied the normal company of girls, were absurdly frustrated. I had met few men beyond my two cousins, Alexander and Tony McMullen. Now I was suddenly surrounded by the 'cream' of the Senior Service. Of course I lost my head or, should I say, my heart, all round. This situation became very bad for me indeed and eventually I fell desperately in love with a subsequent commander who adored women and flirted with me quite a bit. When I realised he had no intention of marrying me in spite of a certain amount of kissing in the back drive, I became ill, collapsed and went to bed. Fortunately my nature was resilient and as my misery waned I began to think that I ought to work.

*

My mind turned again to the theatre. Cyril Maude who had retired to Devon to live, and who with his second wife became our friend, encouraged me to think of going into the theatre, but Mother and Father were still against it. They were sure I hadn't got what it takes to be an actress. I decided that I must get away from home. I suppose I realised that this absurd situation at the RNC was leading me nowhere. I was really too immature to marry and quite unrealistic about it. There had been one serious possibility of marriage with a truly remarkable man, but I wasn't in love with him. I loved him, but to me that was not enough.

Eventually with Cyril Maude's help it was agreed to let me attempt to get into RADA. Cyril Maude retired from the theatre when he was about sixty-five, married his second wife Beatrice and bought a place called Redcap House on the cliffs near Stoke Flemming, about three miles from Dartmouth. It was a lovely place and they were enormously hospitable. They loved people; the house was always full. He and his wife very soon invited us there and we became friends and constant guests. I met among others the late Lady Alexander, then about 80, with a thick enamel-like white make-up, Cyril's daughter Marjorie and his son John, later Judge Maude. Cyril had a barn converted into a room for parties or recitals; the walls were hung with photographs, paintings and caricatures of himself in his various parts. There were huge books full of his theatre and later film cuttings, and he never tired of showing these and talking about the theatre. This fed my ambition, and when I told him about it he was delighted. To Cyril anyone wanting to go into the theatre was worthy of encouragement and he would fan the faintest spark of talent.

At this moment, came the big financial depression. Father's salary was cut by a third. My brothers were still at school and he said he could not afford the RADA fees, absurd as this would seem to the Principal. Cyril suggested I should try for a half scholarship and this I somehow managed to get.

Cyril Maude was my good friend and counsellor. He had started an amateur group which I joined, called the Dartmouth Players, and directed it himself. He also asked me to play Lady Teazle to his Sir Peter in the two quarrel scenes from *The School for Scandal*. He made me follow his every inflection for, he said, you must play Sheridan with the greatest possible style and clarity. It was no good attempting to be realistic. Sir Peter had been one of his favourite parts opposite his first wife Winifred Emery. He gave me every gesture and we rehearsed and rehearsed to get it perfect. He was quite a stern, though encouraging, teacher.

We finally played the scenes in his great barn-room at a large party. I doubt if I was good, but he had somehow made me act it, and he was superb. Also, he had hired the most exquisite costumes, and I think I looked the part. Everyone was delighted, including my parents, and it was that evening that decided them to let me train for the professional theatre.

*

I was in a state of tremendous excitement when I went to London for the entrance test. I chose a speech from 'A Hundred Years Old', one of about five set speeches. I'd worked hard at it, but I know that I was too nervous to be good and it must have sounded a very set recitation. However, with some prodding from Cyril, Kenneth Barnes, the Principal, awarded me a half scholarship. This meant that, instead of paying £35 a term, Father only had to pay £17 odd.

I lived at Aunt Winifred's house in Chelsea. It was not very comfortable because she worked all day at the Chelsea Polytechnic and was in poor health. The house was terribly cold and as I was supposed to have had a hot midday meal at RADA, Aunt Winifred provided a light supper. She was always most loving and intensely interested in my work, and it was much better to have a home to come back to at the end of the day than a bed-sitting-room in a girls' hostel.

At RADA I worked as hard as was possible under the conditions. The school was far too full. Each class was very large, with a great many more girls than boys. This meant at least six girls to every leading part in the plays we rehearsed. Elocution was taught rather than voice production, and mime, movement and fencing; and lectures were given on costume and the history of the theatre.

Father gave me as good an allowance as he could afford, but it wasn't enough. I therefore economised over food in the canteen, eating buns or a sandwich and coffee for lunch, with the consequence that after a year I had become terribly anaemic and often felt giddy and breathless. I had never lacked good food since the convent and didn't realise that it had any relation to strength and health. My sandwich lunch and our snack supper at Aunt Winifred's at night wasn't enough to work on. However, I loved the work and the other students.

The sense of not belonging still persisted here; many of the students had affairs, many lived on their own. Also, most seemed to be able to afford to go to theatres in the evenings, which I also wanted and needed to do, but only managed a few times a term on account of lack of funds. I did see Peggy Ashcroft as Juliet at the Vic, and she freed and inspired me beyond anyone I can think of at the time. She was so young and so completely unmannered. She spoke Juliet's lines with all the poetry, but made them seem as if she had thought them herself at the moment. Her acting was a revelation of truth and I set myself to try to be like her. Marius Goring was her Romeo.

There were various competitions at the end of the term: one for the best performance of a ten-minute one-act play. I went in for and won the prize, tied with a little dark quiet girl called Joan Littlewood. Ida Lupino was in my year – she was only fourteen but her mother had passed her off as sixteen. She had her hair bleached almost white, and was also a student, always surrounded by boys, who seemed to encircle her in a little wall, from inside which one saw her dazzling smile lighting the spaces beyond her.

Chapter Eleven

King Alfonso

The terms at RADA were shorter than ordinary school terms. I always went home to Dartmouth for the holidays.

It was during a spring holiday or 'leave' as it was called at RNC that ex-King Alfonso XIII of Spain visited the college, where he stayed at the Captain's house to arrange for his son Prince Juan to join the following term, just over halfway through the course. The cadets and most of the officers and masters were away on leave. The Captain, Sidney Meyrick, and his wife gave a dinner party on the Saturday night of the royal weekend visit. They invited among others the duty officer, my parents and myself, also the Second Master and his wife. There were a number of young girls, friends of the Meyricks, staying for the weekend. The house was always full of various girl friends of their sons and if I was at home I was often included in their parties.

For this special evening I took a long time getting ready. I had a bath with lots of bath-salts and then spent about three-quarters of an hour over my face. I used very little make-up in those days – Pond's vanishing cream lightly powdered, a pale pink lipstick and a very little mascara on my fair eyelashes. Fairly pleased with the result, I put on my evening dress – shot taffeta with fitted bodice and a skirt made of layers of frills. Finally I practised curtseying in front of my long mirror before going down to the drawing-room to join my mother and father.

It was to be an informal dinner so Father was wearing a black tie and dinner jacket. I don't remember what Mother wore. I suppose I was too taken up with myself. I am sure she looked elegant and as beautiful as always. Mother looked me up and down and pulled at my hair a little to 'soften' it, as she said. She always did this, which annoyed me.

We were invited at 7.45 for dinner at 8. As we only had to cross our garden to the college and Captain's house in the corner by the chapel, we waited until 7.45 exactly. It was a fine evening, so we needed no coats to go the fifty yards along the gravel path to the small door behind the chapel which led to a passage and lobby of the chapel and so to the Captain's front door.

We were shown into the drawing-room. The ex-King stood in front of the fireplace, smoking a Turkish cigarette. He was surely the handsomest of the line of Hapsburgs. He had the slightly drop-ended nose, full mouth and protruding lower lip of the Velazquez portraits of earlier kings. There was a poetic melancholy about his expression which changed to gaiety when he smiled. His hair was black, greying very slightly at the temples, and a moustache like a shadow outlined his upper lip. A group of girls stood near him; also Captain and Mrs Meyrick.

The Captain came forward, and first my mother, then my father and lastly myself were presented. I curtsied low. Drinks were brought round by the Captain's coxswain. Conversation was muted. The King had an easy manner and a look of enjoyment. He asked questions ceaselessly during the quarter of an hour before dinner. We grouped and regrouped ourselves, talking rather self-conscious small-talk. More guests arrived and were presented. Just after 8 o'clock the coxswain announced dinner.

The King took Mrs Meyrick into the dining-room and we all followed, the older guests first and then the younger ones. The dining-room was dimly lit. There were branched silver candelabra at intervals on the mahogany table, the lighted candles reflected in the highly polished surface covered in gleaming silver.

King Alfonso sat on Mrs Meyrick's right, Father on her left. Mother sat on the right of the King. The rest of us sat along the opposite sides down the table length, each girl with a man on either side or vice versa. The coxswain and crew waited at dinner. This was the custom at the Captain's house, where he had his boat's crew as if it were a ship at sea.

The Meyricks had a wonderful social gift for making every occasion seem informal, at the same time observing the necessary formalities. When it came to dessert the electric lights were switched off, leaving the soft candle-light. Voices were lowered to fit the lessened light. Eyes and cheeks softened and glowed. The port was passed round, starting from the Captain who, when all the glasses were filled, proposed the toast of 'The King', which was our own sovereign at that time, King George V. After the toast cigarettes were passed which, if I remember correctly, none of the women took. Women never smoked at table when I was a girl, at any rate not in either the Captain's or Headmaster's house.

Candlelight gave an air of mystery to everyone. I looked towards the Spanish king, who talked animatedly to Mrs Meyrick and my father and mother in almost perfect English. Eventually Mrs Meyrick got up and all the girls and women followed, leaving the men to the port and nuts.

We went into the drawing-room for coffee and while waiting for the men to join us we talked. Soon the Captain brought King Alfonso and the other male guests to rejoin us. Immediately an air of excitement and gaiety filled the room. The King was in excellent spirits. He seemed like a boy on holiday. The Captain asked if he would like to play a game.

'Yes, yes, indeed. What do we play?' he said.

The Captain suggested charades.

The King was delighted. He said he knew the game and that the Captain and he would pick sides at once.

The King had first pick and to my delight he pointed to me and said, 'I will have you.'

When the sides were complete he said, 'We will act first, but we must go out and dress up.'

I cannot remember the word we chose to act, but whatever it was the King said that in the first scene he would play the part of a grandmother surrounded by her children.

'You,' he said, taking my hand, 'will be a boy. Come up to my room and dress up in my clothes.'

I was entranced. He ran up the wide stairs almost dragging me after him and took me into his bedroom, opened a wardrobe and got out a suit, handing me the trousers.

'Now, my dee-ar, take off your dress and dress up as me.'

I was a bit nervous but absolutely thrilled. However, I couldn't bring myself to take off my dress and so I said, 'Oh, Your Majesty, I can't take my dress off but I'll put on your trousers and tuck my dress into them.'

He watched me stuffing the frilled shirt into his immaculate black trousers with great amusement. I must have been a comic sight, but he seemed delighted.

We went down to the hall where Mrs Meyrick had found some odd garments, coats, scarves, etc. King Alfonso put on a cloak which belonged to one of the guests, wrapped a lacy shawl round his head, and put on a pair of spectacles he found on a table.

He then said, 'In this scene I am going to be the grandmother, and you,' looking at the girls but especially at me, 'are to be very loving to your grandmother (grandmos-air) and hug and kiss her a great deal.'

We went into the drawing-room and started the scene which, as I recollect it, was chiefly the King sitting in a winged armchair, looking a most extraordinary sight, with his right arm round me and his left round two of the other girls, holding us very close. We hugged and kissed him and made up a lot of ridiculous dialogue, and so did he, everyone speaking at once. I very much doubt if the word was ever guessed and I'm quite certain he didn't care whether it was or not.

I have no recollection of the rest of the game or what the other side did, but when it was over I took off the black trousers in the hall and shook out the frills of my dress. I went back to the drawing-room and the King called me to him and asked me about myself – my life. I could just see Mother and Father in the background, smiling as was everyone else. When royalty is present, even if it is ex, everyone wears a grin upon their faces, which they keep whether they are amused or not. Should anyone disapprove or feel envious, they smother their feelings and act like automata.

I told the King I was training to be an actress at the Royal Academy of Dramatic Art in London where I lived during the school terms.

He said, 'I wish to take an interest in your artistic career.'

A fairly unlikely statement, but I was naive to the point of idiocy in those days. I had no sophistication whatsoever and to my great disadvantage have very little now. This lack has made life difficult and often painful, but one is as one is. I don't think these things can be learned.

The King asked me for the address of RADA, which I gave him, and he said, more or less dismissing me at last, 'You will hear from me.'

For the rest of the evening he talked in turn to the guests and later retired with the Captain to his study to talk no doubt of the arrangements for his son Prince Juan to join the Royal Naval College.

*

Back in London for the summer term I found in the letter rack one morning a very elegant white envelope addressed to me. It had a very small gold crown on the back. It was from King Alfonso asking me to lunch with him the following week at Claridges, where he was making his headquarters.

I accepted by return of post.

Then came the problem of what to wear. I possessed very few clothes, as my dress allowance of £60 a year did not go very far. I had a pretty new cardigan suit, as they were then called. It was a deep violet colour. I had a white straw boater with a purple ribbon but felt doubtful about my only blouse. I told a more affluent student friend about my invitation and she said she would lend me a white silk blouse-top of hers that she had bought from Rhavis. I had some good shoes and bought a pair of white gloves.

The day arrived at last. I got out of the last morning class and Aminta de Leon helped me to dress in the students' cloakroom. Her white silk blouse certainly put the final touch to the outfit. I made up my face very carefully with a light make-up, a little more mascara than usual perhaps, but except for the stage I didn't know how to do more. Aminta thought the result was very good and so, frankly, did I. She saw me off in the taxi.

It was a lovely day. The sun was shining and yet it was not too hot. I was elated. When the taxi turned into Brook Street I realised I was early, so I told the driver to stop so that I could walk the rest of the way.

I walked very slowly to Claridges and managed to arrive just on one o'clock. Inside I saw a liveried hotel flunkey, and very quietly I said, 'King Alfonso.'

The man bowed and gestured with his white-gloved right hand to another flunkey in similar uniform who, slightly bowing, led me forward across the deep-piled carpet. By now I was able to take in the hushed and lush surroundings: white pillars, many mirrors and finally, a few yards ahead, the King standing with an elderly man at his side. I was flushed and smiling.

When I reached the King I held out my right hand. He took it in his and raised it to his lips. He then introduced me to the Duke of Miranda, his courtier and friend. Our entrance into the restaurant was one of the big moments of my life, a delightful slow progress through bowing waiters to the table.

At lunch the King was entrancing, attentive and gay. The Duke was elderly, distinguished, smiling and quiet. They made me feel like a princess, drawing me out, making me talk about myself, which I did entirely unselfconsciously. When we first sat down the King gave me a red rose for my buttonhole.

He put it in himself and then said, 'Do you know you are wearing the royal colours of Spain?'

I thought, Oh, happy coincidence. I said, 'I am so glad, Your Majesty.'

Lunch was correct, social, gay, perfect. Before I left, King Alfonso said, 'I want to visit your Royal Academy of Dramatic Art and see you at one of your rehearsals of a play you are doing.'

I thought this was a rather difficult request to fulfil, but if he wanted it he should have it. I would have complied with any request except the giving of myself, and that this was what he hoped for had not occurred to me, and did not until some years later.

*

As soon as possible I went to Kenneth Barnes and told him King Alfonso's request. Kenneth was rather tickled by the idea, partly because he was a tremendous snob and this was a 'catch'.

It was early in the term and the only play in which I was rehearsing was some very poor modern comedy in which I had an entirely unsuitable part. If I had had any sense I would have refused to be seen in something so detrimental to myself, but in my naïveté all I could see was that the ex-King's request must at any cost be gratified.

In the early stages of rehearsal we worked in classrooms and Kenneth foolishly decided that King Alfonso should see a classroom rehearsal in all its bareness and lack of illusion. Had he been more sensitive or more of a showman, I think, he would have arranged to have it in one of the two theatres with at least some rough lighting.

The visit was arranged for an afternoon about two weeks after I had lunched at Claridges. I, the cause of the whole thing, was ignored entirely about any of the arrangements, which when I was told about them seemed to be like those for a village fête. The students involved in the rehearsal had to be briefed and we were told that the cast and teacher producer would assemble in the classroom at 3 p.m. We would wait for Kenneth Barnes, his wife, his secretary and a few senior staff to bring the King into the classroom, and at a signal from Kenneth Barnes would start a run-through of an act of the play. I was glazed with nerves and I knew I had no hope of giving anything more than a calculated recitation of my lines without feeling or meaning. My hands were clammy, my cheeks burning.

After I had waited in misery for about twenty minutes, Kenneth and Daphne Barnes with his secretary and others came in with King Alfonso. I dared not look at him. We were told to start. I have no recollection, except of somehow getting through and feeling completely hollow. My artistic career! I was wretched and ashamed.

After this fiasco was over Kenneth Barnes led the King, and we followed, into another classroom where an enormous tea was laid out. There were plates of sandwiches and plates of cakes, but before tea was passed round by the students Kenneth Barnes presented first his wife Daphne and then the staff to King Alfonso.

Daphne Barnes was an extremely handsome but slightly hysterical young woman. She was dressed very smartly in a lightweight dark-blue silk suit, small hat and enormous pearl earrings. When she was presented she giggled as she curtsied and fell over backwards. I wished the earth might swallow me and the whole proceedings.

The rest of the staff were presented. The King was agreeable but I could sense his boredom. I don't think he looked at me again. My shame was so great that the departure of ex-King Alfonso XIII of Spain from the classroom, RADA and my sight or knowledge for ever was eliminated from my mind. I cannot remember any moment for Daphne Barnes's unfortunate behaviour, anything said by anyone then or later.

Let there be no mistake, I was not 'in love'. I had merely been brushed by a fairy-tale dream. It had not affected me in any way except for resentment at Kenneth Barnes's handling of an awkward situation. And so I tried to erase it from my mind.

Chapter Twelve

Stratford 1932

At RADA if you did well enough, in fact if it was thought you had reasonable talent, you were able to get through the whole training in four terms. This I managed, and in my final term for the Public Show, as it was called, in which one was cast in an act or scene from one of about six plays, I was given Rosalind in a scene from *As You Like It*. The late Dorothy Green directed.

At the show I won the Anmer Hall prize and was afterwards sent for by W. Bridges Adams, Director of the Memorial Theatre, Stratford-on-Avon. The result was a contract for £4 a week for the season of 1932. My parts in the first six plays were as follows: first witch in *Macbeth* to be directed by Komisarjevsky; a dancer in his *Merchant of Venice*; Phoebe in *As You Like It*; lady-in-waiting in Tyrone Guthrie's *Richard II*; Virgilia in *Coriolanus*; and Hero in *Much Ado About Nothing*. I understudied Fabia Drake as Rosalind in *As You Like It*; Anew McMaster was the superb Coriolanus, George Hayes Macbeth, Shylock and Richard II. There was a large company. Many were old Bensonians: Stanley Lathbury, Eric Maxon, Gerald Kay Souper. John Wyse was the very golden, handsome juvenile playing Orlando, Bassanio, Malcolm, etc.

Eight days' rehearsal were allotted to each play, two days to each play at a time, so that, for instance, the first three weeks when we were at a large rehearsal room in London we did two days' *As You Like It*, two days' *Richard II* and two days' *Macbeth*, and so on in rotation: a ridiculously inadequate arrangement, quite incomprehensible in such an organisation with money at its disposal even in those times.

My first two days were as first witch in *Macbeth*. It was extremely exciting to work with Komisarjevsky, already a legendary figure, even though my part was very small and for me difficult. The sets and costumes for the production were designed by Komisarjevsky himself, assisted by Leslie Blanche, whose job it was to carry out his ideas by supervision. The scenery was made of strange pillars set on rostrums interchangeable in position and painted a silvery aluminium colour. The men were dressed in grey battle-dress, with German steel helmets, but wearing badges and orders, according to status, made of aluminium kitchen utensils strung into circles or oblongs and looking very effective and not recognisable for what they were. The make-ups were uniform – No. 9 as a foundation left unpowdered, lake mouths and shading. The three witches were rag-picking beggars, and in the opening scene we were picking over the corpses on the battlefield and spoke in Scots dialect.

On the whole the company were enthusiastic and supported the brilliant director well. I mention this because, with the old Bensonians of the company who were deeply rooted in Sir Frank's tradition, innovations were usually greeted, to say the least, cautiously, and at the worst hostilely. George Hayes worshipped Komisarjevksy because Komisarjevsky believed in George and told him he was in advance of his time. Fabia always worked loyally all out, to the limit of her overstrained physique, for each producer, whether she agreed with his ideas or not. Her courage was enormous. She was extremely sensitive and had been grossly overworked for many seasons, culminating in a US tour on which she was so exhausted she had to be dressed by her dresser while she sat in her chair, but she got through and was a lovely Portia, Rosalind and Beatrice, and an excellent Lady Macbeth in this, my first, 1932 season.

*

Richard II was directed by Tyrone Guthrie, then about 28 years old. He conceived the idea of *Richard II* as a primitive icon to look at, but this did not quite fit with acting. However, the young new members of the cast were intensely enthusiastic, including myself. George Hayes as Richard, and already too old for the part, was unhappy and out of sympathy with Guthrie, who had great difficulty directing him. There were continual disagreements, ending in near revolution at the first dress-rehearsal. Guthrie kept his temper and by way of refreshment collected his young supporters together late at night after the dress-rehearsal and taught us most lovely madrigals and rounds: 'Rose, Rose', which we sang in the Queen's Garden scene, 'White Sand and Grey Sand', 'London's Burning' and others. We were at his feet. The old Bensonians all gave him hell by way of laughter behind his back and general non-cooperation. However, Tyrone Guthrie was tough and could take it, and did, without any show of anger.

As You Like It was directed by Bridges Adams in a conventional but charming style.

I was greatly in awe of Anew McMaster. When at the first rehearsal in the rehearsal room without books, it came to the moment of meeting in Act I with mother, wife and child, and Coriolanus after greeting Volumnia, his mother, turns to Virgilia, his wife, saying 'My gracious silence, hail', I averted my mouth when he had to kiss me.

In front of the entire company he said in his resonant voice: 'Dear, will you give me your lips?' Blushing scarlet I did, and was kissed in a most passionate manner.

Later we became excellent friends and I played Ophelia to his Hamlet. Mac had played Coriolanus superbly and the critics applauded him, but he was not suited to the subtleties of the introspective prince and the critics said so in strong terms. I had by then become the 'new find' and whatever I did for a short time was praised. Mac and I quite understood this situation and he, ever resilient, didn't mind at all. We used to laugh together a great deal, and before I went on for one of my scenes in *Hamlet* he would be waiting in the wings for his next scene and used to say: 'Now dear, on you go and hurry up. You're all very well in your tin-pot way but remember, it's me they want to see!' I grew very fond of him. With his huge physique, he was the opposite of The Method, acting always on instinct but filling the stage and the theatre with glowing warmth, a real *actor*.

The Merchant of Venice was another Komisarjevsky production revived from the 1931 season with Fabia Drake as Portia, George Hayes as Shylock and John Wyse a glittering Bassanio. The sets were a brilliantly coloured Commedia del'Arte Venice, all red and gold tumbling palazzos and stanchions for gondolas. There were virtually two scenes, Venice and Belmont. Belmont was set on a lower lift stage, so that Venice set on two sliding stages parted in the middle and Belmont with Portia, Nerissa, maids and negro servants rose in a golden tableau from below. It was breathtaking. The music was Bach's Suite in G for flute and strings. I was one of the Commedia del'Arte dancers who came dancing across the bridges of the Venice canals at the beginning and end of the play. It was a thrilling, warm and highly successful production.

Much Ado About Nothing was directed by Bridges Adams. Fabia was Beatrice, dressed like one of the Infantas of Spain in a Velazquez painting. I, as Hero, was dressed like the little Infanta in white and scarlet. The clothes and wigs were cumbersome and difficult to act in, especially for Beatrice. Fabia said we looked like demented spaniels.

*

After three weeks' rehearsal in London the company went to Stratford for the final three weeks' rehearsal. I lodged at a house called Avon Croft, which was half of the Dower House in Old Town, near Holy

Trinity Church, all timber and sloping floors and full of atmosphere. I had a bed-sitting-room and all meals for 25 shillings a week. Mrs Barnard, my landlady, was a poor cook but a dear, kind woman. I was still terribly anaemic from my undernourishment during my training time at RADA. I felt the cold of March badly, and I became easily exhausted, and yet if I ate too much I got indigestion; so it was a struggle against odds. In the company I suffered the same odd-man-out feeling as always. People were friendly but I didn't feel one of them. However, I settled into my digs quite happily, thanks to Mrs Barnard.

The week of dress-rehearsals was killing. Every night we were in the theatre until four or five in the morning, and the week of six first nights was consequently pretty agonising for an exhausted company. My first night on the professional stage was the opening night of the season as Hero in *Much Ado About Nothing*. I was so excited that I wasn't nervous. I can feel the extraordinary thrill of excitement and dreams fulfilled to this day, as the scarlet curtain rose. This was *it* for me. Here I was at last, appearing on the professional stage. I'd *got there*, after years of longing and discouragement. Exhaustion, anaemia, indigestion, were forgotten that night. I believed myself in love with my Claudio, John Wyse. All seemed perfection.

During the second week with very small parts I recovered from the lack of sleep of the dress-rehearsal week. Once the first six plays were on, conditions for the next three plays were much better; each had a month's rehearsal.

About a week after the opening Bridges Adams sent for me and told me he had decided that I was to be the Juliet in his production, the next, of *Romeo and Juliet*, opposite John Wyse as Romeo.

I felt giddy with the news; it was so fantastic. Feeling faint, I staggered along to the Dirty Duck pub run by Jim; and Mrs Jim, seeing I was groggy, made me sit down quickly while Jim put a mug of Flowers beer in my hand.

'It's fow-ud (food) yer want dear,' he said, 'and beer is fow-ud.'

I drank it down, and another, and felt better, but couldn't eat lunch. I ran back to Avon Croft to tell Mrs Barnard and to write to my parents.

We rehearsed *Romeo* during May. There was a heat wave and I found it terribly tiring. Playing Juliet for the first time was for me like a passionate love affair and equally exhausting.

Bridges decided that to help me avoid straining my voice in the large theatre we would have a permanent set placed forward against the proscenium arch so that most of the action could take place on the apron. There was a permanent balcony right across the stage.

Underneath its pillars were the ballroom, Juliet's bedroom and the tomb in turn, but the action and outdoor scenes were played in front of this on the apron. The costumes were Elizabethan, not the most becoming I think, but from the 'cords' scene onwards I was in a white shift and long, grey, woollen white-lined cloak. Bridges was endlessly patient and loving and nursed me through those rehearsals. I became terribly tired and nervous as the first night approached. Also, although my parts were small in the other plays, I had no night off at all. On Saturday, a week and two days before the dress-rehearsal, I collapsed and felt too weak to get out of bed. I couldn't stop crying. Mrs Barnard sent a message to the theatre to say that I would have to miss morning rehearsal. I asked her to take a telegram to the post office, for my parents. It said, 'Please come. Better Dad than Mother. Rachel.'

Father arrived that afternoon, white and breathless. He had almost run from the station. The sight of him restored me. He went down to the theatre to see Bridges and got me off the matinée and evening performance and promised Bridges he would have me fit for the Monday rehearsal.

On the Sunday we got up very late and he took me to lunch at the Arden and gave me burgundy to drink.

I slept all the afternoon, and then we went and sat in the little garden next to the site of New Place, Shakespeare's last house in Stratford. It was peaceful there, smelling of sun-warmed yew and early roses. Father said he would ask for me to be let out of *The Merchant of Venice*, so that I could have one night off the week before the opening. Bridges was entirely understanding, Father said.

On Monday I went back to rehearsal restored. Father left me provided with a case of red wine. There was one week to go before the first night. I had lunch every day, at the Arden Hotel at Father's expense. My £4 wouldn't stretch to lunches out.

A week later, Monday, was a dress rehearsal all day until 5 o'clock. Mother and Father had arrived with Cyril and Beatrice Maude. Mother and Father stayed at an hotel and he came round to see me for a moment between the dress rehearsal and the first performance. I now quote from his book:

> We found Rachel lying on her bed trying to get rested before the performance. She looked desperately tired and fragile. From all across the room I could see the pulse plunging in her neck.

I didn't sleep in the break before the evening performance but lay still. At 6.45 I went down to the theatre. The beloved dresser who looked after me and other girls, Marie Humphries, or 'Pumfie' as I called her, was dressing me. She was quiet, calm and collected.

As I made up I began to feel some life coming back to my limbs, and by the time I was carefully made up and dressed in my first gold-and-white brocade dress I was feeling well and excited. Fortunately for Juliet, her first entrance is a little delayed and her first two scenes – the one with her mother beginning, 'Madam I am here, what is your will', the second the ball-room scene when she meets Romeo and they speak the sonnet beginning with Romeo's 'If I profane with my unworthy hand' – are small, so that Juliet has a gentle beginning and can ease her way into the play. I was in love and I played Juliet on that entirely. Every word I said I truly meant, and by the end of the balcony scene I was amazedly enjoying myself and said as I passed the stage manager's prompt corner, 'Barbara, I'm enjoying it!'

This was a fatal mistake as she was an envious mischief-maker. She reported my remark to Randle Ayrton, the stage director, who thought I was spoiled and conceited and took it out of me for the rest of the season. However, I was unaware of the effect at the moment and in any case had no time, since one is *on* for the greater part of the play, with almost no break from the 'cords' scene onwards. I went all out emotionally. I hadn't the technique to save myself in any way. It was fortunate for me that we never had to play two performances consecutively, for I could not have managed this physically.

Next day I could hardly move again, but the notices were really lovely, especially *The Times*. And so elation kept me going and the next night I only had to be a lady-in-waiting in *Richard II*.

Mother and Father and Cyril and Beatrice Maude were very happy, and so was I. Mother stayed on for some weeks, which I loved. She had never been a sweeter, gayer companion, and everyone liked her.

The next production was *The Taming of the Shrew*, which I was not in, and so, with my days and one night or matinée a week free and one good meal a day, I began to get much stronger.

At the end of the season Bridges asked me to return the following year and play the juvenile leads. He offered me Ariel in *The Tempest*, the Princess of France in *Love's Labour's Lost*, Olivia in *Twelfth Night*, Titania in *A Midsummer Night's Dream*, Juliet in the revival of *Romeo and Juliet*, and Hero again in *Much Ado About Nothing*. John Wyse was coming back, but not Fabia. Dorothy Black took Fabia's place; she played Beatrice, Viola, Rosalind and Helena. I was out of *Julius Caesar*.

Anmer Hall, the Manager of the Westminster Theatre, asked Bridges if he could have *Romeo and Juliet* with the entire company for a season at the Westminster. I was terribly anxious to play Juliet in London, but Bridges, no doubt wisely, wouldn't let it go. He said it had been carefully planned for the Stratford stage and might not transfer well and if it should fail it would spoil the revival for the 1933 season.

*

I had saved £60 out of my £4 a week and with it I decided to take a room in London and try my luck during the winter months. Anmer Hall put on one of the plays by the Quintero brothers, *The Lady from Alfaqueque*, with Gillian Scaife, John Wyse, Geoffrey Toone and me, but it was a failure and I was soon out of work. With no money coming in it became increasingly difficult to stay in London. I had to be very economical and couldn't afford to go to the theatre, so that the days were spent visiting managers of theatre and films and continually ringing my agent.

I found film interviews particularly humiliating. One was always treated like some animal for market; the interviewers rarely spoke to me but looked me up and down quickly, dismissing me with 'We'll let you know'.

My only humiliating theatre interview was with Gilbert Miller at the St James's. Cyril Maude had given me an introduction to him, and with an appointment I went along one morning. He was a repulsive mountain of flesh with his beady eyes sunk in his puffy face.

He looked at me as if I were a slug and said in an insulting manner, 'What have you come here for?'

I said, 'Mr Maude wrote to you, I think, Mr Miller.'

He went on, 'Well, you're no good to me unless you're a star. I want stars for my shop-window. Don't come to me until you are a star.'

I realised he had only let me come and see him in order to turn me down. If I had had any guts I would have slapped his face, but I was intimidated.

My happiest interview was with Bronson Albery who, though unable to offer me any work, was courteous and kindly and very encouraging.

Some days I just walked in Kensington Gardens to pass the time, feeling lonely and unwanted. It was often said in those days that if you played in Shakespeare no one would want you for a modern play. You became categorised very easily. One day just before the Stratford season I was sent for by Basil Dean about a play called *Touch Wood*.

Dean was very pleasant but said, 'I put young girls through it, you know, Miss Kempson. I make them or break them.'

'I've heard that, Mr Dean,' I said, 'and I'm going back to Stratford.'

I was a great deal more in command of myself at that interview than with Gilbert Miller. Basil Dean had a reputation of being a sadist, and this has been vividly recounted in Moss Hart's *Act One*.

*

Finally, no matter how economical I was, my £60 ran out and I had to give up my bed-sitting-room and return to Dartmouth and wait until it was time to go back to London for the Stratford rehearsals.

I was older now by four years and the theatre was my passion, so that Dartmouth seemed to have lost its magic for me. The horses had been sold and I knew so few of the people except for some masters and their wives. The house was still 'home', but the life of the college, its officers and cadets had gone cold for me, like an exhausted love-affair. I felt terribly sad about this and somehow disloyal.

Beloved Father, however, remained the linchpin and he and I went for long walks together and visited Bozomzeal, the farm where he had his shooting. I followed him and David Foale, the young farmer, as they walked with their guns in search of pheasants or partridges and we would go back for tea in the stone-flagged parlour where old Mrs Foale, David's mother, joined us and was hostess.

We always loved the Foales from the early days of arrival at Dartmouth when Father first made friends with old Mr Foale and hired the shooting. Mrs Foale was small and dark and very pretty with her apple cheeks and slurry Devon voice. David, their son, was very quiet, but he adored the farm and shooting with Father, who loved his companionship more than that of anyone he knew. I think with David he recalled his youth at Birchyfield; Bozomzeal was Father's escape into his romantic world, but a very real one. When I was at home in September we often took a picnic-lunch, and after walking across the fields we would sit on the bramble-covered hillside high above the Dart, eat our sandwiches and then, lying against a sunny bank, talk drowsily in the hot noon sun.

I loved Ellen Foale, and in the Second World War she came and cooked and kept house for us while I was working. She is in my mind a link with the country as it used to be. She told me about her life as a young farmer's bride: how the kitchen was full of men at midday dinner; of the food they ate and the rough cider they drank; of how the swedes and turnips tasted sweet if you cut and ate them raw. She said it was because only farm manure was used: artificial fertilizers were unknown. By the time we first knew them Charlie, her husband, was old and ill and the farm had gone down a good deal. David was determined to farm, but while he was young they sent him to grammar school because they wanted him to be educated. He wouldn't learn schoolbooks, however, and only wanted to get back to the farm and the fields.

When Charlie died of cancer David took over and married a girl who brought a small dowry with her, which put Bozomzeal on its feet again. It was hard for Ellen Foale to take second place, which was why she came away to live with me and our children and Nanny during the Second World War for a while. Ellen was like an apple tree: in her youth she must have been like the blossom; in old age she was the sun-warmed fruit; she was slender to the end of her life, though her hands became gnarled with rheumatism. This may be called a sentimental view, but that is how she was to me. She grieved at her husband's death but accepted it, and Father said that when he went up to the farm he would see her sitting quietly in a field, and she said once, 'I go out there and think of Charlie and my life with him, and it helps me.'

*

In the Christmas holidays, 1932-3, my brothers were at home for a bit: Robin, 16, from Cheltenham, Nicholas on leave from HMS *Erebus*, the training ship for midshipmen who went into the navy by direct entry. Mother was in rather poor shape. Somehow the magic of the college had gone for her too, but she said she was looking forward to my being at Stratford again and coming to stay.

*

In those days the Stratford season was only six months and so we didn't start rehearsals until the end of February for the April opening. At last the dark red Temple Shakespeares arrived with their cuts and I was able to start studying my parts. *The Tempest* was to be the opening play and Neil Porter was cast as Prospero, Gwynne Whitby as Miranda, John Wyse as Ferdinand and myself as Ariel.

We rehearsed in London, as before, for the first weeks. When the time came to go to Stratford, Bridges asked me to go down on the Saturday before the Monday *Tempest* rehearsals on the stage, so that I could practise in my flying harness. It was planned that at the end of the play I should fly up into the air from one of the rocks on the island. There were also one or two other mechanical devices for me to learn to negotiate.

I spent Saturday afternoon in the theatre manoeuvring in the set. It was marvellously enjoyable. I wore shorts and a sweater. Bridges loved the devices as much as I did, and I soon found my flying harness reasonably comfortable and the sensation of flying up high above the proscenium arch intoxicating.

On the Sunday I settled into my digs at Mrs Barnard's at Avon Croft once more, but this time with a salary of £8 a week. I had taken an extra room so that my last year's bed-sitting-room was my sitting-room and I had a lovely sloping-floored bedroom with an Elizabethan heavy wooden bed.

Norman Wilkinson, the designer, had died before completing the designs for *The Tempest* and Rex Whistler took over. The sets and costumes were designed to make *The Tempest* look like a Jacobean masque. As Ariel I wore a short gilded tunic, almost like a golden Roman war tunic. I had small gold wings on my back, and gilded sandals with wings on the ankles, on my head a gilded band with gilded spikes rising out from it like an artificial star. When Ariel during the play transforms himself into a sea nymph to lure Ferdinand with the song 'Come unto these yellow sands' I had a scant covering that looked like green seaweed. The head-dress was a green band with seaweed trailing from it. Ariel's songs were given new settings by Anthony Bernard, and most strange and lovely they were. At that time my voice was high treble like a boy's, so that with my very thin body I could seem neither boy nor girl. Father describes the dress-rehearsal of *The Tempest*:

> It began at 5.30 in the afternoon and ended at three o'clock in the morning. Every one of the actors was completely flaked out, some of them lying about on the floors of corridors, snatching half an hour's sleep, tempers in shreds, only Bridges Adams standing inexorably in the stalls hour after hour, dragging the suffering cast through scene after scene over and over again. Through all those nine and a half hours Bridges never moved, never even went to his room for a drink.

This sounds as if Father had not admired Bridges, which he did. I include it because it gives a vivid picture of all the dress-rehearsals of the first five plays of the season, each one under-rehearsed: only the steel in Bridges could have got the plays on under the circumstances. The first night went extraordinarily well considering the weight and complication of the sets.

We revived *Much Ado About Nothing* and added *Twelfth Night*, in which Dorothy Black played Viola to my slight sadness, as I was greedy and wanted to play Viola as well as all my other parts. I played Olivia. *Julius Caesar* was the fourth revival and *Romeo and Juliet* the fifth. This was heavy, but I was out of *Julius Caesar* and had played Juliet and Hero the previous season. We were to add *A Midsummer*

Night's Dream, Love's Labour's Lost and *Henry V*, which I was not in.

I adored playing Titania in the Norman Wilkinson magic setting and costumes. The forest was all grey-blue and the fairies wore transparent grey-blue over tight-fitting leotards of the same colour with blue hands and faces, so that we seemed almost to become one with the forest. The mortals wore white and scarlet. *The Dream* was a revival from two years back, but the cast was almost entirely new. John Wyse played Oberon and looked glorious. *Love's Labour's Lost* was a brand-new production, with a permanent set consisting of a large tree on a mound which was set on the rolling stage and changed position to indicate other parts of the King of Navarre's park. I played the Princess of France; Dorothy Black, Rosaline; John Wyse, Berowne; and Patricia Hayes, Moth. She seemed exactly like a little boy.

Being out of *Henry V* and *Julius Caesar* gave me two free nights or performances a week once the repertoire was complete. My voice strengthened with the demands upon it and held up well during the openings and first month of the season.

*

Mother came to stay with me at Avon Croft when all the plays were on. I think this was another of the happy times in her life. During the days we went on the river and drove out to Broadway with Gwynne Whitby and her babies and picnicked in the fields above the town. We walked along the river meadows, sometimes sat in Shakespeare's Knot garden and drank beer before lunch at the Dirty Duck, and she and I both absorbed the lovely atmosphere of the old town and the lush Warwickshire country in summer. Some early mornings I used to lean out of a window on the landing at Avon Croft and look at the old timber and plaster of the sleeping house and listen to the birds and imagine that someone looking out of this same window in Shakespeare's day would have seen it all almost exactly as it looked to me – only then the listener would have heard the wheels of the morning carts crunching instead of a distant car.

Mother came to the theatre continually, especially to *Romeo and Juliet*. She relived and satisfied many of her youth's longings in this way, as mothers do, as I know now watching my daughters Vanessa and Lynn.

Towards the end of the season Bridges announced his resignation, much to my sadness. Father wrote:

It was after the 1933 season that Bridges spoke of his doubt as to whether Rachel should go on with the stage: no doubt as to her artistic power, but a feeling that she herself was not of the theatre world, a world which called for something hard-boiled in its citizens, a world where she might never be at home. I know that she found much happiness in her work, but I also know that Bridges was not far out ... I do not believe the theatre is her home.

As I have said, I have never quite belonged anywhere. I think it is to do with my lack of an important ingredient: a tough ego. I hope this does not sound conceited, but I really believe this is true. In order to succeed you must believe in yourself, know exactly what you want and do it. Never be put down by those who do not believe in you as I was only too easily. Of course, if you have in you *greatness*, nothing will stop you, but if you only have talent and the wish to act and perhaps some looks, then you must be tough enough and stand up to all the 'changes and chances of this mortal life' as the prayer says. You also need perfect health. I think that with enough egotism and health a talented or good actor or actress can make a very satisfying career.

The new director, Ben Iden Payne, was appointed and came down to interview people about the 1934 season. He told me I would have to start again. He felt, I am sure rightly, that I had gone too far for my experience and offered me possibly one part and walk-ons and understudies.

I felt I couldn't face being demoted in the same theatre and so I decided to try my luck elsewhere. I met St John Ervine who had given me a lovely notice for Ariel, and he said I ought to get into the Liverpool Repertory Company and work for William Armstrong, and he offered to write to William for me. The Liverpool Playhouse was the most renowned of all the repertory companies and much coveted by young actors and actresses, and consequently hard to get into.

I was very sad at leaving Stratford and Bridges and the company. I knew nothing would ever quite come up to Stratford for me and it never has. Playing Shakespeare in Shakespeare's own town and surrounded by his country has a magic unknown elsewhere.

*

I went up to London for a few weeks, staying in a small bed-sitting-room in a hostel in Queen's Gate Terrace, but no work turned up and as my savings were dwindling I decided to return home to Dartmouth for a holiday while writing around to reps and hoping that a vacancy might come up at Liverpool. After Christmas I was asked to go to Oxford Playhouse and play Anne Pedersdotter in *The Witch* by John Masefield, opposite Stephen Haggard as Martin.

The Witch is a violent play, and the parts of Anne, Martin and old

Pedersdotter, the elderly husband of Anne, are magnificent acting parts. I got on splendidly with Stephen, who was immensely stimulating and full of vitality. He looked terribly pale and fragile but his energy never seemed to flag. We had ten days' rehearsal only.

For the first three days I stayed in London in the hostel where Aunt Winifred had taken a room and so I had her company in the evenings. I was anxious and nervous about the part and missed the security of Bridges and Stratford. I burned up my nervous energy, feeling almost faint with exhaustion in the evenings after the day's rehearsal.

Stephen drove me to Oxford in the morning and back in the evening in an open sports car. After a few days we both decided to take digs at Oxford, so as not to take up time travelling. The Playhouse at Oxford was still in a tin-roofed hall with very small stage and dressing-rooms in a reeking, damp, semi-derelict cottage adjoining it. The stage management lit fires in the dressing-rooms each evening to warm them and dry out the clothes, which absorbed damp from the walls.

I enjoyed playing Anne Pedersdotter almost as much as some of my Shakespeare parts. Arthur Brough played Pedersdotter, the husband. The play went very well and Oxford notices were on the whole excellent. At the end of the week I was asked to stay on and play Stella in *The Sacred Flame* by Somerset Maugham. This I enjoyed less, but it was good for me to try to play a modern part at last. I began to have a lot of pain from violent indigestion and lost my appetite. I met a number of undergraduates who supported the Playhouse and made particular friends with two, Murrough Loftus and his friend 'Trim' Oxford. I never knew his real Christian name. They were such fun and so wonderfully kind, and when I was unwell they went everywhere with me, arranging taxis to and from the theatre.

This wretched stomach trouble seems to follow me through life and overtake me at the most inconvenient times. I recognise the pattern now. It comes when I feel insecure and have a certain amount of nervous strain from anxiety over my work in the theatre. It had its root in my childhood fear of being left alone to face situations or people before I was ready. The feelings I suffered at the large children's parties at the Headmaster's house at Rugby were the same as the feelings of anxiety at facing a first-night audience, but later the fear and strain only became acute if I had not been supported in the preparation of work. So at Stratford there was first Bridges, with his loving, encouraging through critical and strong direction, and secondly Mrs Barnard and my digs, which she made a true home. At Oxford my digs were cold and wretched and in Stanford Holme there was not a feeling of any sort of security.

Here at Oxford in cold weather I began, most unfortunately, to wilt. However, I was never off and completed my engagement. Mother came up at the end of my time and a doctor who had seen me said I ought to go into hospital for a week and have X-rays taken of my inside to make sure there was nothing radically wrong. Meanwhile William Armstrong wrote to say he had suddenly got a vacancy at the Rep. Ena Burrill was leaving to play in the West End and he wanted someone to fill her place just for *Flowers of the Forest* by John Van Druten. He said he was passing through Oxford for one day and would I meet him for a drink at the Randolph Hotel. I was terribly excited, although a little worried at the thought that I had got to go into hospital for a week.

We met and got on marvellously. He was tall, sandy-haired, broad and a little bent. He spoke in a Scots accent and was a little feminine and very amusing. He said he was prepared to take me on St John Ervine's recommendation.

'You look a bit too young,' he said, 'but never mind, you'll be playing opposite a very nice young man, rather inexperienced, but sweet – yes, very nice – Michael Redgrave – and then we have Geoffrey Edwards – dear Geoffrey – brother of my darling Alan.' I had met Alan Webb and admired him enormously.

I told William about having to go into hospital. 'Only for a week. I'm sure I'll be all right.'

He said he would risk it, and added, 'Now you go along and get well and come along up to Liverpool.'

So it was settled, and so was my future, although I had no idea of the consequences of this meeting.

I returned to Dartmouth, was sent to see a doctor in Exeter, who put me into a small nursing home for examination and X-rays. The result was fortunately not an ulcer, as I had feared, but hyper-acidity due to exhaustion and nerves. At the end of a week I returned home and with a diet sheet and medicine left a day later for Liverpool.

Chapter Thirteen

Michael

At Liverpool I was a paying guest with a Mrs Winter in Gambia Terrace, which faced the cathedral. Mrs Winter was a friend of some people we knew in Dartmouth. They had suggested I should stay with her on account of my health.

I arrived late in the evening after a seven-hour journey and took a taxi up the hill to Mrs Winter's. A rather scruffy-looking little girl who was the housemaid opened the door, but standing behind her was Mrs Winter with her yellow-white hair and her eyes smiling behind her gold-rimmed spectacles. We took to each at once. No one could have felt insecure in her company. She took me up to my bedroom where a huge coal fire was giving a tremendous heat into the large, dark room, which looked rather dramatic with its enormously high ceiling, royal blue velvet curtains and a huge screen between the door and the bed to keep out draughts. Having unpacked, I went down to dinner, which was at a long table in the dining-room. There were a number of other paying guests, mostly elderly, a man and three women of Dickensian personalities. I sat next to Mrs Winter, who immediately showed she was going to cosset me delightfully.

From Gambia Terrace you could see beyond the bulky, red cathedral, then half built, down to the Mersey River. The stone birds on the Liver Building near the quay gleamed white in the sun. As it was such a lovely morning I decided to walk down the hill to the Playhouse instead of taking a tram, so I set off along the terrace, turning left into the main street which went straight into the city. It had rained during the night, and so the air was clear and the streets looked washed. There were streets and streets of shabby-looking Georgian houses. Their windows were beautifully proportioned and many doors had fine fanlights, but the buildings were all covered with the black smoke and grime given off by the factory chimneys in all northern towns. Even in the most prosperous streets the houses looked grim and forbidding. However, as I walked down the hill in the sun I felt far from depressed. I was full of that nervous excitement that precedes any new venture in the theatre.

Once in the town, which was noisy with trams, bursting with passengers going to work, I thought everything looked very lively, and quite soon I found my way past the Bon Marché to Williamson Square and the Playhouse. I found the stage-door and as I was forty minutes early I walked round to the front again to look at the entrance. Outside hung two uniform frames containing the photographs of the company, all taken by the same photographer, which was a very good idea and looked much tidier than the usual hotch-potch of frames outside the ordinary commercial theatre, where they have every shape and size of glamorous pictures of those who play within. The name of each actor and actress was printed underneath the photograph.

My eyes were held by the one of Michael Redgrave. He looked as if he might have been a naval officer in civvies, or indeed in any profession except the theatre.

Shortly I returned to the stage door, went in and asked for William Armstrong. I was shown into a little office off a passage and opposite the entrance to the stage. In a few minutes William came in, followed by the tall, extremely goodlooking young man I had seen in the photograph.

'Rachel, this is Michael, your leading man,' he said.

Michael and I shook hands and he said, 'Oh good, you're tall. I thought you were going to be tiny.'

*

William took us on to the stage and I was introduced to the rest of the company: Lloyd Pearson, Deirdre Doyle, Louise Frodsham, Valerie Tudor, Geoffrey Webb and others. From the stage I saw the perfect little auditorium. It was horseshoe-shaped with two circles, with lots of scroll decoration on the plaster-work, which was painted white, picked out in gilt. The walls were dark green, and there were footlights, which I have always loved and which have now largely gone out of fashion.

Chairs were placed in a circle on the stage and I sat next to Michael. We read *Flowers of the Forest* during the morning. Although I was nervous at first I soon forgot and became absorbed in reading the long part of Naomi, who starts the play aged 40 and in Act II goes back to about 20. William seemed pleased and said that as I looked very young we would have to take especial care over my dresses for the middle-aged part. 'But don't worry, it'll all be all right,' he said in his delightful optimistic way.

Michael asked me to have lunch with him and took me to the restaurant of the Bon Marché. The lunch was slightly overshadowed by my shameful indigestion powder, which I had to take at the end of meals.

Finally I said, 'It's rather a nuisance, but I have to have some medicine.'

Michael's face lit up. He called a waitress and asked for a spoon and water, and the whole thing became rather amusing. He told me later how this had pleased him because, he said, 'I am an awful hypochondriac and keep taking things, and it's wonderful to find someone else who does too.' We left the restaurant singing Polly and Macheath duets from *The Beggar's Opera*. We felt happy; he started singing and I joined in.

Rehearsals were mostly enjoyable. William was a most loving and amusing director, always over-praising: 'So moving, so moving … oh! I have such a clever company,' etc. etc.

My life was changed now and I entirely forgot my wretched stomach, which suddenly behaved perfectly. The only difficulty was that, having been told never to drink *with* meals and there being no possible opportunity of drinking *between* meals, I drank almost no liquids at all. However, I was too busy to worry about that.

At Mrs Winter's I was spoiled. In the theatre I loved the work and the daily lunches with Michael. One day Michael asked me to tea at his room at 23 Faulkner Street to go through our scenes together. I was already falling in love. We had two scenes which were flashbacks to the First World War, when Naomi was in love with Richard, a young officer in the army (Michael). The first scene in Act II is when Richard tells Naomi how he loves her and the second scene is when Richard comes back from the front, bitter and disillusioned, and Naomi is pregnant and they know they must marry although he'll go back to the front and probably never return, as is the case.

We had tea, and then in the dusk light in his sitting-room we went over our words. They were so real to me that I dared not look at Michael but gazed out of the window, so that he shouldn't see the truth in my eyes.

The following Sunday he asked me to lunch at his rooms. When I got there he had lost his voice and asked me if I could go and fetch some medicine for him from a chemist he knew was open. I was delighted and ran all the way there and back. He gave me Grenadine to drink, and because he gave it me I broke my rule of diet and drank a tumblerful *with* lunch and so had violent indigestion afterwards. Nothing mattered now but to please Michael.

One Sunday morning, a week before our final dress-rehearsal, I awoke in bad pain. Mrs Winter called a doctor, who said the symptoms were probably a stone in the kidney, and this was seen quite clearly in an X-ray. The specialist who was consulted said he didn't know what could be done without an operation. I told Mrs Winter my horror with the opening night coming up. 'I *must* be well *at once*,' I said.

Mrs Winter asked me if I could put myself in her hands and see what she could do with what she called 'electro-homeopathy'. 'Don't on any account mention this to the doctor,' she said. So, very secretly, she popped what she called 'globules' in my tea and rubbed me with various lotions which she called 'electricity'. In twenty-four hours the symptoms had all subsided, and at the second X-ray I was pronounced free. The specialist said that it was an incomprehensible miracle. Mrs Winter and I laughed together. Years later, when during some illness in a hospital the house surgeon asked me my medical history and I told him about this episode, he said, 'We'd better put down "resolved by witchcraft".'

I now drank pints of water all day long and felt extremely well and more in love with Michael every day. We lunched together continually. Michael gave a party at his rooms after the evening performance of the current play, which was *Libel*. Valerie Tudor asked me to spend the evening at her digs while waiting to go to the party and held forth quite a bit on Michael's inability to give a party properly.

'He doesn't have gin,' she said.

I wasn't at all bothered by this as until then I had always been quite pleased with beer, and so apparently had he. I was extremely angry at her criticism, which I thought very cheap.

All her fears were dispelled at the party, as Michael provided plenty of gin. He played and sang beautifully and I was more in love than ever. The song I still remember was 'The Lass with the Delicate Air' and I wished he thought of me as her.

*

We opened the play on Wednesday, March 27th, 1935. I was extremely nervous, but Michael had asked me to go to the Adelphi for supper after the performance, with Geoffrey Edwards and Valerie Tudor. He had also given me a white camellia to wear on my black velvet evening dress, and so pleasure nourished nerves.

Act I, in which I was the older Naomi, went well. Then came Act II, which flashed back twenty years, ending in the love scene with Michael. Michael and I, as Richard and Naomi, stood in the embrasure of a window, centre stage. At a certain moment in the scene I had to switch off the lights in the room on the dummy switch and pressed it up, but the electrician did not lower the stage lights simultaneously. With my heart beating a little faster I kept my hand on the switch and after a second's pause we went on with the dialogue.

Then came the moment when Richard puts his arms round Naomi and tells her that he loves her, and she puts her arms round him and they kiss. I thought, better take one's hand off the switch and hope that, in spite of the lighting effects of the scene having gone to pot, it would be safe to continue as if one hadn't meant to put the lights out. So I took my hand off the switch. As we kissed, the lights went out and there was a big laugh from the audience. Michael held me a little closer and we held the kiss; the audience quietened and we finished the scene, which to us had been ruined.

There was no time to say anything between scenes as I had a quick change from my 1914 green dress to a VAD's uniform for Scene II. In the interval I had another change and had to age twenty years, so again no time to speak to Michael, but at the end of the play he came to my dressing-room and said how horrifying it had been. I changed quickly into a black velvet evening dress and pinned on the white camellia. When I was ready I went to his room. I suppose I looked rather pretty and alight because I was so in love; he held out his arms and I was in them and we were kissing in reality.

'Oh, darling, darling,' he said, 'it was awful those lights going wrong.'

I said, 'Oh Mike, I love you so.'

Eventually we went off to the Adelphi with Geoffrey and Valerie, who looked at my flower and said, 'It's almost dead.' I saw that it had been crushed and was turning brown, but I didn't care since it was Michael's embrace that had killed it.

*

The plays were always put on for three weeks, so that each play had three weeks' rehearsal. *Hamlet* followed *Flowers of the Forest*, with Geoffrey Edwards as the prince, Michael as Horatio and Valerie Tudor as Ophelia. I felt terribly envious, having played Ophelia at Stratford. I couldn't resist trying to talk to Valerie about the part, but she quickly stopped me by saying, 'I haven't made up my mind what I'm going to do with it yet.'

Michael was extremely patient about playing Horatio, which was a slight agony as he had had a tremendous success as Hamlet, including good notices from London critics, while still a schoolmaster at Cranleigh. However, he showed nothing of his feelings except to me.

We were together in every possible spare moment and after about a fortnight he asked me if I would come and live with him at Faulkner Street next season. Had I been less strictly brought up I would certainly have agreed, and we might never have married, but I was very fearful, especially as I was still a virgin.

At night after the play I went back to his rooms and we lay together on the divan in his little living-room. I loved him passionately but I did not *dare* to be his with my body; I ached with longing, but I still had no knowledge and didn't know how to prevent a baby. I couldn't bring myself to go to a doctor to find out what to do before marriage. Indeed who would have told me in those days? I was Michael's first close experience of a virgin in love.

One day after lunch we lay on the hearth-rug by the fire and suddenly my bursting heart made me say, 'Couldn't we get married?'

He was worried. He said that there were difficulties in his nature and that he felt he ought not to marry.

'I understand,' I said, 'it doesn't matter to me – I love you so.'

After a long pause: 'Very well, if you are sure, we will,' he said.

We both burst out laughing – it seemed such a lovely, funny way to get engaged.

Although I came from a very sheltered background, I knew what Michael meant by 'difficulties'. During my seasons at Stratford, I had fallen in love with my Romeo, John Wyse, who was bisexual. And there were many like him in the company. The fact that I loved Michael so much meant that I was sure I could overcome his difficulties. I would have done anything for him. And indeed it was probably this sensitivity in his nature that made me love him so, as I was very scared of the macho type. It was partly his beauty that entranced me; also his un-actorish appearance, and the fact that he didn't behave in the elaborate fashion that many 'laddie actors' adopt. His conversation was not sprinkled with 'dears' and 'darlings', as was that of so many others. Any woman in love thinks that her love will change the man she cares for, and also she wants to change for him. Up to a point I think that husbands and wives do grow a little like each other and gradually take on the same points of view. In his autobiography Mike admits to having had cold feet before our wedding, but I think he had always wanted to marry and indeed he had been engaged to an American girl while at Cambridge. The fact that he had happily consented to marry me made me sure that he and I would be forever faithful. Doesn't every young couple feel that way? Of course it proves to be almost an impossibility.

Next day we told William, who was not too happy at the idea of our marriage. He explained that it spoiled things for the audience, who imagined themselves in love with Michael or me according to their sex. However, he warmed to it gradually, and later we proved his theory wrong as, during the next season, after our marriage, the audience adored the fact that we really were married if we had love scenes together.

I was delirious with joy – absolutely light-headed. We didn't manage to keep it secret for long. Michael wrote to the girl whose photograph on the mantelpiece I had wondered about. He told me that she had been his mistress for a year but that it was over for him before he had met me. I felt sorry for her but thought to myself, 'She could never have loved him like me or she wouldn't have lost him.' How arrogant I was about love.

Father wrote that he would like to come up to Liverpool and meet Michael. My mother wrote that it was a shock but she was sure if I loved him it was all right, etc. Michael's mother, Margaret Scudamore, wrote that she thought we ought to wait at least a year before deciding and that if we still loved each other at the end of that time we should marry. We both wrote back that we had no intention of waiting but would get married during the break between the two seasons very quietly at a register office.

Mother wrote saying that I must surely give her and 'your father' the pleasure of seeing me married in white – in church – and preferably in the chapel of the Royal Naval College at Dartmouth, where I had been christened. Michael longed to take his own line; I wanted to please Mother, and so after some more letter-writing it was agreed that it should be the RNC chapel.

Meanwhile Margaret Scudamore wrote and asked what I would like to call her; if I had no mother would I call her Mother? I was slightly on the defensive and wrote back saying that I had a mother and would call her whatever she liked. She replied that I had better call her Margaret. All this began slightly to spoil things, but Father's arrival for the weekend restored my elation.

*

Father arrived at Lime Street Station about six o'clock and I was able to meet him before going to the theatre. We were, as always, delighted to see each other. He was as warm and smiling and full of security and giving unfailingly of himself as ever. Whatever his private feelings were he showed nothing of them. I don't remember what we said; it is of no importance. When I had to go to the theatre we decided we would go back to Mrs Winter's together after the play which, of course, he watched, and meet Michael for lunch on Sunday.

I told him what a fine person Michael was, and he never asked the usual questions: were we suited? etc. The truth is, neither of us *knew* the other at all. Michael was very well educated and fairly politically minded; that is to say he read the *New Statesman*, which I had never heard of. I was badly educated and politically totally ignorant. I had read a little and knew a certain amount of Shakespeare from having played the two seasons at Stratford. I had heard very little music but had an ear and a natural love for the little I knew. Michael was, for those days, unconventional in his mind, in spite of his conventional background from the time Margaret had married J.P. Anderson, Michael's stepfather, when Michael was about nine years old. My background and upbringing were conventional from birth. Considering all this, Margaret was the wise one in suggesting we should wait for a year. However, she didn't know the urgency of marriage to a girl who is forbidden to taste love without. I swept Michael into marriage against his doubts. Yet, who would ever marry young if they judged wisely?

On Sunday Father and I walked round to Faulkner Street to lunch with Michael. For a few moments they were both a bit embarrassed, and then suddenly Father laughed his great Rabelaisian laugh and said he couldn't think of any of the proper things to say; I had told him we loved each other, and that seemed to be that. We all laughed, and drank, and ate lunch, and thoroughly enjoyed ourselves. Father invited Michael and me to supper at the Stork, a commercial hotel in Williamson Square where they used to have a most wonderful cold buffet. The table was laden with huge hams, turkey, beef, veal, lamb and pies. Supper went well too, and I know that Michael took a liking to Father. Father noticed with great pleasure that I was well; to me it was a miracle wrought by my young god.

*

When *Flowers of the Forest* ended its run I stayed for the first night *Hamlet* to adore Michael as Horatio and then returned home to Dartmouth. The announcement of my engagement was put in *The Times* and everyone I knew asked me to show them my ring, which I did not have, and I rather gloried in shocking them. That would show the old fuddy-duddies what a fine, free modern young man I'd got!

Betty Jefferies, my friend since our convent schooldays, came to stay; she was to be chief bridesmaid and she helped me cut out and begin to make underclothes for my trousseau. As usual there was very little money and my trousseau was made by a local dressmaker, Mrs Armstrong, who had made my clothes for me since my return from Paris in 1927. Until I started to earn I had £60 a year to dress on, and it didn't go far. In loyalty to her, I said she was to make my wedding-dress. It never occurred to me to ask for a well-cut, smart garment. Fortunately my figure was good enough to carry off most things and it was only a few months after we were married that I realised how provincial my clothes were.

I wrote to Michael most days, and he to me. After *Hamlet* was over he got a free week and asked Mother and me to come to London to stay at Margaret and Andy's house, No.9 Chapel Street. I rather looked forward to this, and very much looked forward to a weekend in London with Michael. Margaret was in a play called *The Aunt of England* with Haidee Wright, and arranged for Mother and Michael and me to go to the evening performance.

Mother and I arrived at Chapel Street at teatime on an afternoon at the end of May, while Margaret was still at her matinée. We were met by his half-sister Peggy Anderson. She was engaged to a young doctor. I was surprised at the bitterness and envy of her conversation about Michael, which seemed calculated to show him in a bad light to Mother who had not yet met him.

No.9 Chapel Street was a charming little London house, rather heavily decorated but to me very sophisticated-looking. The drawing-room upstairs was L-shaped and had gold wallpaper, comfortable chairs and sofa, a great many attractive china ornaments, photographs, pictures, miniatures, a grand piano, and heavy curtains lightened by cream net curtains, which slightly billowed into the room with the warm spring breeze, blowing through the open french windows.

Peggy took us upstairs to the top floor to show us our bedrooms. On the way up on a little half-landing she pointed out Michael's room and told us he would arrive about six o'clock. After we had washed and unpacked our things we came down to the drawing-room and tea was brought in by the pretty parlour-maid. Margaret and Andy kept three excellent staff.

A very lovely blue-white-and-gold tea-set was laid on a gleaming silver tray. On a cake-stand were a plate of tiny cucumber sandwiches and a Victoria sandwich cake.

Peggy was very handsome. She had a tall, generous figure, glowing skin, corn-coloured hair very neatly brushed close to her head. Her nose was a little aquiline and long for beauty, but she had large brown eyes. She spoiled herself by her sarcastic manner and talk directed against Michael, whom she appeared to dislike. Jealousy, I thought. However, I was charmed by the elegance of the house, and so was Mother, and we were much looking forward to meeting Margaret.

*

Margaret came sailing and bustling in at about 5.30 p.m. She was rather plump. Her hands were small and rather plump too, her skin was almost perfect, and she had the same corn-coloured hair as Peggy. She was very welcoming with her slightly wheezy, gruff voice. At first sight I found her charming. She had the old pro, theatrical habit of those days of calling one 'dear' a good deal, and the 'dear' was pronounced in what I can only describe as the old pro accent. Nowadays 'darling' is more the fashion, or 'love', and I find that you can tell the vintage of actors by the sprinkling of 'dears', 'darlings' or 'loves' in their conversation. Margaret was, as I say, very bustling and welcoming, and very sweet to Peggy, who was rather sulky in return.

Margaret said she had arranged complimentary tickets for her play, *The Aunt of England*, playing at the Piccadilly and that Michael would go with us.

Presently we heard a 'Hell-oh-oh' from the hall and Michael came bounding up the stairs and into the room with his light, almost dancing, step. He threw his arms round Margaret and she made happy little purring sounds as she asked him how he was. Then he kissed me and I introduced him to Mother. He was beaming and warm.

The introducing of in-laws-to-be for the first time is one of the most difficult situations in life. Everyone is overdoing everything, trying to be at their best, trying to sum each other up at a glance, talking too effusively, too fast, too much; no one listens to a word the other says and in a very few minutes all this can't possibly be kept up and anti-climax sets in, as it did on this occasion. However, Margaret was helpful and said she must rest before her performance and suggested that Mother do the same. Peggy wandered off.

At that moment Andy – J.P. Anderson – came in and there were introductions again. Andy was a heavy man of medium height with a large paunchy stomach. He was balding, his remaining hair dark and greying. He had brown twinkling eyes and a slightly drop-ended nose. He was kindly and jovial and inclined to make a great many puns, especially to ladies. He soon made jokes mostly aimed at Michael and me, the engaged pair, whom he, kindly, regarded as a fitting target. He shortly suggested that Michael and I might like to be left alone together, to our embarrassment because it seemed forced. Everyone dispersed and Michael took me to see his room.

'I love your mother,' he said, 'she's *charming.*'

'So is yours,' I said.

We didn't quite know what to say to each other. Somehow everything seemed different from Liverpool, and of course it *was* different. We were now subjected to each other in the presence of each other's parents, all anxious and ill at ease. Presently I went up to change for dinner.

I looked in on Mother in her room and at once asked her if she didn't think Michael a marvellous person. She said she found him very charming to meet but added, 'Of course, I don't know him yet, but he *seems* charming.'

I went to my room feeling strange and unreal.

*

At seven o'clock we all met again in the drawing-room and Margaret rang for a taxi and departed for her theatre. Andy, Peggy, Mother, Michael and I went down to the dining-room for dinner. The dining-room was rather dark. The wallpaper was dark gold; there were heavy dark curtains. The oval dining-table was mahogany and highly polished, laid with delicate lace mats and perfect cut glass. Silver candlesticks gleamed on the highly-polished mahogany sideboard. Everything was dark and shining.

Peggy was a bit caustic, Andy making heavy puns, Michael a bit remote. I was reacting too much and Mother too little. The parlour-maid stayed in the room all the time. When dinner was over Michael said we should leave for the theatre. He telephoned for a taxi and he and Mother and I set off together.

The play wasn't very good, a pastiche Victorian drama. Margaret was one of the middle-aged daughters-in-law. Barry K. Barnes was the young hero and Diana Churchill (not Winston Churchill's daughter) the young heroine with whom he eloped by moonlight. Margaret made the very best of a poor part. We went round afterwards and were loyally enthusiastic. Then, with Margaret, we went back to 9 Chapel Street for sandwiches and drinks.

Margaret talked critically of the theatre in general and her fellow-actors. I listened attentively and, although irritated by the way she talked, I was at the same time impressed, because she and Michael were from old theatrical families. Mother was terribly bored, especially as we sat up until one o'clock. I was never referred to. Mother was terribly proud of my work during my two seasons at Stratford and, I think, felt that I should be brought into the conversation. Eventually we went to bed.

*

On Sunday there was a hot roast family lunch, and Margaret told us that she had asked two very special friends to spend the evening. She described them as a particularly devoted married pair, an actress and her husband. She told us that the actress was at the moment teaching and to a certain extent reorganising a school of acting.

I don't remember anything about the day. The evening came and the two guests arrived. We were all introduced and said how-do-you-dos. I don't know if they knew anything of our background at the RNC or anything of Father, but not one referred to it in any way at all, which hurt Mother as she was proud of our home life, even though she didn't entirely enjoy it. As soon as introductions were over, the actress started talking about her work at the drama school. Her conversation was an endless tirade of criticism. She talked before, during and after dinner about the absurdity of the methods, the absurdity of the two principals and the absurdity of all the teachers, except herself, who it seemed to me had in her own view been sent to bring light into their darkness. Margaret roared with laughter as the horrors were unfolded. The husband nodded and smiled happy agreement. Andy sat by the fire, smoking and grunting occasionally. Mother became more and more stony. Finally she could bear the monopoly no longer and ventured, by way of a change, to suggest that it would be 'so delightful' if Michael and I could play *Romeo and Juliet* together some time.

Margaret and her friend, by now fairly ginned up, metaphorically fell upon Mother. It was a ridiculous idea they said. Success at Stratford meant absolutely *nothing*, the standard was appalling, it wasn't good, almost amateur, etc., etc.

'No, no, if Michael played Romeo and of course he would, then he must play opposite Edith Evans as Juliet.'

Although I knew that Edith Evans was our greatest actress in the fullest sense, Juliet was not, as I think she would agree, one of her parts. Poor Mother in the face of this assured statement by two established members of the theatre, was unable to explain her feelings coherently. Her feelings were that it would be delightful, and quite possible, that Mike and I should play it together, but, to say the least, unsuitable for him to play it with Edith Evans. He played Orlando to Edith Evans's triumphant Rosalind a few years later, but Rosalind is a maturer heroine than the fourteen-year-old Juliet. Edith Evans played Rosalind brilliantly, radiantly, with all her sparkling comedy and wit.

To go back. I wilted and could not say a word. Poor silly simpleton, as Tyrone Guthrie once called me during rehearsals of his play *Top of the Ladder* years later. Michael too was silent. This was the first big blow to such confidence as I had. I had the confidence of youth, and that had carried me through the ordeals of some of the big parts before I was qualified to play them. Actors are easily put down in their own estimation, and if the necessary confidence is taken away much of their strength in our difficult and transient work is destroyed. Mine, foolishly on my part, was destroyed at that moment. Every word of praise I had ever received was blotted out by the two older women. Margaret suffered an agony of jealousy that Michael should marry, and I think that perhaps her friend was somewhat in love with him and unconsciously they wanted to put me down.

Mother was terribly hurt and angry, and later, in her room, told me exactly what she thought of Margaret, her friend and also Michael who, she felt, should have championed me. I stood up for him violently, of course. Mother said I was a fool with no spirit. I said they were real theatre people and *knew* what they were talking about. I excused Michael to myself by saying in my mind that, to him, Mother's suggestion of our playing *Romeo and Juliet* together was as foolish as Margaret's and her friend's suggestion that Edith Evans play it, and so, as has always been his way when he thinks people are being foolish, he had said nothing. Mother's attacking Michael made me champion him.

*

We left next day politely, but the joy had gone. We returned to Dartmouth and the wedding arrangements, which seemed formal, tiresome, and very laborious. Michael and I continued to write.

Chapter Fourteen

The Wedding

Presents poured in. A few weeks before the wedding Michael asked me to come to London to stay at Chapel Street for one more weekend. I went on my own. I wasn't looking forward to it, but enjoyed it much more than I had expected. He took me to the Army and Navy Stores to buy my wedding ring and arranged a little dinner-party at a Spanish restaurant in Air Street to introduce me to two of his many friends. They seemed to take to me and this obviously pleased Michael. We returned late to Chapel Street. Andy and Margaret had gone to bed and so we went into Michael's room and he held me in his arms and we kissed and lay side by side on his divan as we had done in Liverpool, and I felt reassured.

Next day I had an appointment with a doctor to whom I had an introduction from my friend Betty Jefferies. I had told Betty of my ignorance of the facts of life, and indeed of all the fears which had so far preserved my virginity. As Mike and I would have very little money at first it was necessary not to start a baby at once. Betty very wisely thought a doctor would be the best person to instruct me. Unfortunately the particular doctor was on the verge of a nervous breakdown from overwork and the whole consultation was a near-disaster. It was extremely damaging and temporarily destroyed all romance. I remember at some point in the interview I laughed hysterically to prevent myself from crying and when I came out Michael, who had accompanied me and waited in the waiting-room, said he imagined I was having great fun because he had heard me laughing. I was absolutely wretched and I couldn't let him know of my unhappiness. I just felt as if I would like the earth to swallow me up. Michael unwittingly had suddenly become a stranger.

*

I returned to Dartmouth that afternoon. As I crossed from Kingswear in the *Mew* the sun shone and the gulls wheeled overhead. Little white-sailed dinghies glided up and down. The beloved college shone in the sun and, I thought, I am going to give all this up of my own free will to marry a young man from whom I now feel divided.

Father met me in the car and asked if I had enjoyed myself.

'Oh, yes – yes, very much,' I said brightly.

It was hot, and we had tea on the veranda. Afterwards when my father had gone into the college to work, and Mother was pottering indoors, I walked alone on the lawn and noticed acutely the sounds and sights and scents around me. Father's 'American Pillar' roses, his great pride, were all out, a mass of crimson flowers on their pergola. The Judas-tree was in flower. I could hear the sounds of the harbour below and was as aware of them all as I had been years ago on my first visit to Aunt Maudie at The Keep when I sat at tea in the nursery with Tony and Miss Cameron and the sounds of gulls and the occasional hoot of a steamer or chugging of a motor-boat would be heard through the wide-open windows.

My throat ached. My innocent life was gone. I knew about the facts of life, and what a wretched knowledge it seemed to be. Every familiar sound from the college – the feel and look of the green lawn – was intensified so that I seemed to hear and see it all for the first time. How lovely it was, and in two weeks' time I must leave it all and only return occasionally as a visitor. I thought, I can't go through with this. I can't leave this place and the dear familiar sight of Father's receding bent back, dressed in his black gown and mortar-board as he went each day down the garden path and disappeared through the door beside the chapel into the college. But then I said to myself, 'This is ridiculous. You don't even want to stay at home, that too would be disaster.' I must go forward, I thought. I must keep in mind those weeks when I rehearsed and played *The Flowers of the Forest* and lunched and supped and made love and talked with Michael. I had already lived, and kept myself, in the theatre for three years.

Next morning I woke early and went to Father's bedroom. I knocked on his door; he was awake and reading. I sat on the end of his bed and tearfully told him my fears. He was distressed, of course, and said he thought it might be a reaction on my part just before having to face a large wedding. I agreed that this was so.

'I try to keep my feelings, when Michael and I were first engaged, fresh in my memory and I try to remember that then it seemed so right to marry,' I said, 'and yet now my heart seems so heavy and I don't know how to go on with it, and equally I don't know how to draw back.' I didn't tell him about the visit to the doctor.

Father said I must realise that, with two weeks to go, masses of presents received, over a hundred guests invited, it would be difficult, but if I really felt in my heart that it was impossible to go through with it, I must say, and he would call the whole thing off. But I would have to make up my mind as soon as possible.

'No, no,' I said. 'No, I am sure I should go on with it. This is just nerves.'

Beloved Father, how he worked to make the wedding go well and smoothly and how little he wanted to lose me. Always, always his thoughts were for our good.

So the preparations went on and I was without feelings, except of going through with it and of course keeping a happy smile on my face in front of the cadets and officers and masters and all our friends.

I am sure that many brides-to-be have felt just as I did during the weeks before a large wedding. What of Michael's thoughts? I have known since that he was far from happy, indeed very frightened, but at the time I was so deadened by my own lack of feeling that I couldn't think of him at all, except as a name and a shape. I remember his wedding trousers and coat and waistcoat arriving and his grey tie. I unpacked them and pressed the trousers and I remember thinking, 'These garments have been close to his body; will they not rekindle something in me?' But they didn't. They were just clothes. I had them taken over to the Captain's house, where Michael was to spend the night before our marriage.

*

On July 16th Michael arrived by train and I met him at Kingswear at 4.15. The hot sunny spell was continuing and I wore a cotton frock and sandals and a rough straw hat to shield my neck from the sun. I thought he looked very handsome in his light-grey flannel suit, but he still seemed a stranger.

We crossed to Dartmouth in the *Mew*, and he was charmed by the estuary harbour and all the sailing boats and other craft plying up and down. I drove him up to our house in Father's car, an old Morris which he was going to lend us for the honeymoon. Mother had gone out, Father was in the College and so tea was put for the two of us in the drawing-room.

I wanted it to seem happy and nice for Michael and I sat and poured tea, but to my slight discomfort he wouldn't sit at all. He walked about the room, talking and gesticulating with a teacup in his hand. All my life tea in our family had been a rather pretty little ceremony. The silver tray, the silver teapot and the silver kettle with its methylated spirit flame under it to keep the water just on the boil. The dainty sandwiches and little cakes. We always sat for tea and held out cups and saucers or put them beside us on some little table provided.

My husband-to-be left his saucer on the table and walked about the room non-stop, waving his cup, which he finally put down on the mantelpiece without its saucer. I was absurdly disturbed by this. Most young girls would have loved it, but as yet I had not rebelled against the ordinary conventions and ceremonies of home-life. I had only rebelled in my heart against the cruelty of the enforced rule of chastity which I felt instinctively was wrong, not against any of the other conventions.

When I had gulped my tea, and eaten nothing, since in any case I wasn't hungry and Michael's restlessness made me feel I was being a bit of a bore, I got up and suggested we should go out. We went on to the veranda and then walked on the lawn, whereupon a lot of curious faces appeared at the windows of the dormitory of C Block, overlooking the garden. The cadets who were invited to the wedding were naturally wild with curiosity about the bridegroom. Very soon I suggested we should go into The Captain's Woods and down to the river, which we did. Michael seemed quite enthusiastic about it all and I began to feel a bit more real.

Eventually we returned to the house to find Mother and Father there. There were greetings, and Mother appeared rather strained. Michael said he'd brought some presents down with him and Father suggested he would unpack them and add them to the display on the long table in the dining-room. There were some books – and then he unwrapped a Maillol nude, very beautifully framed.

Mother became stony and said, 'We shall have to hide that.'

Poor Michael looked amazed and once more I, the 'poor silly simpleton', was completely flummoxed and said nothing. Michael put the picture, very carefully, standing on the floor, propped against the table. Mother said to me in a whisper later, 'We'll have to hide it or something, before the guests arrive tomorrow.'

Looking back, this was extraordinary. The drawing was a lovely one – a sketch, for a sculpture, of a young nude figure. Mother, the daughter of a painter, was *horrified* by pictures of nudes, and I daresay she may have been right in thinking that many of the guests to our wedding would also be shocked.

The atmosphere at dinner that night was a bit difficult and afterwards Michael and I went for a little walk in the warm night air with brilliant stars studding the indigo-blue sky. Next day, July 17th, was filled with preparation. A marquee went up on the lawn for the wedding reception. I went to Dartmouth to have my hair done during the morning. In the afternoon at four o'clock Michael and I went down to Dartmouth to meet Margaret, Andy and Peggy, Dick Green, his best man, Betty Jefferies, chief bridesmaid, and a few others.

Margaret, Andy and Peggy were all to stay at the Captain's house where Mike was staying, but Father had arranged a little family dinner-party to be served in the marquee. It was still very hot. We all assembled on the veranda of our house at about 7.30. After a few drinks even Mother and Margaret began to get on quite well, and after champagne for dinner everyone was quite gay. I was still in my remote dream and Michael seemed a stranger. Mother didn't help the situation, perhaps she was too unhappy, but she never lost an opportunity to say how difficult and strange she found Michael. Had she been a more mature person I am sure she could have helped both him and me. Margaret and Andy complained a good deal about their hostess, the Captain's wife, who *was* a little eccentric; the Captain, and many of the choir due to sing at the wedding service, had been delayed on a cruise in the college sailing yacht *Amaryllis* and in fact only got back late at night on the 17th. The Captain, a cantankerous character, was in no mood for my in-laws Margaret and Andy, and they all took an immediate dislike to each other.

I went fairly early to bed that night, terribly relieved to get to my room. My luggage stood packed, but the cases were unclosed. One, a dressing-case with blue enamel and silver brush set, a present from Maudie, was a great pride to me. In the midst of confusion I began to feel that the status of marriage would hold certain compensations.

*

Next morning, July 18th, dawned bright and warm again. Father worked terribly hard all morning moving furniture and making all look nice for the wedding. He completely exhausted himself. Mother did flowers, and both looked pretty drained and sad. The only actual indication Father gave me of his feelings was when he came to me and said, 'Only one thing, darling – don't press my arm as we go up the aisle. I can only get through it if we behave quite impersonally.' I knew what he meant, and felt the same, and agreed with him.

At last it was time to dress. Mrs Armstrong arrived with an assistant. I was thankful to have the 'old cosy' to help me. I put on a very little make up, feeling it wasn't suitable to be made up much as a bride. I wore all-white underclothes, brand-new white silk camiknickers, silk stockings, and then in my dressing-gown I was given a little light lunch which I could only just swallow. I thought continually of behaving perfectly and of my determination to show no sign of my sadness at leaving home. This would be impossibly cruel to Michael, and fatal all round. I sipped a little champagne. This done, I was helped into my white and silver brocade princess-style dress with its train from the waist and, last of all, my veil held by a little wreath of silver leaves. I looked in the mirror. My spirits suddenly took a leap and soared up. I'll enjoy myself, I thought. Whatever his family may think or not think of me as an actress, I *am* the star of this particular scene and I'll *play* it.

Betty Jefferies, chief bridesmaid, came in ready-dressed in peach-pink organdie, ground-length, full-skirted, with a wreath of rosebuds on her chestnut-brown hair.

She kissed me and said, 'You look lovely.'

'So do you, Betty darling,' I said.

She then went off to join the other bridesmaids: my cousin Violet, her cousin Charmian Spencer Phillips, and Peggy Anderson (Mike's half-sister), who had made a fuss the night before, saying she wanted to back out because I had not sent her the right amount of material for her dress. Michael told her she could have thought of that before and to shut up – or words to that effect.

Mother came into my room when she was ready herself. She looked really beautiful in an ankle-length chiffon dress with a pattern of blue flowers on a white ground, and a picture hat. She was exquisitely made up and now her sense of the theatrical in the proceedings came to her aid. She behaved perfectly. She kissed me lightly and went ahead to take her place in the chapel escorted by Nicky in his summer naval dress uniform, white trousers and short naval bum-freezer jacket (he was a midshipman) and Robin, who was not very well, wearing morning-dress, and in spite of being very thin, looking beautiful in his shining black topper with his, now, pale freckled face and red hair.

It was time for me to go and join Father downstairs. He was very quiet. I took his arm and old Mrs Armstrong and her assistant came across the garden with us to support my train until I met my bridesmaids at the chapel door. The door was opened wide, the church thronged with many uniforms. The cadet choir all in their places, the two parsons, one the college chaplain, the other an old friend of my Father's and Mother's, Dick Simpson, stood at the altar steps. Michael, with Dick Green beside him, stood looking towards me. Mr Piggot at the organ started the voluntary and very slowly on my father's arm with my veil over my face I walked up the aisle. I was shaking like a leaf inwardly but somehow enjoying the eyes upon me just as I had enjoyed my first night playing Juliet when the moment came, and the curtain was up.

Michael looked really beautiful, and I think we both acted our parts to the full. The cadets sang 'Jerusalem' gloriously while we signed the register. We were the first couple in the book as ours was the first wedding since the chapel had been licensed for marriage. Other couples before us had had a civil wedding first at a register office.

Michael and I came down the church arm in arm, smiling, and so out into the sunshine on to the lawn, and prepared to shake hands with our guests. Champagne flowed, photographs were taken and it all grew very merry. I have seen by photographs, especially one snapshot of Mike and me and old Cyril Maude together, that we appeared happy and relaxed. In fact, speaking for myself, I was in my remote dream of unreality: it was a first-night performance as far as I was concerned. I do however remember that I was now rather excited at the thought of our actual first night together. I had a sort of 'Well, here goes, come what may' attitude towards the rest of the day, and I began to long for the moment to come when Michael and I could be entirely alone away from all the fuss and strain and behaviour of everyone.

At last Father said it was time for Michael and me to change. Father had had his old Morris car driven over to Exeter in the morning and had hired a chauffeur-driven car so that we could drive off and go as far as Exeter in luxury.

When I was ready my luggage was brought down by our housemaid and I found Michael and a huge crowd of guests in the hall. Mike and I went out of the front door together. Betty and the other bridesmaids and Mother and Father, Margaret and Andy were all by the car. We kissed good-bye very quickly and got into the back seat. Rose-petals were thrown, the chauffeur started the engine and away we went.

*

Now a weight began to lift from my heart. Was it the final loosening of Mother's long domination? I think it was. I looked at Michael – he smiled – we laughed – and I thought, 'He is my husband and I am going to love him and it will be a good marriage.' We had some champagne with us and drank it on the way and grew very gay, and by the time we got to Exeter we were both thoroughly enjoying ourselves. At an hotel in Exeter, where Father's car was parked, we transferred our luggage to the Morris, said good-bye to our chauffeur and, with Mike driving, an L-plate tied to the bumpers, set off for Lyme Regis where we had arranged to spend our first night en route for Hamble and the house lent to us by Lady Helen Best and Miss Fullerton, sister of Mrs Sidney Meyrick, in whose time King Alfonso visited Dartmouth.

It was a beautiful golden evening, and we went happily along, Michael driving carefully but most courageously, as he had only had a few lessons. He decided that he wasn't going to let me drive on our honeymoon. We arrived at Lyme Regis at about seven o'clock. The two of us and our brand-new luggage were taken up to our double-bedded room. I immediately unpacked my pride and joy, the blue enamel and silver hair-brushes and mirror and laid them out on the dressing-table. We changed rather shyly and Mike suggested a drink before dinner, with which I eagerly agreed.

After a while we went into the dining-room and had a slightly subdued dinner. I know because Michael has told me since that he was feeling terribly oppressed and nervous at the thought of his first night with his virgin bride. By now I was feeling pretty carefree. If I thought about it – and I did, of course – I thought that, as he was quite experienced, all would be absolutely fine, and probably rather exciting. It was the 'great adventure' to me now. After dinner Mike suggested a walk and we went along the Mole in the dusk. I began to wonder if we might not go back to bed, and eventually we did.

The night, due to his knowledge and my determination, was a moderate success and I remember how I laughed with pride to think that, whether I'd enjoyed it or not, I was, for better or worse, no longer a virgin. I was a married woman.

Next day was rather overcast but we decided to go for a swim. Before lunch we played some of our records on the gramophone given us as a present by Bridges Adams and after lunch set off for Hamble.

We arrived about six o'clock and it was all sheer enchantment. The lovely mature garden full of flowers smelling heavenly after a shower, the old house, the charming maids left to look after us, all the welcoming kindness given to us by our dear absent hostesses and their present servants conspired to restore us, and heal all the difficulties and intervening strains. We sank into that house as into the arms of some friend and comforter, and from that night, for the ten days we were there, happiness and relaxation began to take over. In the day we would lie about the garden or drive to some beach and bathe, and at night after dinner we played and played our lovely records of Brahms and Mozart with the windows wide open and the scents from the garden coming in. We became happy in the big double-bed in the pretty bow-windowed bedroom. The ten days came to an end and we drove on to Malvern where the Festival was on and then to Stratford-on-Avon and finally back to Dartmouth for a few days before finishing up at Chapel Street and so to Liverpool.

*

Dartmouth was hopeless. Mother enveloped me again. Father and Michael and Nicky were terribly distressed. We all breathed a sigh of relief when Mike and I got into the London train at Kingswear, seen off by darling, sensible Father. No.9 Chapel Street was all right, except for some visits from the actress friend who at Margaret's suggestion started giving us lessons in movement!

Margaret gave a large evening party. I foolishly wore my wedding-dress because Mother had said it was the right thing to do. Ena Burrill, an old Playhouse friend of Mike's, arrived very smartly dressed and it was then that I realised how terribly provincial my dress was. She was very nice to me, but she and Mike had a lot of rather smart talk and jokes between them and I felt insignificant and desperately aware of my lack of sophistication.

During the week we saw a very gay musical and finally returned to Liverpool for the new season together. We had decided to go on living at Miss Rankin's, at 23 Faulkner Street, and had taken three extra rooms, so that we now had Mike's old room on the ground floor as a small dining-room, a sitting-room with two large windows on the first floor and on the top floor a bedroom with our own huge double bed, Margaret's wedding present, and a small dressing-room for Michael. It was a perfect arrangement, as with continuing rehearsals and performances it was good not to have to cook and housekeep as well.

Chapter Fifteen

Love's Labour's Not Lost

Our salaries were £7 and £8 a week respectively, £15 in all, which although not riches made it possible for us to live very comfortably.

Geoffrey Edwards and Valerie Tudor had left the company. Jane Baxter, guest artist for two plays, Harold Scott and Megs Jenkins, aged 17, were the newcomers. The season opened with *Youth at the Helm*, a comedy by Hubert Griffith in which Michael played the leading part, followed by *A Hundred Years Old* with Michael as Trino. I played small parts in both. We rehearsed from 10.30 a.m. to 4.30 p.m. The curtain rose on the evening performance at 8 p.m. There was time for studying lines and a rest and a meal between the end of rehearsal and making up for the evening performance. Michael, who was enormously strong and energetic, usually walked in part of the break. I would often take the tram up the hill and have a rest. At night, after the play, we usually walked home if I hadn't arranged for supper and we bought fish and chips from the shop at the corner of Faulkner Street and took them home wrapped in newspaper.

The first few months of marriage could have been very difficult without the unifying work. We had known each other only for three weeks and two weekends before we married and the short honeymoon afterwards. There was so much to do to adjust our lives and ways of thought to each other.

I was very conservative. Michael was progressive. He tried hard to educate me and, in spite of some resistance at first, made good progress.

Our nights in our large double-bed helped to resolve daytime disagreements. To me a very important facet of marriage is the sharing of a bed. It is in part a symbol, but I think symbols are important. Even if you haven't everything in common, which is in any case impossible, provided you love each other the bed with its warmth and nightly companionship can draw you closer.

For us there was the work, to which we were both dedicated, and the company, who were like a large family. Of course there were a few jealousies and heartaches when one didn't get the hoped-for part in a play, occasionally quarrels; but on the whole we worked well together, fathered by William who helped us to accept disappointments.

A fresh production was put on every three weeks, mostly London successes with a new play from time to time. There were two new plays that season. *Miss Linley of Bath* and *Boyd's Shop* by St John Ervine. *Miss Linley of Bath* was a poor play about the runaway marriage of Richard Brinsley Sheridan and Elizabeth Linley. It proved to be successful chiefly because of the marriage scene between Sheridan and Miss Linley, Michael and myself. The audience loved this scene because they felt they were not only seeing the stage wedding but our own. Whatever it was, they applauded loudly and came in numbers. The second new play, *Boyd's Shop*, was attended by the author but did not, as he had hoped, transfer to London.

The play I enjoyed most of all that seaon was *Richard of Bordeaux* by Gordon Daviot which had been a big London success with John Gielgud and Gwen Ffrangçon Davies. Michael played Richard II and I Anne of Bohemia, the first wife who died of the plague. Michael was a glorious golden Richard. The production was as nearly as possible a replica of the London one with the beautifully simple Motley sets and rich costumes. It ran for eight weeks since it was a big success and packed the theatre through Christmas. We were preparing the children's play for matinées written by Michael, *Circus Boy*. Patricia Hayes, in those days a brilliant boy impersonator who had been with me during my second Stratford season playing the boys' parts, came up to play Ludo the gypsy boy. The play was about the adventures of the boy, aided by two upper-class children from the circus audience who go off with him to discover the secret of his birth, and finally his legitimate ownership of the travelling circus which had been taken from him by a villainous prospector. William put it on superbly. It has never been played in London but at various theatres in the provinces. I saw it very well done at the Belgrade Theatre, Coventry, some years ago.

During the run of *Richard of Bordeaux* Michael had a letter from Bill Linnit of Linnit and Dunfee, the big theatre agents, saying that he was intending to drive up to Liverpool bringing Hugh 'Binkie' Beaumont to see him with a view to a West End offer. We were terribly excited by this news, and when Bill Linnit arranged for their tickets we decided to invite them to supper at our digs, since we couldn't afford the Adelphi and thought it would be nicer to give them supper by candlelight in our own place, however small. I was preparing all day and also very much hoping they might like me as the Queen and perhaps give me work in the future.

We felt we gave our best performance that night. At the end they came round and back to supper but told us that, alas, they had only seen the last scene of the play when Richard is in prison as they had lost their way driving. It was an awful blow to me that they had missed all my part, and Michael was terribly disappointed too. They were both charming to us and the visit resulted in an offer for Michael.

*

A few weeks later, towards the end of the season, Tyrone Guthrie came up to see us in *Storm in a Teacup* by James Bridie. He was on his way to Ireland. He asked us if we would like to consider coming to the Old Vic to play young leads the following season. He told us not to make up our minds immediately but to let him know our decisions on his return from Ireland, when he would come to see us again in *Twelfth Night*, in which I was to play Viola and Michael, Malvolio. There was never the slightest doubt in our minds. We knew we wanted to go to the Vic more than anything in the world.

By the time Guthrie returned from Ireland I realised with dismay that I was pregnant. Guthrie arrived at our digs for breakfast and holding back my tears I told him the news. He was charming but disappointed. Michael of course said how much he wanted to join the Vic and it was settled. It was a severe setback for my career.

Before we left Liverpool Guthrie wrote suggesting that perhaps I would like to come for the first play, *Love's Labour's Lost*, and play the Princess of France. Michael was to play the King of Navarre; Alec Clunes, Berowne; Margaretta Scott, Rosaline; and Alec Guinness, Boyet. It was a great alleviation to me to be able to take part in the first production of the season. It seems, looking back, wasteful and unnatural to have been so upset by the pregnancy, but young leading parts at the Vic were a tremendous chance. I was to have played Ophelia to Olivier's *Hamlet*, Alethea in *The Country Wife* with Ruth Gordon and Edith Evans, and Viola in *Twelfth Night*, and so it was hard to be reconciled, to visualise not the reality of the baby, only the reality of the loss of the most marvellous work – and a foothold on a major theatrical stepping-stone.

*

At the end of the Liverpool season we packed all our possessions and Miss Rankin kindly offered to keep them while we found a flat in London. We stayed at an hotel in Buckingham Palace Road and were lucky quickly to find an unfurnished flat in Greycoat Mansions, Westminster, behind the Army and Navy Stores. It was on the ground floor. The back looked onto the playground of the Greycoat Girls School. We arranged for a moving van to collect our things from Liverpool. Margaret was very kind in helping to shop for various necessities. I was disgracefully undomestic. I had never learned to cook when I lived at home; however little Father's income, there had always been someone to cook. During my time at RADA and in my various theatre engagements I had always lived in digs with Aunt Winifred and so had been cooked for. Now, after nearly a year of marriage, I was faced for the first time in my life with housekeeping and cooking and was at a loss.

Fortunately we had about three weeks before rehearsals started at the Vic in which to settle into our first home. We found a nice fat Cockney lady to come in and clean. In the early stages of my pregnancy I felt terribly sick a lot of the time and this made me tearful over small things such as washing up and trying very unsuccessfully to cook. Michael was extremely patient and tried to laugh me out of my depression and by the time rehearsals started for *Love's Labour's Lost* I was feeling much better although beginning to lose my figure.

On a beautiful late August morning we set off for our first reading. Tyrone Guthrie was directing; Molly MacArthur designed the set and costumes, which were all made in the wardrobe. On the first day we assembled on the stage and were welcomed by Lilian Baylis. Miss Baylis was, at first sight, rather formidable. She was a devout Christian who seemed to have God at her elbow, and on her side, over all decisions. For instance the story goes that when an actor asked for a rise in salary Miss Baylis said she would ask advice. The reply was, 'I've asked God, dear, and he says "No".' I was extremly fortunate in gaining her liking, chiefly I suspect because of my condition. I am certain she thought pregnancy was heaven-sent and therefore, since God had seen fit to smile on me, she did too.

The stage door and passages at the Vic are very rough, but we thought it all wonderful. For the reading there was a circle of chairs placed on the stage. The curtain was up so that I saw the auditorium, where I had watched Peggy Ashcroft as Juliet, for the first time. The Vic was shabby in those days but less so than when my father had taken me fifteen years earlier to see *Twelfth Night* and we had sat on bare benches from which I had almost fallen with laughter.

Miss Baylis went and sat in her box on stage left. After introducing the company Tyrone Guthrie gave a talk on the production and we settled down to the first reading. I felt fortunate to have played the Princess of France at Stratford so that I was familiar with the text. Indeed, I still knew the words by heart. My problem was to think of it as if for the first time. I was also fortunate in having worked with

Tyrone Guthrie before; it was only in the tiny part of a lady-in-waiting in *Richard II*, but I was familiar with his way of working. He was enormously stimulating and quick in inventiveness, to which we all responded. I was glad that he never spared me or made any reference to my pregnancy. Lilian Baylis in her anxiety was vigilant enough for two. She watched most of the rehearsals and when we practised the final dance, at the moment when we all had to sweep across the front of the stage close to the edge of the orchestra pit, I could hear her saying, 'Oh, Tony! Oh, the dear lovely child – take care …' etc.

Guthrie's production of *Love's Labour's Lost* was played in a simple permanent set. There were two small tent pavilions, one on each side of the stage, one for the King of Navarre and courtiers, the other for the Princess of France and her ladies. Two or three steps led to a rostrum at the back of the stage on which were delicate trellis arches. I found the voluminous costumes comfortably disguising except at the moment when Costard comes up to the Princess and says, 'You're the thickest here', and I knew I *was* and wondered if the audience might find it too true.

Michael found the King of Navarre difficult because there seemed no character to get hold of. He had to present *himself* with a difference, and Michael always preferred a character in which to sink his own personality, never being quite sure who 'himself' was. He had always had a chameleon quality and changed according to whom he was with, even to changing his intonation of voice and pronunciation. Another small difficulty for him at that time was that he was conscious that his front teeth were irregular and had grown a habit of smiling without parting his lips. This inhibited him. Later, when he could afford it, he had his teeth capped.

The first night of *Love's Labour's Lost* seemed to go well, but the notices were mixed, which was disappointing. Shortly after it was on, rehearsals for *The Country Wife* by Wycherly started. The cast was dazzling and Michael felt terribly excited to be acting for the first time with Edith Evans. I hated not to be playing Alethea and to know that I must leave the Company so soon. However, during the run I felt the first movements of the baby in my womb and from that moment onwards I began to become absorbed by the thoughts of the child to come. The nausea disappeared and I felt extremely well. During my time at the Vic we started flat-hunting again, as we realised that our Greycoat Mansions place wasn't big enough for a baby and Nanny and cook-general, which we could well afford on Mike's salary of £20 a week. A trained Nanny got 25 shillings a week and a cook-general about £1 a week.

We found a large flat with six rooms and two bathrooms in a block called Pembridge Mansions in Moscow Road, Bayswater. It was on the top floor, with no lift, and it had a view across roof-tops to Kensington Gardens. I think the rent was about £180 a year.

By now I was getting much larger; the baby was a perceptible bulge. Michael was hard at rehearsal. Ursula Jeans was playing Alethea, and Ruth Gordon had come over to play *The Country Wife*. Edith Evans was Lady Fidget.

Although I was playing in *Love's Labour's Lost* I did not come in much contact with *The Country Wife* cast and felt terribly envious of them and Michael especially. He was swept off his feet by them all, quite naturally. The whole set-up was so glamorous and distinguished. Oliver Messel, already a big name, designed the sets. Part of the money had been put up by Gilbert Miller with the arrangement that if successful the production was to go to New York with Ruth Gordon and part of the cast.

One of the difficulties of marriage in the theatre is that the work comes before everything else in life to a dedicated artist. There is nothing more absorbing than really good work in the theatre. Wife, mistress, child, husband, lover come second; I think the reason I have not realised my early ambitions is that I soon felt private life to be the more important. I loved the work but it has taken second place, and human relationships first place. Who is to say that either is right or wrong? It is as it is. For marriage to survive is a miracle and, looking around our profession, I am afraid that not many do.

*

One day during one of the first dress-rehearsals of *The Country Wife* Michael tripped off the rostrum in the dark and sprained his ankle very badly. He was in agony and telephoned me to come down to the theatre. Margaret had gone to the dress-rehearsal and been very critical of him and this, combined with the pain, reduced him to tears. I was, as always, terribly moved when something hurt him. He was so big and strong but so vulnerable. I found him at the side of the stage still in costume, with his heavy restoration wig slightly awry on his head, the tears running down his face and spoiling his make up. With our arms round each other we went up to his dressing-room and he said he didn't know how he could play the performance that night. It was clear that if he was to open in *The Country Wife* he would have to rest his foot; so he went home and called the doctor, and an understudy played Navarre.

After the performance I went home and found him sitting disconsolately with his foot in a basin of water and a chaos of books and dirty crockery around him. The broken toe was not diagnosed by the doctor, but the pain subsided and Michael was able to do the dress-rehearsals and play that glittering first night. His painful foot, and his fear of smiling fully, did slightly take the edge off his performance, but the production was an enormous success and, as the run went on, helped by Edith Evans, Michael steadily improved. His teeth were capped during the run and by the end of the eight weeks' season he was a superb Mr Horner.

The third production was *The Witch of Edmonton* by Dekker. The director was Michel St Denis. Edith Evans was the witch. Michael had a very small part in which he was not happy and he felt that St Denis didn't think him good. This distressed him, since he was an enormous admirer of Michel and had looked forward to working with him. It was only a moderate success.

The fourth production was *Hamlet*. Laurence Olivier was Hamlet and the play was given in its entirety: four and a half hours. Michael played Laertes and was very remarkable. He made a fascinating character of a part that can be – and often is – played as a rather ordinary juvenile. He chose a wig of straight, longish auburn hair. His face was made up pale: he used green in the foundation to give his complexion an olive tone. He was full of fire and passion.

I went to the first dress-rehearsal. By now we thought the baby was due, so Lilian Baylis asked me to sit with her in her box. During the duel in the last scene between Hamlet and Laertes, which Laurence Olivier and Michael fought with great reality, Michael accidentally knocked the sword out of Larry's hand and it shot straight into the box where I was sitting with Miss Baylis, who caught it and handed it back. Lilian was rather alarmed but noted that God was with us, no doubt sitting in the back of the box. Larry had apparently said to Michael just before, 'We'll frighten that baby out of her', and they nearly had; but it was not ordained, as I had evidently miscalculated the time by a month and, unknown to us at that time, still had four weeks to go.

At our flat I spent the days sewing. Father had given me a simple Singer sewing machine and I made all the first baby clothes. I knitted four vests and made four flannels, four petticoats and four dresses. I was given numberless jackets. Michael was by now rehearsing *As You Like It*, playing Orlando to Edith Evans's Rosalind. Ursula Jeans played Celia and my brother Robin was Silvius.

I was alone all day and evening, but the preparations for the baby were absorbing. I got everything ready, marked and packed well before the time. On Sundays Michael helped me with the nursery. We bought a canvas screen and began to cover it with scraps. Aunt

My mother, Beatrice Ashwell, married Eric Kempson in 1908

My father and I, aged 3

Hero in Much Ado about Nothing, *1933*

Ariel in The Tempest, *1934*

Our Wedding at the Royal Naval College, Dartmouth, 18 July 1935

Portrait by Cecil Beaton

My father and mother at my wedding

Candida in Candida, *1940*

Michael, Ordinary Seaman R.N.

With Michael and Corin at Pinewood Studios, 1941

Wartime portrait by Anthony Devas

*'Robin'. Eric John Kempson, R.N.
Reserve, killed in action in 1942*

*Portrait of Michael
by Augustus John, 1945*

The family at Bedford House, 1946

Wilks Water Cottage, Odiham, 1958

The family at Bedford House, late 1940s

Tour to Moscow, 1958–9. Angela Baddeley, Michael, Dorothy Tutin, our tour guide, Coral Browne, myself and Geraldine McEwan

Lady Capulet in Romeo & Juliet

Dionyza in Pericles

The family at Lynn's première of Smashing Time *in 1968*

The Seagull, *1964. Top row, left to right: Peter McEnery, George Devine, Philip Locke, Mark Dignam, myself. Middle row: Peter Finch, Peggy Ash-croft, Paul Rogers. Bottom row: Ann Beach, Vanessa.*

With Susannah York in Jane Eyre

With Vanessa, Natasha and Barney, 1965

Vanessa and her son, Carlo Nero, 1969

With Michael at Lower Belgrave Street, early 1970s

With Meryl Streep in Out of Africa

With Jemma by the pool in Nairobi, on location for Out of Africa, *1985*

With Vanessa and her daughters Joely and Natasha

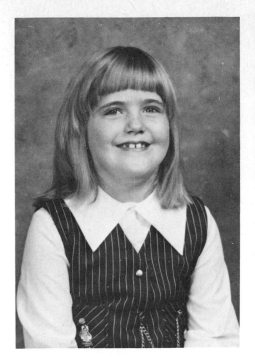
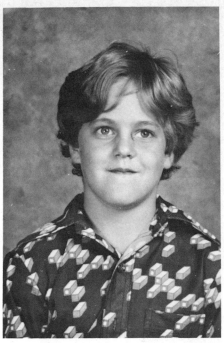

Lynn's children Kelly and Benjamin

Corin's children Harvey and Arden

With Lynn at Michael's funeral, 1985

Maudie gave me a chintz of little roses on a white ground for curtains for the three big windows. The nursery was on the corner of the building, light and sunny. We walked in Kensington Gardens on Sunday mornings and looked in all the prams at the little babies snuggled under blankets, thinking of our own to come.

In one's first pregnancy it is often hard to realise the child at all. One grows larger and larger and there are the movements inside, but one still cannot visualise the *baby*. Margaret's great woman friend, the one who had helped her to destroy my confidence as an actress on that awful visit before our wedding, had advised a vegetarian nursing home at Blackheath, run by two obstetricians – Drs Pink and White, of all improbable names. I was Dr Pink's patient and he insisted on the vegetarian diet. This might have been good, but in my case the result was a degree of malnutrition and towards the end of my time I began to feel very weak and sometimes giddy. He gave no instruction on childbirth and so I was entirely ignorant of the real stages of birth. I knew one had to expect pains and that the baby would finally emerge. This I kept pushing into the back of my mind as, again, I could not visualise the reality.

It was during my pregnancy that we got to know Stephen Haggard and his wife Morna. She was also pregnant for the first time. We visited them in their house in Horbury Mews, converted from stable and harness-room with its flat above. Horbury Mews is just beyond the Mercury Theatre at Notting Hill Gate. Stephen, whose father was at the time British Consul in Berlin, was very fond of Germany and German ways. He and Morna spent holidays there. They told us that whereas here in England we always thought of pregnancy as something to hide and disguise, in Germany it was much honoured. Mothers-to-be swam and sat around open-air pools in summer, proud of their shape. I was envious of this because in my day disguise was considered modest and necessary.

We had also made friends with Angela Baddeley and Glen Byam Shaw, and one night they invited us to supper and dancing at the Gargoyle Night Club.

Michael wasn't very keen on my appearing in restaurants at this moment, but they insisted and we went. Glen asked me to dance. I said I couldn't, but he said, 'Nonsense. I love pregnant women. You dance and rest your child against me.' This was the most wonderful thing he could have said to me, and so we danced and, instead of feeling ugly and bulging, I felt attractive and light again and remembered him with real love.

We spent Christmas Evening 1936 with Stephen and Morna. Stephen lit candles on the enormous Christmas tree and ran out to the pub to get bottles of beer. They had a German maid who kept the house immaculately clean. They always had a clean white table cloth for every meal. The maid laundered the cloths after every using. Stephen was very slim and pale in colouring but with a burning vitality. He loved discussions and argument and we spent many fascinating evenings with them, sometimes getting really angry with each other.

Ursula Jeans and Roger Livesey, Michel St Denis and Vera Poliakoff and many others spent evenings at our flat, but Stephen and Morna were our most constant visitors.

*

Towards the end of January it was certain that the baby was due and that at any moment of the day or night, it would start to make its entry into the world. Mother came to stay to keep me company as Michael was at the Vic from morning till night and she wanted to be with me when the first pains started. The baby's suitcase with the clothes and nappies had been packed a month before and waited in the nursery.

On January 29th, 1937 I had gone to bed early. Michael wasn't back. I quickly fell asleep, to wake about an hour later. At first I wondered what had woken me. The sound of Michael's key in the lock? I listened, but there was silence. Mother was fast asleep in the night nursery-to-be at the other end of the flat. I lay still and then was aware of an almost imperceptible tightening of my muscles and the smallest pain, which subsided almost immediately. Strangely enough I didn't jump to the obvious conclusion. I know I am not alone in this. Vanessa and my daughter-in-law Deirdre told me that although they knew when their first babies were due, the very first warning took them by surprise. It was some hours before they could believe the birth had started.

However, I was wide awake. After an interval of about twenty minutes the same thing happened again and twenty minutes later was repeated. I looked at my watch. It was about midnight. Then I heard Michael coming in and I called out. He came into my room surprised to find me awake.

'Darling, I think it's started,' I said. 'I'm not sure but I think it must be *it*.'

He sat on the bed looking anxious and excited. At about one o'clock, after the same slight pains were repeated, he said he thought he ought to ring the maternity home. The night sister told him that, since it would take their car quite a while to reach us and bring me back, she thought it would be advisable to come as soon as possible.

I got dressed, packed and woke Mother to tell her the news. She was so deeply asleep it was difficult to wake her. I felt sad to see her startled look when she was awake enough to understand that the moment had arrived. Mike and I were shortly going off. He said he would come with me in spite of two performances ahead of him the next day.

I know Mother was in agony for me and worried and unhappy that she was going to be at our flat without me. Relations between Michael and her, having been strained at the start of our marriage, could never completely recover. In fact, I think she hardly saw him at all during her stay and felt like the lost child which she was all her life.

The car arrived about 1.45 a.m. and we set off excitedly, driving through the now deserted streets. Snow was falling. It was very cold, but we didn't mind, sitting close together under a rug. A night nurse opened the door when we arrived at Stonefield Nursing Home and we were shown up to a large bedroom on the top floor. There was a fire burning in the grate, the bed turned down ready for me and a little cot made up to receive the baby. Mike waited outside while I undressed and had my pulse taken. Then the nurse called him back into the room. He sat by the fire while she unpacked the baby clothes, laying out a set on the cot. This brought reality closer. As I have said, I had no prenatal preparation of any sort and could not believe that these secret distant pains and little contractions meant that shortly, inevitably, the baby would come out of me and no longer be in my imagination.

The nurse told me to ring for her when and if the pains became stronger and more frequent. Then she left Michael and me together. She didn't suggest that I should be quiet or try to get some sleep. I thought the baby would be born very soon. Meanwhile we just couldn't stop talking and conjecturing.

I think Michael finally left at five o'clock in the morning to make his way home and try to get some rest before his two performances of the 'eternity' *Hamlet*, as actors call the full-length version. The nurse said that Mike could ring for news whenever he liked and that of course he would be telephoned as soon as the baby was born.

I didn't sleep at all that night. By morning my labour was becoming hard. By evening, after a day when pain obliterated thought, except perhaps the thought that I would die, I only longed for oblivion. At last I was helped down the stairs dragging my legs and pushed on to an operating table. A mask was put over my face and I passed thankfully into unconsciousness.

When I came round the doctor and the New Zealand nurse whose charge I was stood by me. The doctor said, 'Look, there she is, a little girl.'

I was lying on the delivery table. It was very still. I felt calm and free and light, pain and fear forgotten; and there in a basket lay a small bundle from which protruded a perfect little head, the face like a flushed peach, the eyes open and deep blue. She sucked at the thumb of her minute hand, which looked like a starfish. Vanessa had been born at six o'clock in the evening of January 30th, 1937.

The performance at the old Vic was over too late for Michael to come to see us that night, so he celebrated with Larry Olivier and others. Olivier made a speech at the curtain call of *Hamlet* saying: 'Ladies and Gentlemen, a new star has been born tonight', and after a slight pause he continued, 'Laertes has had a daughter.' The warm Vic audience, so loving of the company, cheered and cheered. The Vic students bought all the flowers off a stall in the Waterloo Road and gave them to Michael with a note saying 'Love's Labour's Not Lost'. Olivier took Michael and some others out to supper at the Moulin d'Or restaurant in Romilly Street, chanting as they entered, 'He's got a daughter, he's got a daughter', and so in spite of the exhaustion of a sleepless night he was able to have a marvellous evening and told me that the evening performance of *Hamlet* almost turned into a comedy. The whole company had rejoiced with him once Vanessa was safely in the world.

*

Michael came down to Blackheath the next day and was in tears of joy over our enchanting little daughter. The birth of the first child must forever be one of the most wonderful experiences of marriage.

At the end of the month Vanessa had thrived in spite of a few setbacks due to exhaustion on my part. The vegetarian diet had been good for her but left me depleted in energy. However, we returned home to Moscow Road very happy. It made home complete to have a baby in the cradle in the nursery. On fine days the sun filled the room, and if we weren't out of doors I used to put the cradle close to one of the windows so that the sun shone on her limbs. She would lie kicking and making happy sounds and playing with a set of coloured beads stretched across the cradle. She grew plump and golden brown with the sun.

Chapter Sixteen

Oxford Idyll

The Nanny we had was a rather depressing character, always smoking. I adored the days when she was out and I could have Vanessa to myself, although I was terribly nervous at first when she screamed while I was undressing her. Indeed I worried far too much over her, fretting at every cry. The Nanny was no help in reassuring me. However, as the days went on we all settled down.

Michael was now rehearsing for *As You Like It*, playing Orlando to Edith Evans's Rosalind. Esmé Church directed; the settings and costumes were by Molly MacArthur, after Watteau. The first night was an unforgettable experience. Edith Evans gave an astonishing performance. She and Michael were 'in love'. It was a tender, brave, gay and brilliantly witty performance. The lines 'Oh coz, coz, coz, my pretty little coz, if thou didst know how many fathoms deep I am in love' sounds in my ears until this day: also the first meeting with Orlando when she puts her golden chain round his neck and says, 'Gentleman, wear this for me.' She gave the words the magic, fresh wondering tenderness of a girl in love at first sight and for the first time. Edith Evans was fifty then but looked a girl, and in disguise made a lovely boy. Michael, at 28, was the most handsome Orlando I have ever seen, but he was more than handsome. He made it a real character. The notices next day were raves, with headlines such as 'Ring the Bells'.

I imagine that anybody seeing the performances of Michael and Edith as Orlando and Rosalind might have assumed they were in love, but as usual in such cases it was the wife who was the last to realise. Of course both Romeos and Juliets and Rosalinds and Orlandos are very prone to fall in love – also Antonys and Cleopatras and Desdemonas and Othellos. I certainly fell in love with my first Romeo, John Wyse. The first inkling I had of their romance was when I discovered that Michael returned with her to her elegant Pont Street flat after the performance.

One Sunday evening Michael and I were having supper together at Pembridge Mansions. A silly argument broke out and Michael stormed out into the night. As time went on and he didn't return, I began to get worried. At about eleven I thought I should ring Edith in case he might be with her. She said he wasn't, and that she would come straight round and we would try and find out what had happened to him. At about one in the morning we called the police, who reassured us that any accident that occurred was always reported to Scotland Yard and they had had no news of him. Edith stayed the night with me, clearly as worried as I was. In the morning she rang her chauffeur and asked him to go round to 9 Chapel Street, Michael's mother's home, in case he had stayed there. There was no reply. At about nine o'clock Michael breezed in, finding me distraught and Edith extremely anxious.

'What's the matter?' he asked.

'Where have you been?' we asked.

'Nowhere particular,' he replied.

He was clearly very annoyed that I had rung Edith since it might disrupt the relationship. I was innocent because I didn't realise that they were in love. By now I was used to Michael having a wandering eye, and being out a great deal. This new relationship, therefore, surprising as it may seem, didn't upset me too much.

*

During that spring I often took Vanessa into Kensington Gardens. One afternoon when Michael had some free time he came too. It was May during a hot sunny spell. I put Vanessa into a tiny bathing suit so that she could get plenty of sun. She lay on a rug opened on the grass and Mike nuzzled her tummy with his face to make her laugh. She was just four months old and chuckled delightedly each time he did it. Suddenly her mouth turned down and she started to cry hysterically and wildly. We were very alarmed because we couldn't seem to comfort her, even though I rocked her in my arms. Eventually the cries subsided but she kept sobbing and her face became mottled. I realised that this was the first sign of a very sensitive and temperamental nature and that we must be careful not to overtire or strain her already active brain. At fourteen months she used to have violent fits of crying if she couldn't make one understand something she wanted. One day when I brought her in from a walk we went into the night-nursery to take off her outdoor clothes and she flew into a screaming rage and crawled under the Nanny's bed where, scarlet in the face, she screamed and screamed. It took quite a time to get her out and I never knew the cause, except that perhaps she always longed to stay out in the air to be free for much longer and so used up her enormous energy.

When she was eighteen months old Edith Evans came out walking with us. Vanessa had a black rage, as I called them, when I put her back in her pram after she had been enjoying shuffling through the mounds of dry autumn leaves. She went stiff and lay across the pram so that I was unable to put her into it. She screamed until she was purple in the face. Edith and I were terribly worried, especially as a crowd soon gathered round and watched us.

Edith in a voice trembling with emotion said, 'Wallop her, Rachel, wallop her and I'll stand by and witness you only did it in kindness.'

Feeling cruel and daring, but exasperated, I walloped. She collapsed into the pram.

Edith and I almost ran as we pushed the weeping Vanessa out of Kensington Gardens as fast as possible. We went to a toyshop in Notting Hill Gate where Edith bought her a wooden horse to comfort her.

*

In May 1937 I was asked to play Viola in the OUDS summer production of *Twelfth Night*. It was the custom in those days for the Oxford University Dramatic Society to cast professional actresses for the women's parts. It was for the OUDS some years earlier that Peggy Ashcroft had first played Juliet with Edith Evans as the Nurse. George Devine, then an undergraduate, played Mercurio; John Gielgud directed. The costumes were by the newly formed trio of young designers called Motley: Sophia and Elizabeth Harris and Elizabeth Montgomery.

Esmé Church who had directed the Edith Evans *As You Like It* for the Vic season was to direct *Twelfth Night*. I accepted with great excitement and pleasure. I had played twice in *Twelfth Night* – Olivia at Stratford in 1934 and Viola at Liverpool in 1936 when, pregnant with Vanessa, I had not really been able to enjoy the production because of the continual nausea I suffered.

Having a nanny it was possible for me to leave home for the four weeks at Oxford, for rehearsals and one week of performance which were to be in Exeter College garden. We had a very nice girl as general help who had come to us from Liverpool where she had helped at Miss Rankin's, our digs. She could cook simple things and did the housework, so Michael would be looked after.

I went to Oxford for rehearsals in the third week in May. The first-night was to be June 16th. Phyllis Konstam, wife of the famous tennis-player Bunny Austin, played Olivia, and Alexis France played Maria. We three with Esmé Church were given rooms at the expense of the OUDS in a private hotel a little way out of the town just off the Woodstock Road. We were only there for bed and breakfast. The rest of the day we rehearsed and had lunch and dinner, if we liked, at the OUDS Club. Our undergraduate cast were delightful to us and we soon loved them. Peter Potter, now a well-known director, walked on, and Willoughby Grey played Antonio the sea-captain. Robertson Davies played Malvolio with brilliance. Michael Dennison walked on as a sailor; Jack Merivale played Viola's twin brother Sebastian. Esmé Church was a perfect director for the cast of inexperienced amateurs and three professional actresses, welding us together most happily. We were all fired with tremendous enthusiasm, which was sparked off partly by the desire of the girls not to let the boys down and vice versa. For the last week whenever it was fine we rehearsed in Exeter garden which was a perfect setting for *Twelfth Night*.

Two long flights of stone steps at right angles to each other led down from a curving bank secluded among beech and lime trees into a green arena. A barred door in the bank served for Malvolio's prison, and for the back of the kitchen in which Sir Toby sings his catches, and a tall silver birch in the middle of the arena was used for Olivia's House and the Palace of Orsino. *The Times* notice said:

> Add the great stone buttresses of the Bodleian on the other side of this natural stage, and when the lamps are lit and the shadows work their magic on leaf and stone, the scene is as Elysian as any that fancy could paint.

There was a paved half-courtyard at the back to one side and under the Bodleian walls where the small undergraduate orchestra in costume played for the songs and music for Orsino's court. Our entrances had all to be from a distance and Esmé directed us to act our way on and off with much inventive business. For example in the second Orsino court scene, which begins with Orsino saying 'Saw you Cesareo?' to one of the courtiers, Esmé had me and a courtier run on down opposite flights of stone steps, throwing a ball to each other so that by the time we were on the grass and racing across to the birch tree Orsino and the Court were entering down the stairs, Orsino speaking his line as he entered.

Except for one evening the weather was fine. On the wet night we started the play before it was actually pouring and by the interval we were drenched. We had a conference about continuing and decided we would play it through if the audience could face it. The stage manager announced this and the audience, mostly with umbrellas up, nobly stayed until the end. Water squelched out of our shoes and ran down our necks, soaking our costumes, but it was a challenge we enjoyed.

Some evenings after rehearsal we took punts up the river. It was terribly frustrating for the boys that we were all married and, I must confess, a little for us; but I think we all rather enjoyed our mutual attractions and had the absorption of our wonderful play. On the last night there was a party, ending with breakfast in the morning. Peter Potter felt faint at breakfast and went blue round the mouth. I held his head between his knees and we comforted him as best we could, since he indicated that his faintness wasn't all from exhaustion but partly from love. We were leaving that day and so this idyll had to end. We all felt very sad – it had been such a lovely and unique experience and we had lived it in a state of emotional euphoria.

I was delighted to be home again. Vanessa had grown and changed in the four weeks I was away. She was now nearly five months old.

Chapter Seventeen

White Roding

In the autumn of 1937 John Gielgud formed a company to play at the Queen's Theatre for a season of four plays to open with *Richard II*. *Richard II* was to be followed by Sheridan's *The School for Scandal*, Chekhov's *The Three Sisters* and *The Merchant of Venice*. He invited Michael to join the company in which were Peggy Ashcroft, Leon Quatermaine, Harcourt Williams, Glen Byam Shaw and many others. The Motleys were the designers. Gielgud played Richard II, Peggy Ashcroft the Queen, and Leon Quatermaine John of Gaunt. Michael played Bolingbroke, son of John of Gaunt, who succeeds as Duke of Lancaster and forces Richard to resign the crown, which he usurps as Henry IV.

Gielgud was probably the greatest Richard II of our time, perhaps of any time. He was royal, weak, lovable and tragic and 'mystic wonderful'. He spoke the poetry to perfection. Michael was superb as Bolingbroke, which was unexpected since physically he is more suited to Richard, which he played fourteen years later at Stratford. Indeed he had admired John Gielgud so enormously in the part that although his Richard was his interpretation it owed much to John's. As Michael said, 'If you have seen a performance which you consider definitive you cannot help being influenced by it – and why not?' This is often found in composers of music and in painters.

In spite of Michael's lightness of physique and voice he made Bolingbroke a formidable lion of an opponent: in the deposition scene especially, when Richard asks for the looking-glass and has speech after speech on the condition he has been brought to by Bolingbroke. Michael used that silence in a remarkable way. One felt his authority, weight and bored patience. He knew, and made the audience feel, that he was allowing Richard this last fling because of his sickness and being the victor. This was epitomised in the way he said the line 'Go, one of you, and fetch a looking-glass'. It was said as if he might yawn, but didn't. The production was a wonderful success.

*

When *The School for Scandal* was being cast there was no one in the company to play the part of Maria, the young ward of Sir Peter Teazle, and Michael came home one evening and told me that Glen Byam Shaw had suggested that I should be engaged to join the company for this production. John Gielgud accepted the idea. At the time I was understudying at the Royalty Theatre in J.B. Priestley's *I Have Been Here Before*. The management of the Royalty agreed, provided they could have first call on my services in the event of the leading actress Patricia Hillyard being off. It was a glowing prospect. John Gielgud was one of the great men of the theatre. The company was one of the most distinguished one could ever hope to be with. At that period I always dreamed of us being able to make a theatrical partnership. With the difficulties of marriage in the theatre I used to think that to act together would be a way of keeping an important contact.

Tyrone Guthrie directed *The School for Scandal*. It received mixed notices. I was rather overawed by the company but on the whole happy, although Maria is a difficult small part. I think I tended to want to blow it up into something better than it was. In my young days I had been taught to feel that you had to make something of every part, whereas trying a little less and accepting a small part for what it was worth and no more succeeds better.

During the run of *The School for Scandal* I was asked to play Celia in Ben Jonson's *Volpone* which Donald Wolfit was to play for a limited season at the Westminster Theatre. I found myself in the unique position of understudying at one theatre, playing in a second and rehearsing in a third. Although there was help at home it wasn't very adequate and the strain began to tell.

One night during a performance of *The School for Scandal* I suddenly found my mind a blank. I heard the prompter say the line, but for a few seconds I seemed to have almost blacked out. I didn't know where I was and I couldn't take the prompt. The prompter gave the line again. I said it then stopped. The prompter gave me the next line. I said it and stopped. After the third line I gained consciousness, as it were, and carried on. It was an awful shock – something I had never experienced before. In all my parts at Stratford the possibility of 'drying' had never entered my comprehension. This was a second blow to confidence and a severe one. I ought not to have been so easily put down, but lack of confidence in myself has been my Achilles' heel.

*

At the end of the run of *The School for Scandal* I regretfully left the company, who had been rehearsing *The Three Sisters* directed by

Michel St Denis. This was a production which no one who saw it could forget as long as they live. Consequently no production since has succeeded in the same way, as yet. I longed to have been part of it. It was a wonderful cast, with Masha played by Carol Goodner and Olga by Gwen Ffrangçon Davies, who both joined the company for the production. Peggy Ashcroft played Irina; John Gielgud, Vershinin; Michael Baron, Tusenbach; George Devine, Andrei; Angela Baddeley, his wife Natasha; and Glen Byam Shaw, Solyony. Harry Andrews and Alec Guinness were in two small parts.

They rehearsed for six weeks and by the time the first night came, instead of feeling nervous as actors always do after the customary four weeks' rehearsal, they all felt ready and longing to play to an audience. From the moment the curtain rose when the three sisters are on the stage – Masha reading, Olga correcting exercises, Irina standing in a white dress, her long hair tied back with a ribbon – Olga says, 'Father died a year ago today.' To the fall of the curtain when the three sisters are left standing with their arms round each other and you hear the sound of the army band receding, the audience were held in an almost breathless silence, not watching acting but looking into and sharing in the lives of the family and their friends shown in the play. One had complete belief in the people, who no longer seemed actors playing parts.

Michael's Baron was one of the greatest performances he has ever given, until his Vanya thirty years later. He said he had great difficulty during rehearsals. He tried, as one had been taught to do, to make the meaning of the lines clear, and Michel St Denis and he made the character a clumsy, slightly ridiculous figure, with a pale spotty face, with gold-rimmed spectacles, looking almost absurd in his uniform and worse in his civilian dress when he gives up the army and is going to marry Irina. The moment in the last act just before he goes off to fight the duel with Solyony and stands with his straw boater on his head looking at Irina, saying 'Say something to me', was one of the most heart-rending of his moving performances. Two of the three sisters themselves – Peggy Ashcroft as Irina, and Gwen Ffrangçon Davies as Olga – were perfection. Carol Goodner as Masha was good, but not perfectly cast. Angela Baddeley was wonderful as Natasha. She arrives during the first act for Irina's party gauche, wrongly dressed, terribly eager, half-acting shyness and is proposed to by Andrei, the large awkward brother of the three sisters. As the play goes on she becomes more and more boss of the household – a plump, boring, house-proud woman filling the house with discord, henpecking her husband Andrei, flirting behind his back with a character one never sees called Propopotov. Angela played the development quite perfectly and by the last act you knew she had taken over the household by sheer force and determination. George Devine as Andrei, one of his most memorable performances, began as a rather large, eager, anxious, longing character deceived into thinking he is in love with Natasha, gradually sinking under her domination, pushing the baby in the pram, and finally falling into a hopeless despondency. John Gielgud was not really right as Vershinin, the Battery Commander, although he did not harm the ensemble. Somehow one didn't quite believe in him and his desperate falling in love with Masha. He was too self-conscious and perhaps couldn't quite believe in himself in the part.

*

During *The Three Sisters* Michael was offered a long-term contract with Gainsborough Films. He should have played Bassanio in *The Merchant of Venice*, but as it was the last play of the season and the film contract was five years with big money and he wanted to break into films – chiefly, I think, to make himself financially independent so that he could afford to do the best and less well paid work in the theatre – John Gielgud released him.

When he started filming in *The Lady Vanishes* with Margaret Lockwood we felt tremendously rich with his film salary and decided to move and generally branch out. We had had a series of very indifferent nannies for Vanessa which had worried me a good deal, but now we had found a really delightful girl, Norland-trained, gentle and understanding. She had a true vocation for looking after children. Vanessa became happy at last, where she had been irritable and difficult. I felt guilty and unhappy that I had not managed to get the right person sooner. However, Sybil Russell was exactly right and I could also feel she would help me to give the next baby the right start. I was pregnant for the second time.

We now began to long for a cottage in the country to go to at weekends. We saw an advertisement of a cottage and derelict windmill for sale in a village in Essex called White Roding. I was fond of Essex by association. Michael and I were both attracted to the photograph of the house with the huge mill beside it.

Although we didn't like it at first, while looking over it we gradually began to feel that something might be made of it, like actors reading over a part that didn't seem very good at first sight.

*

In the spring of 1938 we had our first visitors: Michel St Denis, Vera Poliakoff, George Devine and Angela Baddeley. Michel was very much taken with the place and said it had an 'air maritime', which in a way it had, because the flat fields stretched away to a distance that could have been the sea. Indeed the winds from the marshes and sea beyond blew over us, forever flapping the sails of the mill, making them creak continually except on windless days.

Michel St Denis and Vera found and bought a small Elizabethan farmhouse called Clobbs a few miles away from our mill-house, and he and Vera often stayed with us while they were preparing it. We spent many happy Sunday evenings there. Sophia Harris, one of the Motley partnership, later to marry George Devine, usually stayed there at weekends and cooked delicious dinners which we ate by candlelight in the big brick-floored living-room.

I have always admired intensely the way Michel and George lived, a style that George carried on to the end of his life, especially in the last years in the perfect partnership with Jocelyn Herbert. Wherever they have had a house or studio, in the country or in London, they have given their rooms the simplest furnishing, the walls painted white, with few pictures. Floors of brick would be scrubbed, with one rug by the fire. George and Jocelyn would not have curtains at the windows, and yet even in winter their living-rooms always glowed with the big log-fire burning and usually a large divan and easy chairs, white linen covered, perhaps a big writing desk for work and one low wooden table in front of the fire, and that would be it. They ate in the kitchen off a scrubbed wooden table. Yet, much as I have admired it, I have always gone in for a more cluttered living, curtains and carpets, glazed chintzes in the country – conventional, really, but somehow I need to be more 'tucked in' to a house. The house is the womb from which I have never quite escaped. I am certainly not unique in this, but I wish I didn't need so many trappings and cushioning to help me feel secure. My early dream of the white mist surrounding me on the long breakwater has always affected me, so that I have to upholster my background.

We did not see Michel St Denis for many years, due mainly to the separation of the war and then the disgraceful disbanding by the Old Vic governors of his Old Vic Theatre School, the best theatre school of our time in this country. He had started it before the war with George Devine, Glen Byam Shaw, the Motleys and Suria Majito, now Madame St Denis. It was called the London Theatre Studio and was housed in Islington. After the war they reopened it at Dulwich as the Old Vic Theatre School. They restored the Old Vic, and the governors treated them in such a way as to force their resignations.

Michel started again at Strasbourg, which broke his health. George founded the Royal Court Theatre and the whole new movement in the theatre, creating work and finding new playwrights, directors and designers.

Chapter Eighteen

War

1938 – the year of the Munich Crisis. Neville Chamberlain's 'peace in our time' message when he came back after talks with Hitler gave the country an elated sense of security – short-lived and false, as it turned out.

At the beginning of my pregnancy I was rehearsing for Ben Jonson's *The Shoemaker's Holiday* for Nancy Price's management at the Playhouse Theatre in Northumberland Avenue. The cast was not starry but good. I played the part of Jane. The work was once more a hard struggle against the daily nausea of pregnancy and so I could not really enjoy it although in a way it was good to have the work to do because it took my mind off the wretched sickness. Nancy Price was a remarkable woman. She was of the genre of Lilian Baylis, quite undaunted by lack of money and somehow putting on play after play on a shoestring. She had made a great success with *Whiteoaks* which paid for a number of subsequent productions. She directed *The Shoemaker's Holiday* herself. It couldn't have made a penny but she kept it on for a month, by which time being four months pregnant I had no time to go into another play.

Once more our flat was not big enough for two children and so we decided to move again. 'Peace in our time' and Michael's salary had gone to our heads. We found a pleasant house in Clifton Hill, St John's Wood with a basement and three floors above, which we were able to rent on a longish lease. There was a small garden at the back with a pear tree. We had all the rooms painted white. We launched out far too lavishly on the decorations but the result was very elegant and we enjoyed it.

*

Michael was in the first production of T.S. Eliot's *The Family Reunion* and went and stayed in an hotel while I packed up and supervised the move. Sybil Russell, Vanessa and I moved into the house on the morning of the first night, to which I was being taken by the late John

Garret. Why we moved house on a first night I cannot now remember. It was a very stupid arrangement since I was eight and a half months pregnant. Michael also asked me to give a first-night-and-house-warming-party. I had found a rather indifferent man and wife to come as cook and houseman, and somehow or other they got the house straight in one day. I felt so exhausted by the evening I didn't know how I could sit through Michael's performance, let alone be hostess for a large party afterwards. John Garret arrived at about 6.30 to take me out for dinner before the play, drove me to the Goring Hotel and ordered champagne immediately, and over a quiet dinner I recovered.

The move, with its usual accompaniment of packing cases and impossible junk you forgot you had ever possessed, the hoovering and dusting and lumping of furniture, and finally preparing for a party of about thirty people, quite finished the new-found couple, although Sybil and I worked with them. However, that night Michael and the guests seemed delighted and one or two congratulated me on the feat of doing it at all. Dear John Garret said he remembered it all his life. I certainly remembered his kindness, without which I think I would have collapsed.

I had decided to have the baby at home and engaged the same maternity nurse who had looked after me at the cranky home where Vanessa was born. We found a very nice local GP who said he would deliver the baby. The first couple having left, we found a rather grand temporary pair who said they would stay for a couple of months to see me through the birth. The cook was splendid. The 'butler', as he called himself, did almost nothing but sit cleaning a small amount of silver and look grand and tell us of the fine places he had been used to and generally frighten Michael and me so that we felt we were being employed by them.

However, I think Michael enjoyed giving lunch and dinner parties and showing off our house. Looking back it all seems rather a *folie de grandeur*, but the value of one's income was about ten times what it is now and we could afford it. In any case that period of apparent affluence was extremely short-lived. It was July 1939 and 'peace in our time' was coming to an abrupt end. I have always found any sort of household staff an embarrassment. The various couples or whoever we had sensed this immediately and nearly always made life difficult with moods and complaints which I tried to appease quite unsuccessfully.

Mackie, the maternity nurse, came to stay a few days before the baby was due. It was nice to have her company in the last heavy days, which seemed unending. She was a big happy young woman who filled one with confidence. Michael was out a great deal. Vanessa had been taken to the Mill House by Sybil Russell for a fortnight. I stayed with them for a few days and then went back to London to wait with Mackie. Vanessa spent a lot of time playing about in the barns, collecting the eggs each day and watching the cows being milked. Sybil gave her a very happy time.

*

It was a hot July and the days seemed to pass very slowly, but late in the evening of July 15th the first, this time unmistakable, contractions started. I had only just gone to bed. I got up and told Mackie, who immediately dressed in her white uniform – cap and all. She laid out the baby-clothes and nappies and prepared the same basket cot used for Vanessa, and then she insisted that I sleep as much as possible between the contractions. She never left me all night, and this time having experienced it all before I relaxed and slept quite a bit for the first hours, and when towards morning my labour got hard Mackie told me how to breathe and relax. I trusted her completely. She made me feel as if we were doing a job together.

About 7 a.m. she telephoned for the doctor, who arrived fifteen minutes later dressed in a tussore shirt, grey flannels and high wellington boots. Near the end he told Mackie to give me a mask, on which she sprayed a little chloroform so that I could use it myself. In that way I never quite lost consciousness because as soon as I began to go under I dropped the mask.

Corin was born at 8 a.m. on July 16th, 1939. Michael had been anxiously hovering about the stairs and the minute after the birth came running into the room. We were both delighted to have a boy. The doctor, H.G. Broadbridge, later coroner for the Kilburn district, I believe, seemed as pleased as we were. He told me that however many times he delivered a baby he always felt the same thrill of pleasure and at that time a little envy too, since he and his wife had no children. They parted later and he married again and to his great joy had a family of his own.

Mackie bathed Corin in my room. Michael watched, beaming with pride, describing every little move he made. When he was dressed and wrapped in a shawl Mackie gave him into my arms for his first feed. There wasn't a moment's difficulty. He opened his mouth and literally grabbed my nipple and started sucking with enormous strength as if he had been doing it for days. He was quite unlike Vanessa. He had a very male, almost poised, determined look with his straight and pronounced nose.

In those days it was the custom to stay in bed for ten days after the birth and then get up a little longer each day following. One was very cossetted, if one could afford it. Being at home was much nicer than a nursing home or hospital.

Vanessa and Sybil soon came back, Vanessa having picked up a broad Essex accent in three weeks. Then trouble started. The couple who had agreed to stay for two months said they had too much to do and gave notice. It's true we entertained a great deal and the weather was extremely hot. Just before Corin was a month old the news of the likelihood of war began to get serious. The couple left and we decided it would be wise to close the house and go to the cottage at White Roding. It was an anxious and fearful time, so the kind and stalwart Mackie said she would stay an extra week and go down to Essex with us. Sybil had become engaged to be married to a doctor who worked at the Romford Hospital but said that since life was so unsettled she would stay on for six months to help give Corin a good start.

*

On September 3rd war was declared. The following morning, awakened by a roar of planes, we sprang out of bed and ran to the window saying, 'They're here!' We thought the first German bombers had arrived. We soon realised they were six of our 'few' airforce on an exercise. Then the government, expecting large-scale bombing attacks, announced the mass evacuation of London for children and expectant mothers and asked everyone in the country to house as many as they could possibly fit in. They offered five shillings a week for each child's keep. Trainload after trainload of children with labels tied to their arms left the London termini every half hour to arrive at country stations all over England.

Our nearest station was Bishop's Stortford, where buses waited, and gradually through the day vast numbers of children and expectant mothers were deposited at the adjoining villages, ours at the small village hall, really a large shed opposite our house. It was a chaotic situation. We in our four-small-bedroomed cottage already housing Michael and myself, Sybil Russell, Vanessa and Corin, took two expectant mothers to whom we gave our double spare room and a mother with a very young child to whom we gave one of the two sitting-rooms. We were full to bursting. All day Michael and I, between the meals and feeding Corin, went across to the village hall to try to help sort out the chaos and to allocate the women and children to the various houses and cottages in and around White Roding village. We kept ferrying little parties in our car and sort of hawking them around. In some cases the householder was co-operative and welcoming; in others they were possibly overworked with their own families and couldn't face extra mouths to feed and for a few shillings a week. Some quite simply refused. By midnight that night the dull lamp-lit hall was full of exhausted, homesick, hungry people clutching little bundles of clothes and the remains of a packet of sandwiches.

Some called out, 'Oh, fer Gawd's sake let's go back 'ome. They don't want us 'ere.' By about two o'clock in the morning we forced the last of this sad group, three very dirty little boys, onto a farmer and his wife about two miles out of the village, who were wonderfully pleasant, though woken in the small hours of the morning, and made up some sort of makeshift sleeping places with rugs and cushions on the floor of the front room. Mike and I returned home exhausted to try to sleep.

Next day the difficulties started. The village only contained two small shops, the post office/grocery store and a tiny butcher; so the first problem was catering. We had our car but petrol was immediately rationed, so driving to Bishop's Stortford for provisions had to be limited. For about three days our guests were very co-operative, helping to cut up large quantities of runner beans and peel potatoes, which were plentiful. For the rest we laid out our dwindling money on meat and milk and eggs and it was abundantly clear that their meagre allowance per head was going to be completely inadequate for the expenses incurred. All day long the evacuees wandered up and down the village collecting into little grumbling groups. One afternoon, when Michael and I had gone to the town to buy more stores, our own little contingent, the three women, collected large sticks which they threw at our one pear tree until they had knocked down its entire crop. We were terribly dispirited when we got back.

After ten days of an impossible situation throughout the country most of the evacuees returned to their homes in London, since there was no sign of the expected air-raids. Through all this Sybil kept calm and good-tempered. Vanessa, at two-and-a-half, was happy playing with the evacuees. Corin fed happily, rarely cried and, with a composure that has marked his character through all crises until this very day and I hope always will, thrived.

*

We realised that Michael must get back to work as soon as possible. Essex was probably very vulnerable and the cottage was clearly not a practical place to live with Corin aged six weeks and Vanessa two and a half.

Old friends, Mr and Mrs Bashford, invited us to send Sybil and the children to Dartmouth for a while which, from a safety point of view, we felt glad of. 'Bash', who had known me as a child and cried on the picnic, was now married to Elena, the Italian widow of Bertie Sullivan, great-nephew of the great Sullivan of the operas, who had died leaving Elena very well off with an income of royalties. Bash, still a master at the College, and Elena had one daughter. They all lived in a beautiful house in the country just outside Dartmouth, with a nice Norland Nanny, and so Sybil could be very happy there.

Michael and I were asked to go on tour with a farcical comedy by Ben Levy called *Springtime for Henry*, to be joined by Ursula Jeans and Roger Livesey. It was a wonderful play and, with only four characters and one set, cheap to put on. My part of Miss Smith was enormous, and I was terribly nervous during rehearsals because I felt completely unfunny. I tried to get the truth as well as the comedy but seemed to be getting neither.

Michael, directing, was overanxious for me and cramped me with too many ideas. One day, within ten days of opening, he suggested I should change parts with Ursula Jeans. She was an accomplished actress and excellent in her own part, and although she could have played mine I really knew I was too young and unsophisticated to play hers. I was in a state of terrible anxiety over the whole thing. Finally Ursula said why didn't we ask the author, Benn Levy, to come down and watch a run-through and suggest either a way of helping me to play my part or a quick replacement. He came and watched and at the end very cleverly and courageously said, 'I don't know what you are worrying about, ducky, you can play it on your head.' And from that moment I could and had a great success. It seemed like magic to me. I am quite certain he didn't think what he saw was good, but he knew we hadn't time for a replacement so he dared a kind of bluff, which worked.

I know that from the moment I met Margaret Scudamore and her friend Molly Terraine who, although they had never seen me act, made it clear to Mother and me that they thought I had been over-praised at Stratford and was not likely to be much good compared to Michael, I had lost confidence and confidence is entirely necessary. Talent and hard work with a lack of confidence are not enough.

I was happy on the stage at night during the tour but missed Vanessa and Corin. We only toured the play for eight weeks, so as soon as we closed went off to Dartmouth to the children. They were both well. Corin, by now four months old, had changed out of recognition. Sybil had been wonderful, hardly going out at all throughout the time I was away. Then, happily for her but unhappily for us, she was anxious to be married and leave. Parting from her was terribly sad and yet I was happy for her happiness in marrying the man she loved with the prospect of children of their own. I sent her for a holiday to see her John and looked after the children myself. It was a happy time. Elena, crippled with arthritis, never made the slightest fuss, but she would sit on the terrace in the glorious garden and watch the children running around. Vanessa had a lovely time going ferreting with Ruth, Elena's daughter, riding on the haycarts with Ruth and Nursie. Corin was still a baby in arms.

I had found another Norland nurse, a middle-aged woman, very experienced but, as it soon turned out, with a passion for religion and baby boys. She was not unkind to Vanessa but lacked real warmth and understanding of little girls. I was soon very worried by this, especially when I had to be away. Corin thrived. So did Vanessa, but she used to come creeping into my bed in the morning, whispering, 'Don't let Nursie hear me', which I knew was wrong. They stayed on at Dartmouth for a month or two. Then, since there was no bombing, we all returned to Clifton Hill.

When there was a threat of raids again Mother and Father invited the children and Sybil to stay at their house at the Royal Naval College. Sybil came with us to settle the children, but now her marriage with John was fixed.

*

During the tour of *Springtime for Henry* Michael was asked to play Macheath in a production of *The Beggar's Opera* to be put on by John Christie with the Glyndebourne Company at the Haymarket Theatre. They said they required an actor/singer in the leading part rather than a singer who might not be able to act. John Gielgud was to direct it.

The manager, Rudolf Bing, suggested sending their brilliant singing coach Jani Strasser on tour for about four hours a day – Jani, a Hungarian, who spoke very good English, was not only a brilliant teacher of voice but an amusing and witty companion. This, I know, made the work even more enjoyable. He taught Michael an entirely new way of breathing and by the time the tour ended and rehearsals started Michael's charming singing voice was strengthened and in good control. Audrey Mildmay played Polly Peachum and Linda Grey was a magnificent Lucy. The set and dress designers were the Motleys, who set it in the Regency period. It opened after a short tour in March and was an enormous success. Michael was a dazzlingly attractive Macheath with his weight enhanced by the beautiful caped coat and top-hat. His make-up was brilliant; he lifted the corners of his eyes to an upward slant which gave him a glittering, slightly devilish look. Macheath is a devil-may-care highwayman with such charm that all the women fall in love with him.

This was a difficult period for our marriage; we were able to be together very little since I was spending my time between the children in the country and Michael in London. Naturally he made many new friends in the shifting population of wartime London, especially during the year's respite from the expected bombing. I was bound to drop out from his social activities.

When I went to performances of *The Beggar's Opera* I was filled with a mixture of love and jealousy and longed to be closer to this devastatingly attractive Macheath. I had learned no wisdom as yet. I was still a young woman in love and very possessive, with little sense of how to behave without continually wearing my heart on my sleeve.

*

In the summer we all went back to Clifton Hill once again. This time it was a short stay because the first big raids started in the last week of August 1940. On the afternoon of the bombing of the City and the docks Nurse and I, Vanessa and Corin, all sat in the basement. We listened to the planes and the horrific swish of the bombs passing over our area of St John's Wood. That night the sky was alight from the fires burning in the City. Each night there was a raid lasting many hours. We had our basement shored up with large beams of wood supported by upright wooden pillars because we felt safer that way. Perhaps, if a neighbouring house had been bombed and our house had fallen with the blast, our basement *might* have kept us safe – a direct hit would have been death in any case. All night sitting by candlelight in that basement with Vanessa lying on a mattress and Corin held by either Nurse or me was the most unnerving and frightening experience of my life. The falling bombs made such an eerie whine before the explosion. The explosion itself was almost a relief, because in hearing it you knew that you and yours were safe that time. But I kept saying: Why not us?

At the end of that week Nurse was completely exhausted and said she didn't know how to go on. Once again the children must return to the country. This time my father's cousin, Lucy Wedgwood Kempson, offered a home for us all at Whitegate, her house in Bromyard, Herefordshire, close to Birchyfield, Father's old home. I felt worried at leaving Michael on his own, but he said he could always get a friend to stay if he needed. In fact he took a room at Athenaeum Court in Piccadilly where Carol Reed and Diana Wynyard were living.

As the train drew out of Paddington Station a weight seemed to fall off me. Corin sat on my knee quite happily looking about him, calm and collected as always. Vanessa was full of excitement at going somewhere new to stay. The train was very full, as trains were throughout the war, with troops on the move and evacuees who, like ourselves, had gone home to London during the calm period of the phoney war, as it came to be called, but now were off again to find homes in the country. Country people were wonderfully generous to the town children and families often became so fond of their foster children that they hated parting with them when the war was over.

*

We arrived at Bromyard's tiny station after a journey of three and a half hours to find Cousin Lucy's chauffeur/gardener, William Hodges, waiting for us with her car. She had an extra allowance of petrol on account of housing a family, which was very helpful since Bromyard was a very small town and it was nice occasionally to be able to drive to Hereford or Worcester, both two miles away. William Hodges had known me and Nicholas and Robin as small children when he was assistant to his father in the garden. Cousin Lucy and her brother, Cousin John, shared Birchyfield for quite a long time, after my grandparents had given it up. Indeed they lived there until about 1919 when they decided to cut down expenses and build Whitegate.

Whitegate is very ugly but has one of the loveliest views in Herefordshire. It stands on a hill overlooking a large plain beyond which is the whole range of the Malvern hills. It was curiously designed to meet the needs of Lucy, John and Hester Richardson, their younger married sister, for which reason they had a large central sitting-hall off which were a study, a drawing-room, a dining-room and servants' sitting-room, and beyond that the kitchen, scullery and larder. At this time John and Hester were many years dead and Lucy, retired from being warden of Bedford College in London, lived there alone. She still had a cook, Frances, and a young housemaid, Joyce; also an old woman for rough cleaning, called Mrs Mason, whom Corin later called Mrs Masement.

On arrival at the house there was a wonderful tea with scones and two sorts of home-made cakes and shortbread, all laid out on a round table in the hall. Tea was almost a ritual with Cousin Lucy; it was the one meal when everyone met together. The children ate breakfast and lunch in Frances's sitting-room, which was small but cosy. It was a good arrangement, because it isn't easy to live in another person's house or for another person to have a houseful of permanent or semi-permanent guests. Lucy was mother and grandmother to us all. She had a big shelf full of her childhood books, which Vanessa gradually got to know, as I had done in my childhood. After tea that first day it was fine and sunny and we all went out into the garden, Vanessa carrying Sammy, the female Siamese cat, so named because Lucy said she wouldn't have had her if she'd known she was a female. Corin crawled at a great rate across the lawn and sat in a rose bed, doing the same again each time we pulled him out. We slept in safety and peace that night, while the grandfather clock in the hall ticked away the hours of war, now seemingly remote from us.

The furnishing of Whitegate was mostly Victorian; even the later armchairs and sofas were pretty worn. The stair carpet and rugs on the polished floors were almost threadbare. The curtains were mostly thick woollen in dark colours, with the 'blackout' curtains hanging behind them to cut out all light at night.

The drawing-room was quite pretty with its iron hobbed fireplace surrounded by blue-and-white Dutch tiles. The curtains were flowered cretonne for summer, brown velvet in winter. Lucy had a beautiful gramophone, or 'record-player' as it is now called, a present from the staff of Bedford College when she retired. She had a fine collection of classical records, since she was a music lover and had sung in the London Bach Choir as a younger woman.

Lucy had been among the first women of her generation to want and to get a university education. She was at Oxford in her youth in company with Dorothy Sayers. Her mother was Louisa Wedgwood, who had married my grandfather's brother, Alfred Kempson, my great uncle. Alfred died young, leaving Lucy's mother Louisa with four young children, Jessie, John, Lucy and Hester (Hetty). Louisa started to go blind from cataract quite early, a disease which Lucy inherited but which was treated and successfully operated on when she was about 80. Lucy told me that because her mother was an early widow they spent most of their time with their Wedgwood and Darwin relations. Lucy cared very little for the Kempsons, except for my father. She thought my grandfather a fool for losing his money and my aunts – her first cousins – narrow on account of their lack of education. To my father she was as devoted as to a brother, and he was fond of her, and he helped and advised in their many crises, such as Cousin John's alcoholism. John might have married but for this disease. A great friend of Lucy's was much in love with him but since she had an excellent job as a senior mistress at St Andrews Girls' School in Scotland, I imagine she felt that her independence was preferable to life tied to an alcoholic who, although she loved him, was too weak a character to change. I remember him as a kindly man who, when I stayed, aged 9, tried to teach me to play golf.

Cousin Jessie I had hated. She was a sexually repressed, unhappy and rather cruel woman. Cousin Hester, the only married one, I

hardly knew. Cousin Lucy sublimated sex in her passionate love of
education, music and all the arts, especially the theatre, which was
what drew her to me and to Michael and finally to our children. How
much I wish she had lived to see their success. She always predicted
great things for them, especially Corin.

*

Thunder Rock by Robert Ardney was put on at the Neighbourhood
Theatre in South Kensington on June 18th, 1940. The theatre was
tiny and improvised from a hall shaped rather like a tunnel. A great
deal has been written about this fine play. Michael played Charleston,
the lighthousekeeper, and the message was inspiring at a time of war.
This was that all periods of history have had their black years, but if
you go after what you believe in wholeheartedly you will win in the
long run. Hope must never be quenched, even if some are quenched in
their efforts.

Duff Cooper came to see it and was instrumental in persuading the
Treasury to give some money to put it on in the West End. This
gesture was the beginning of grants to the theatre. The play was
transferred to the Haymarket Theatre on July 18th, but the Blitz
started two days before the opening and all London theatres were
closed. Michael later played Charleston in the film, but though the
film reached a greater public the play was the perfect thing with its one
set of the interior of the lighthouse.

*

A quite regular life with a daily pattern continued for about three
years for the children, but for Michael and me, for my father and
mother and Nicholas and Robin it was lived in daily uncertainty and
some danger. Nicholas was in destroyers. I used to lie awake on
stormy nights thinking of his small ship in rough seas. He took it all
with complete calm, as they all did. He had visited us in Edinburgh
while his ship was in and we were playing in *Springtime for Henry*. He
and his fellow officers gave a big party one night at the Caledonian
Hotel in Edinburgh. When officers of the navy or army got leave their
relief was so great that the gaiety and the temporary freedom went to
everyone's head like champagne. The truth seems to be that life is at
its most precious and perfect when the possibility of death is near. At
such times, as in war, the moments of freedom from fear are enjoyed
to their bubbling limit, and so it was that night.

Robin went into the navy with a commission as sub-lieutenant

RNVR. He was in torpedo-boats and badly wounded and shell-shocked quite early. His nerves were all to pieces; in fact he had a slight nervous breakdown and he was on leave at the RNC with Father and Mother when Dartmouth was raided for the first time and completely collapsed. Father wrote to me and asked if I could accompany Robin to an hotel on Dartmoor for a week or two so that he could recuperate. I went, leaving the children at Whitegate with the nurse and Lucy, and Nicholas on leave joined us. Robin was outwardly calm but the sound of planes overhead affected him badly. There was an old doctor staying at the hotel who noticed Robin's illness and talked to him and me about it. He suggested that Robin ought to have a long leave with freedom from the anxiety of his own fear of going back to sea and facing dangers for which he was clearly unfit, before his nervous exhaustion and shock were completely cured. He suggested that Robin should go to see the neurologist Sir Farquhar Buzzard, Regius Professor of Medicine at Oxford. I wrote to Cousin Lucy to ask if she could take Robin into the household for a while and she, as always, generously agreed. Nicholas had to return to his ship and so I travelled with Robin to Bromyard, going by train from Plymouth via Bristol. At Bristol there was an air-raid warning; the train stopped and Robin sank into a corner but said nothing. Fortunately it was only an alarm; the all-clear soon sounded and the train continued the journey. We got out at Hereford, where William met us. We arrived at the house in time for tea.

Corin was sitting at the foot of the stairs in the hall and said, 'I go up and downstairs by myself, I do.' It was the first time he had spoken sentences. He seemed as delighted as I was and kept up a stream of sentences: 'I do (so and so), I do.'

*

After the run of *The Beggar's Opera* Michael was called up and decided to follow in the footsteps of Nicholas and Robin and go into the Navy. He joined HMS *Raleigh* training school at Devonport as an ordinary seaman, while I stayed at a farm nearby. He came for the odd night.

It was primitive, but I was happy with the farm life. I learned to wash and iron Mike's uniform, collars and tops. If the blue ran into the white, the whole outfit had to be washed again in the copper and ironed with a flat-iron heated on the grid of the black kitchen range.

During his training Michael was asked to get up concerts for the seamen and officers. Having been a friend of Noel Coward's, he sang many of Noel's numbers, 'Mad Dogs and Englishmen' being a favourite with everyone. I sat in the front row with the Commander and his wife, feeling very privileged.

At the end of the three months' training, Michael was asked by Lord Louis Mountbatten to join HMS *Illustrious* in Norfolk, Virginia. (Noel, a mutual friend of Michael and Lord Louis, was instrumental in this arrangement.) Michael went out in a troop-carrier. Most of the troops were seasick, he told me, but fortunately he was a good sailor, and so was made to do the cleaning up!

On HMS *Illustrious* he was soon put to 'painting ship', sitting on a plank slung over the side. While the ship was coaling he injured his right arm and later was invalided out of the Navy.

Ruth Gordon, an actress friend, invited him to stay at her house near New York. He was much fêted in New York and, although disappointed at leaving the Navy, realised that there was so much that he could do as an actor and entertainer to help the war effort.

Chapter Nineteen

Venice & Bedford House

Michael was away at HMS *Raleigh*. We managed to meet at weekends and would stay at the Cavendish, Rosa Lewis's famous hotel. Rosa would sit dispensing champagne in the lobby and would keep saying to us, 'They are all waiting for you.' Who, we didn't know. The place was a muddle but full of valuable antiques supposedly left to her by Edward VII whose mistress she was reputed to have been. She was a pretty woman, white-haired, rosy-faced and slender, often slightly tight. Her illegitimate daughter Edith made the bookings and tried to maintain some order in a totally disorganised hotel. It was no good ringing for anything because there was never anyone to answer.

I became pregnant again. It wasn't a very good time for it. Rationing was still acute, and it was before the time that pregnant women were given extra rations, but we could get rabbits and the odd black-market chicken. We also received the occasional parcel from America from Aunt Nora Mellon, mother of the famous race-horse trainer and art-collector Paul Mellon.

On March 8th, 1943, Lynny was born. We were living at Rivermead Court. I went to the London Clinic for the birth because at that time there was an air-raid shelter in the basement. Vanessa got whooping cough very badly, so I had to stay at the London Clinic for a month! It was an easy birth, needing little anaesthetic. Michael had wanted another boy, but I didn't mind at all. Lynn was born with dark hair, and was round and healthy. She was easy to feed, and I tried not to let the nurses know when I had finished so that she would stay by me in her cot all day.

Eventually I returned with Lynny to Rivermead Court. Vanessa and Nanny were delighted, but Corin was 'not amused'. Nanny put Lynn on the nursery table to change her nappies, and instructed Corin not to touch her in case she fell off. Corin said crossly, 'Would it matter?'

When there was an air-raid warning we all trooped down to a ground-floor flat belonging to two kind elderly ladies for shelter. Corin used to take his teddy bear by the arm, saying, 'Come along, my

147

child.' Lynny lay in her carry cot, gurgling, and Nanny, Vanessa and I used to talk to our two women friends until the all-clear went.

On Sunday afternoons we often had tea parties for our friends. One Sunday Edith Evans came because she said she wanted to see the 'new ba-by'. We all sat round a large table. Edith said she was going to sit next to Corin, who looked very cross.

'He's not talking now,' she said, 'but we are going to be great frie-nds.'

Corin was scarlet in the face. He looked at her and said, 'Wot a lot of teeth you've got.'

'Yes, and thank God they're all me ow-n,' replied Edith, thus triumphantly carrying off the tricky situation.

*

In 1944 Michael was asked to play in *Uncle Harry* by Thomas Job. It was a murder thriller. He played Harry, Beatrix Lehmann the older sister and Ena Burrill the younger. I played the young girl whom Harry was said to be keen on. We played it for nearly a year at the Garrick Theatre. Quite often the air-raid siren would go during a performance. There was a pause to allow anyone to leave who wished to, but mostly the audiences seemed to feel safer in the theatre. By then nowhere was safe and people began to get philosophical. If the sirens went during an evening performance at any theatre, people were told to leave if they liked, or to stay while actors from adjoining theatres gave an impromptu concert performance until the raid was over.

Edith Hargreaves, Mike's dresser and 'friend' during the run of *Uncle Harry*, had been introduced to Mike by Edith Evans. She always remained his greatest fan.

I got to know Beatrix Lehmann very well during the run of *Uncle Harry*. She used to come and visit us at our flat in Rivermead Court, and later at our cottage at Wilks Water. She had a wonderful sense of humour, but at the same time was very down to earth.

One day, while she was working with Charles Laughton, he had said to her, 'Beatrix, has anyone ever told you that I am repulsive and ugly?'

She, in order to be kind and tactful, replied, 'No, Charles dear, *of course* not.'

'Well,' he said, 'lots of people have told me that *you* are.'

Fortunately Beatrix's sense of humour got her through. She was very intelligent and witty, and her personality was enchanting. When she came to stay at Wilks Water, she was a delightful guest. She knew a great deal about wild life, especially birds, and would explain how robins had their own territory and would fight if one crossed into the other's patch. She had a garden in her house in Islington which she had made quite beautiful. She was wonderful with children and played endlessly with Corin, amusing him by pretending to be a lion. She adored her dog, and always insisted on bringing him to rehearsal; he would wait for her in her dressing-room during a performance. She was a really good friend, loyal and understanding.

At the end of the year's run Michael was getting tired and fed up and said he must have some time on his own. He went to stay at the Savoy Hotel for a month. Father stayed with me and we watched the V1s from a bedroom window, realising for the first time that there was no pilot.

One day during the run of *Uncle Harry* I was lunching alone before a matinée, feeling a little low, when an American officer at the next table introduced himself to me. He asked me what I was doing that evening and when I told him I was in a play at the Garrick Theatre he asked me to reserve him a seat, which I did. He came round afterwards and we left together. Hand-in-hand we walked to Victoria Station. He wanted to come home with me, and I would have liked him to, but with the children there it was not possible. I rang him next day at his hotel before he went back to the States. He sounded bitter and angry, but there was nothing I could do about it. He was a very attractive man and, like so many American servicemen in England at that time, very lonely. Recently I was reminded of this episode when I saw Vanessa in the film *Yanks*, the difference being, I thought rather wistfully, that her character had had an affair and I hadn't.

*

In the autumn of 1945 Mike took me to Venice for the first time. As it was the end of the war, everything looked very shabby. We were not allowed to take much sterling, but we had a suite at the Danieli Hotel looking across to Santa Maria del Salute. The day before we had flown to Milan and booked seats at La Scala. The Opera House had been damaged but repair was going on successfully; mirrors glittered and it had been repainted inside. The opera was *Werther*. A rather elderly couple were singing the young leads; the costumes were frowsty, the sets terribly old-fashioned, with festoons of pink roses. However, the singing had such intense passion that we were completely carried away by the end.

During the interval a fair-haired man came into the stalls where we were sitting. It was Stephen Tennant, a member of the

Glenconner family. He was with the American novelist Willa Cather, who was shy and elderly. He asked us to meet him next day at the Danieli.

The next day we went on by train to Venice, a beautiful journey across the Mole. The main station at Venice was crowded and exciting. A porter took our bags to a motor boat which chugged quietly down the Grand Canal past the beautiful *palazzos* on either side.

That evening Stephen arrived at our suite. Throwing handfuls of lire into the air, he said, 'Let's not worry about money. Let's all have a good time.'

This nicely resolved our sterling crisis. Like all visitors to that beautiful city we took gondolas, visited the Accademia museum and went in a lift up the tower of the Santa Maria del Salute, one of the most beautiful monuments. We were entranced by all we saw. We also saw the famous Palazzo Casa d'Oro, the atmosphere of which so intrigued Michael that he based his palazzo on it in his adaptation for the theatre of Henry James's *The Aspern Papers*.

Mike and I were very happy in Venice. I loved the feeling of the soft air blowing off the sea. After the austerity of the war, the city seemed to be a magic place. I loved the sight of the marriage parties in gondolas, with the bride dressed in white, floating along the water. They stacked flowers on the prow of the boat. The bridegroom would wear black, with a black gondolier's hat and a scarlet sash around his waist. One of the guests would be playing a mandolin, and the whole party would sing its way to the church. Many of the weddings took place at Santa Maria del Salute.

The lovely thing about Venice is that you can walk everywhere: over bridges, through arcades, past the cafés – the only sounds being the lapping of the water against the quay, and the not too unpleasant noise of the *vaporetti* taking people up and down the canals.

*

After our return from Venice, Stephen Tennant and we became friends and met again. I was once invited on my own to stay at his house in Wiltshire. It was extremely luxurious. He told me that he had invited two friends for lunch the next day – Juliet Duff and her gentleman friend.

I was shown to my suite of rooms. The walls were covered with wonderful paintings, and a maid unpacked and laid out my clothes. The room was full of flowers.

That evening we had a wonderful dinner. Next morning, as I was about to go downstairs, a note arrived at my bedroom, delivered by the housekeeper, which said: 'Dear Rachel, amuse yourself. Read, write, get up when you like, go into the garden, until the guests arrive. I cannot come down for a while because inspiration has struck, and I am compelled to go on writing.'

I went down to the sitting-room where the butler, Parry, brought in sheaves of flowers which, he said, the master wished to be placed in the middle of the room on the floor. It was very curious. I wandered into the gardens: marvellous lawns, gilded gates, great banks of flowers. Parry gave me vases and we put the flowers where Stephen wanted them, in the middle of the room on the carpet.

When Juliet and her friend arrived for lunch, I was in the large drawing-room. I had to explain that Stephen was still inspired and would come down as soon as possible. Parry was rung for, and we all had drinks.

Juliet was amused, and said: 'Typical Stephen! He's a dear person, but extremely vague about time.'

We all got on very well together and chatted away until Stephen, in full pancake make-up, arrived. He took a flying leap into the middle of the floor and landed on one knee, with the words, 'My darlings, how wonderful to see you.'

Lunch was eventually served in the dining-room where there were exquisite shell decorations with plants and flowers on the table, fine lace mats, and lots of crystal and silver.

After coffee and liqueurs, Stephen asked me to entertain his guests for a while.

Juliet Duff said, 'Now I want Stephen to bring you over to me. The Lunts are coming and various friends.'

Her gentleman friend said to me discreetly, 'I want you to come to a fancy-dress dance with me, and I think it would be fun if you dressed up as a boy. We'll have masks and nobody will be able to tell one from another.'

Finally we said goodbye, agreeing to go to Juliet's the following day. I spent the afternoon sitting by an enormous log fire reading, and Parry brought in a delicious tea.

A good deal later Stephen joined me. 'Now, darling,' he said, 'I want to talk and talk and talk, I have so much I want to hear about you, and so much I want to tell you, I want you to be my inspiration.' He added: 'When I took you to lunch at the Dorchester last week and you wore a pillbox hat you looked like a Botticelli angel.'

We talked by the fire for a long time. Stephen was then about fifty and I was in my mid-thirties. He had dyed golden hair, and at that period always wore full make-up. Somehow this didn't matter to me, he was so welcoming, kind and fun to be with.

We went to Juliet's for the evening. There were lots of guests, and I wandered from room to room, admiring the paintings and furniture. I was introduced to the Lunts. During the war, they had offered to have Vanessa and Corin to live with them in United States, and we had named Lynn after Lynn Fontanne. Michael had got to know them through Ruth Gordon when he was in New York during the war. Although Lynn Fontanne was middle-aged, she was one of the most elegant and attractive women I have ever seen. Alfred Lunt was a fine, tall, distinguished-looking man, and they were an absolutely devoted partnership, offstage and on. Their life was the theatre. They were dedicated to work and their friends.

*

One day, Nicky, Michael and I were having lunch at a restaurant in Romilly Street called the Moulin d'Or with John Fowler, the brilliant interior designer of Colefax Fowler, who had become a close friend and often stayed with us during the bombing. He told us that he had seen a beautiful seventeenth-century house for sale on Chiswick Mall.

John had the keys, and as we went in the front door the house seemed to say, 'I've been waiting for you.' It was the most beautiful house we had ever seen, but it too had suffered from the bomb-blasting. A sheet of corrugated iron covered a front window, and matted couch grass grew up to the windows and doors like a thick green carpet. The state of disrepair did nothing to put us off. On the contrary. But I realised that we would need professional help to restore it to its former glory. John was the obvious choice. The price was £12,000, a fortune in 1945. Our lawyer, Fay Blackett-Gill, said that we could borrow or raise a mortgage. She settled the whole thing in three days. Bedford House now belonged to us.

Since we were still living at Rivermead Court, we went over to Chiswick on Sundays and picnicked in the drawing-room looking on to the river and the wide garden which was overgrown with a rough lawn. One day when we were there with Vanessa and Corin Drs Mary and Tom Nelson from Eynham House next door called on us and said we must come into their house if we were cold or needed any help. They were two of the dearest doctors and friends we had ever known in our lives.

We eventually moved in, in 1946. We all loved it. 'It is such a lovely place,' Michael said, 'that I think I shall want to stay at home more.' I hoped that this would prove true.

The party of the year on Chiswick Mall was the Oxford and

Cambridge Boat Race in the spring. It was often fine and warm so that our guests, Laurence and beautiful Vivien Olivier, John and Mary Mills, Binkie Beaumont, Roger and Ursula Livesey, and many others, could walk on the lawn, champagne in hand, and later crowd onto the balconies and the front garden to watch the famous race. Television was beginning to improve, so we hired a set so that our guests could watch the start and finish of the race, which ran from Putney to Mortlake.

Vivien Leigh was a great friend, and had been to visit me in the London Clinic when Lynn was born. When she came into my room it seemed to light up with her beauty. She and Larry were at that time radiantly happy.

After the move, Michael directed and acted continuously. He put on a production of *Jacobowsky and the Colonel*, at the Piccadilly Theatre, with Michael as the Colonel, myself as Marianne and our dear friend Diana Gould, now Lady Menuhin, in the cast. Michael was working so hard that he had to have a secretary, and that is how Joan Hirst first came into our lives. She had a son, Robin, the same age as Corin, and they amused each other in the garden during their school holidays. Joan has worked for us devotedly ever since.

Gradually we began to restore the house. John Fowler bought book-binding canvas for the curtains, and we had some beautiful silk fringe made by his firm into edgings: all delightful and very inexpensive. Luckily the interior of the house was in good condition and needed little doing to it. The garden was the main problem. I worked hard at rolling back the matted couch grass, revealing paths and flower beds. An elderly gardener, Mr Owers, from Essex, came to live in the adjoining cottage. He stoked the old-fashioned coke boiler and cleaned the paths and flowerbeds and scythed the lawn outside the drawing-room.

I bought a mermaid rose and trained it along the wall dividing Eynham House from Bedford House. Owers and I dug the borders. I planted lupins, stocks, delphiniums and other herbaceous plants in the long border. Irises were in the square beds at the far end of the lawn. There was a derelict tennis court, which we were able to restore more or less, a greenhouse for tomato plants and a chicken coop. Nanny looked after the chickens, and Owers wrung a neck when we needed a chicken for the pot. There was a pergola near the drawing-room with grey paving stones, and a garden seat, chairs and a summer table.

The nursery upstairs looked out onto the river. It was lovely in summer, when the reflections from the water seemed to flicker on the nursery walls, the rocking horse and the doll's house. There were eight bedrooms and three bathrooms. On the ground floor was a hall, an oval library and a very large drawing-room with a huge fireplace. Corin's bedroom had a balcony with an iron balustrade, upon which I later discovered many hidden cigarette stubs. Corin smoked secretly from the age of eleven!

I used to play Halma, Snakes and Ladders and Happy Families with the children by the fire after tea in the oval library. Michael was rarely there, since he was working most of that time and had to leave early.

We had our first children's party just before Christmas with a large Christmas tree with real candles, which Nanny snuffed out as they burned down. Because of the rationing I got a caterer to do the tea, and we hired a conjuror. We invited Matthew Guinness, son of Alec and Merula, and the Lousada family, children of designer Jocelyn Herbert and Anthony Lousada, and many others who joined with ours for lessons with a governess. Corin and Matthew teased the governess, who was really very nice, unmercifully.

*

In the spring of 1946 both Michael and I were cast in *The Captive Heart*, a film to be made by Ealing Studios. Margaret Genn was the casting director for Ealing Films and thought I would be suitable for the part of the young girl. Michael was cast in the leading role as a Czechoslovakian officer attached to the British Army in the war. We started filming in the studios at Ealing. Other members of the cast included Basil Radford, Guy Middleton and Gladys Henson. It was a tremendously successful film, and after it I quite imagined I would become a famous film star! They finished the shooting in a real prisoner of war camp in Germany. Nicky happened to be there as he was attached to the Navy in Hamburg. Michael said it was extraordinary being in an actual camp and seeing the ghastly conditions the inmates had had to endure. The cast party was given at the Atlantic Hotel, Hamburg, attended by the male members of the cast. Max Adrian, who happened to be in Hamburg, was invited to attend. He arrived extremely late, and the cast and officers were all left hanging around waiting to go into dinner. At last he arrived full of apologies. 'I'm so sorry we're so late,' he said, 'but actually we think it's rather chic', which started the evening on an amusing note.

At about this time Glen Byam Shaw asked me to play Octavia in his production of *Antony and Cleopatra*. Edith Evans was Cleopatra and Leslie Banks, Antony. Neither was quite right. Perhaps foolishly, I refused. I think Glen found it hard to forgive me. I hadn't done a great deal then and he felt it would have helped my career. Later he told me he thought I had turned it down because I was too grand to play a small part. In fact I would have liked to play it in repertory, but not for a long run.

Chapter Twenty

Difficulties

Corin and Vanessa went to a nearby day-school when they and the others had outgrown the governess. When Corin was eight we decided to send him to a boarding prep school at Malvern Wells, Wells House. The school had a fine reputation and had been good for my father, my cousins Tony and Alexander McMullen, Dick Green, our best man, and John Marshall, a friend of the family, so we thought it a good idea.

Corin and I went to have a look at it. Malvern Wells is a lovely place. The school was on the hills in fine country. We met the headmaster, who talked a great deal in praise of the school and his methods. He seemed amiable and breezy, if a little pleased with himself. Corin thought it a pleasant place, and it was decided that he should join in the autumn term of 1947.

He duly went off, happily enough, but it proved a disaster for him. The headmaster insisted that the beds in each dormitory should be moved to new positions every night so that no boy had his niche or was next to the same boy as the night before. As I remember, children like a 'home' corner, where they feel secure at night. A bell clanged for every class; all movement was done at a run. The whole place was over-spartan, over-disciplined. Corin became increasingly unhappy. At the end of his first term he looked very tired but happy to be back for the Christmas holidays. Lynn, aged four, met him outside the front door. He put out his arms and she ran into them. They hugged each other with affection and a deep mutual love.

Corin didn't talk much about school, and Christmas was a happy time. We called on A.P. Herbert and his wife Gwen. They lived in a large spacious house on Chiswick Mall where they gave parties at which A.P. played the piano and we all sang. Gwen was always very twinkly and adoring of A.P.

*

At the end of the holidays, Corin returned to Wells House for the spring term. When I saw him off at Paddington Station he didn't seem too unhappy. His letters home revealed nothing of his school life. However, I did have doubts but didn't think I could do anything about it at the time.

The crunch came in the spring holidays. The day before he was due to return to Wells House, he begged us to let him stay at home. He was desperately unhappy at school as I had suspected. I kept him at home and comforted him at night for an extra day.

Then Michael took him to Paddington. 'If you really can't bear it at the end of this term,' he said to Corin, 'we will take you away.' He put him in the charge of a pleasant-looking woman on the train, and gave her his ticket so that she would see that he got off at Malvern Wells station.

Two days later we received a letter from her which said that Corin had been so distressed during the journey that he told her he didn't know where he was going. She also said that she had telephoned the school to make sure that somebody would meet him. The letter worried us both greatly. I wrote and said that I would go down and see him at half-term.

At the time I was playing in *The Paragon* at the Fortune Theatre with Hugh Burden and Walter Fitzgerald, directed by Norman Marshall. After the Saturday night performance I was driven through the night by our chauffeur, Kenneth. I arrived at an hotel at 1.30 in the morning and went to bed. Corin arrived at about eight next morning and leapt onto my bed. After breakfast we went out for a walk. It was a beautiful day. As we were going along we met some of the boys from the school. Corin deliberately avoided looking at them, and appeared shy and unhappy. I asked him if they were friends of his and he didn't answer and turned his head away. I realised that things were far from well with him. We carried on walking and returned to the hotel for lunch. He didn't eat much. We went for another walk and returned for tea. Again he didn't want to eat. Eventually it was time for me to return him to the school. We kissed goodbye, and he walked silently in through the back door. I returned to London, extremely worried about him, and discussed the matter with Michael on the Sunday night. Michael said he would write to the headmaster, Mr Darvall. He feared he wouldn't get much response, but promised to go down before the end of the term to find out the true situation.

Michael eventually arrived down on the last day of term to find Corin quite cheerful. It was a fine day, and boys were playing cricket on the field. Michael asked Corin what he had decided.

Corin said, 'I hope you won't be disappointed, Dad.' Michael thought he was going to say that he would like to stay on at the school, but he said, 'Dad, I have quite decided. I want to leave.'

Michael reassured him and told him it would be perfectly all right by us.

Michael went to see Darvall in his office and told him what he had decided.

Darvall said, 'You are just giving way and spoiling the boy. All the others are perfectly happy.' Michael knew for a fact that this wasn't true, as a second cousin of Corin's also went there and felt very much as Corin did. It was finally settled that Corin should leave, Darvall having informed Michael that an intelligence test had shown Corin to be of only medium intelligence. Years later when Corin, who had got into Westminster, took a classics scholarship to King's College Cambridge, where he went on to get a double first, Michael wrote to Darvall to ask him what he thought of this. Darvall pig-headedly replied that this did not alter his opinion in any way.

At the end of the term I met Corin at Paddington station. He looked exhausted. I took him in a taxi to Victoria to catch a train to Bexhill-on-Sea where we had taken a cottage for the summer. We got into the carriage, and Corin lay down and fell instantly asleep for the duration of the journey to Bexhill. His relief at being freed from Wells House was obvious. The summer was a happy one for us all. I could only stay at weekends because I was still playing in *The Paragon*, but the children had a healthy time playing on the beach, swimming and shrimping. It was there that we met John Counsell, the director of the theatre at Windsor and his wife Mary Kerridge and their two children, with whom we used to go shrimping in the rock pools.

Back in London, we selected Eaton House as a suitable prep school for Corin. This was a day school, and the headmaster was delightful. On the first day of term I took Corin by tube from Chiswick to Sloane Square. When we got out of the tube he said he felt sick. I said we would walk round the bomb sites to see if he felt better, and he soon said he didn't feel any better and must go home. I said we could go back today, but tomorrow he would have to face up to it, go to school and stick it out. We went back home and Corin immediately felt perfectly well, and ate a good lunch. Next day, we set off again on the tube, I saw him to the front door of the school and to my surprise he walked in without a qualm. Clearly the problem had been solved. Indeed he became so independent he would go to school on his own without worrying if I was there or not.

Vanessa and Lynn never went to boarding school. They both attended Queen's Gate School in central London, where Vanessa was happy, but Lynn felt in the shadow of her elder sister.

*

During the run of *The Paragon*, which I enjoyed, at home I felt in low spirits. Michael was rarely around, which made me insecure.

The governess noticed my unhappiness and said, 'I have grown so fond of you all, I don't like to see you like this.'

'I don't know what is the matter with me,' I replied. 'I feel like one of those figures that you see in glass bubbles that you shake and the snow rises and falls around. Isolated and cold.'

The fact that somebody else had observed my state of mind made me feel I needed help. I rang John Fowler and we met at his house. He told me that he knew, and had had help from, a wonderful doctor of psychiatry called Charlotte Wolff.

'You couldn't do better than see her,' he said. 'She has been the greatest help to me with my problems. She has changed my outlook on life, and she might help to change yours.' He gave me her telephone number, and I left to consider the matter.

One evening, when I was feeling extremely lonely and despairing, I found myself wandering about the streets in the vague direction of Earl's Court where I knew Dr Wolff lived. I went into a telephone box and rang her up. I told her who I was and that John Fowler had introduced me, and asked her if I could come round.

Her voice sounded gentle and encouraging, 'Come round immediately,' she said, 'and we can talk together for as long as you need.'

I went to her flat at 11 Redcliffe Place. She was small and fragile, with a great inner strength. She asked me up to her sitting-room, told me to sit down and relax, not to hurry, but to take my time and start to talk when I felt calm enough.

I looked around and saw that there were many paintings on the walls. As soon as I felt calm enough I began to talk, gradually spilling out my troubles of loneliness and my feeling of being imprisoned. I described to her the feeling of the snowman in the glass bubble. She said this was very usual, and that I must visit her for many sessions, so that in time I would become more outgoing and be able to make friends and contacts. I was quite frank about my situation at home. She told me that to speak the truth to her, from whom it would go no further, was most necessary. I went home that night feeling more cheerful and relaxed than I had for many months.

Dr Wolff also suggested that Michael should come and see her, if I could persuade him. He agreed to go, but only went once. He returned saying that he knew all about himself and didn't need a psychiatrist to tell him. I feared, and so did she, that he was wrong. He was a deeply troubled man, and could have benefited from help. But I think it was easier for him to stay as he was. This meant that he was often moody and unpredictable with both me and the children. I sometimes felt that I was partly to blame for his inconsiderate attitude towards others. I had always given way to him in everything. I had seen how my mother had seemed uncaring of my father, and I had resolved at an early age that, however my husband behaved, I would never criticise him. Even if he got drunk, behaved badly, left me alone, my husband could do what he liked. A very unwise decision.

Charlotte Wolff was a great help to me over the years. I became more outgoing and friendly to other people. She helped me to see myself as an individual, rather than just as an appendage of Michael. I began to make friends of my own, and wasn't so dependent on his, who often filled our house. He had many admirers who monopolised his attention and who paid scant heed to me. I began to realise that the possibility of other relationships would not be out of the question.

Chapter Twenty-One

Hollywood & Stratford

In January of 1947 I took my first trip to America to join Michael, who was filming in Hollywood. I went by sea on the *Queen Elizabeth* in the company of a friend, Jenny Nicholson, the daughter of Robert Graves.

On the train we met Margaret, Duchess of Argyll, one of the great beauties of her time. She looked at Jenny and me and said, 'Oh, you poor English, with your cold blue hands. I feel so sorry for you.'

We didn't mind a bit since we were heading for sunny California. I did worry about leaving the children in one of the bitterest foggy winters, but I trusted Nanny completely and, much as I would miss them, I knew that they would be all right.

On the *Queen Elizabeth* Jenny suffered from sea sickness. I used to visit her in her cabin where she lay groaning, eating the odd grape and drinking ginger ale. The stewardess was extremely worried about her. By resting in the day I managed to get up and dance in the evening, sit at the Captain's table and attend his cocktail parties. All in all, for me it was a very enjoyable journey.

On the morning of our arrival I went to Jenny's cabin and told her she must come out on deck to see the New York skyline rising out of the mists in the early morning sun. She looked at it, turned away and said, 'Ugh, how horrible!' But, by the time we landed with swaying sea-legs, she cheered up. We were to stay a week and were tremendously entertained the whole time.

I went to California by train, the 'Superchief', stopping for one day in Chicago, where I had lunch in a restaurant filled with blue-haired ladies in feathered hats. I continued the journey to California on the night train, and was again lavishly entertained by some delightful American couples. We arrived at Union Station in the morning. There were wild roses all along the railway track. It was a beautiful sunny day and Michael met me. He was temporarily staying at the Bel Air Hotel, which was extremely luxurious with its own swimming pool and suites of rooms. He introduced me to a handsome young man, Robert Michel. Michael said, 'This is my best friend in California.'

Later we went to lunch with Gladys Cooper at her house overlooking a golf course near Pacific Palisades. She was exquisitely beautiful, and she welcomed us warmly. Another guest was Evelyn Waugh, whom I found it interesting to meet as I had read many of his books. He was a small, pale, unprepossessing and slightly intimidating man. Michael and he got on very well and talked animatedly.

Gladys, then married to actor Philip Merrivale, provided a wonderful lunch which we ate outside in the garden, by the pool. I felt then that I was going to be very happy in California. But I soon realized that problems remained. Michael was working very hard and, as in England, was often out late. So once again I found myself turning to other people for company.

We had moved to an attractive house on Angelo Drive with a swimming pool and a pretty garden surrounding it. Every Sunday we gave a lunch party for our friends, including Gladys Cooper, Dame May Whitty, Greta Garbo, Ivor Novello, of whom I was extremely fond, and many others.

*

One Sunday, Margaret Genn, our friend, came to lunch with her husband Leo, a dark, handsome man with a charming deep voice whom I liked immediately. He and Margaret became frequent visitors. Leo and Michael were both working on *Mourning Becomes Electra*, directed by Dudley Nichols and co-staring Katina Paxinou and Kirk Douglas.

After a while it occurred to me that Leo and I were spending a great deal of time in each other's company, alone. Michael, as usual, was often otherwise occupied, but Margaret seemed to be deliberately pushing us together. I heard later from a friend of hers that this was indeed the case, as her affections, at that time, lay elsewhere.

Leo and I went for long drives in the mountains, spent many afternoons sitting by the pool and were often invited together to lunch at a house on Malibu beach owned by Eileen Erskine and her husband Philip Friend. After lunch we all swam in the ocean and played rounders on the beach. I was aware that he was watching me all the time and that I was beginning to find him disturbingly attractive. I realised that we were becoming infatuated with each other. It was a wonderful feeling, and I began to feel beautiful, desirable and loved. We continued to meet where and when we could and were very happy together. He was careful not to reveal his feelings for me in front of other people in case gossip might hurt his wife. He once gave me a present of a book of poetry in which he had written: 'To

Rachel, with love from Leo, from the city of love which knows so little about it.' It was difficult when Leo, Maggie, Michael and I were all together. Michael didn't admire Leo as an actor, though he liked him well enough. I exaggerated my admiration for him as an actor, because of my infatuation.

Michael returned to England when he had finished filming, but I remained behind, having been offered a role in *A Woman's Vengeance* (based on *A Giaconda Smile* by Aldous Huxley), co-starring Jessica Tandy and Charles Boyer at Universal International Studios. I rented an apartment of my own and hired a car. Leo and Maggie had also returned to England, when suddenly he was recalled to Hollywood for a part in *The Snake Pit* with Olivia de Havilland.

As soon as he arrived he sent me a message asking me to meet him. I was thrilled by his return. From then on, for the rest of my time in Hollywood, we met every evening, and at weekends we stayed in his apartment at the Château Marmont. This was the first time we had been able to be completely alone together. At the end of the day's filming I parked my car by his apartment and spent the evening with him, though if I was working the next day I didn't stay the night. We were invited out a lot but continued to be careful in front of other people. Many probably guessed our relationship and were sympathetic, but there was no need to be indiscreet.

When the day finally came when I had to leave for England I was distressed, because it seemed an end to two months' happiness. Having returned to England and resumed my life with the family, Leo asked me to meet him, but somehow the magic had gone out of it. It was never the same again.

*

In 1951 Michael was asked by Anthony Quayle to join the Shakespeare Memorial Theatre Company to play Richard II, Hotspur in *Henry IV Part I*, Chorus in *Henry V*, and Prospero in *The Tempest*, to be directed by Michael Benthall.

It had been suggested that I should play the Queen in *Richard II*, which I very much wanted to do. But Anthony Quayle engaged Heather Stannard to play Doll Tearsheet and other parts, and he asked me if I would give up the Queen so that she could have a reasonable season. I agreed, rather foolishly. Michael felt that I should have stuck to my guns as I was in Stratford anyway and had been originally offered the part.

A marvellous young actress called Barbara Jefford played Lady Percy in *Henry IV Parts I and II*. She was very beautiful, and she and

Michael played their scenes extremely well together: she played as if she was really in love with Hotspur.

It was young Richard Burton's first season at Stratford. He played Prince Hal and Henry V to great acclaim, and also Ferdinand in *The Tempest*. His charming wife Sybil had a small part as Prince Hal's wife and there was a scene where she sang beautifully in Welsh. It was apparent to us all that Burton was destined to become a great star. At the end of the season Tony wanted him to stay on and consolidate his success. This was the view he expressed to Alexander Korda, who was luring Richard away to Hollywood.

'He will have too much money and too many wives,' said Tony.

'My dear friend,' Korda replied, 'it is sometimes nice to have too much money and too many wives.'

Hugh Griffith, another Welsh actor, was also at Stratford that season, and Michael confessed to me that he got somewhat irritated by the 'Welsh contingent', who were always wandering about quoting *Under Milk Wood* and the like at the tops of their Welsh voices. Michael certainly did not share their view that the Welsh have the monopoly on poetry. I had in fact worked with Hugh Griffith in a play at the Arts Theatre called *Fatal Curiosity*, and later in *Tom Jones*. He was a difficult man to work with but a fascinating personality.

Although I was not part of the Company, I enjoyed my stay in Stratford. I was able to make myself useful by acting as Mike's dresser when his was ill. I dressed Michael in *Richard II*, holding his train at the side of the stage so that it would sweep on majestically. The sets that year were original and quite magnificent. In the opening scene of *Richard II* pages, wearing tabards with Richard's emblem, the white hart, flung open massive wooden doors to a fanfare of trumpets. It was an electrifying moment.

The Tempest was magical. It was a personal triumph for Michael. His Prospero was both poetic and imposing, with Hugh Griffith's Caliban the perfect foil. Alan Badel was one of the first male Ariels. I had played it myself at Stratford in 1933.

During this season the children, now aged, fourteen, twelve and eight, used to come and stay with us in their school holidays. They all loved the plays, and I remember Lynny, during a performance of *Richard II*, holding my hand and crying, saying, 'It is so sad, Mummy, it is so sad.'

By now, I think, Vanessa had set her heart on going on the stage. At Queen's Gate School she had played Shaw's Saint Joan wonderfully well. One of the other mothers sitting next to me said, 'I don't believe what I have seen.' This was after a moment when Vanessa with the light shining upon her said 'How long, O Lord, how long.'

*

At Bedford House the children borrowed Michael's tape recorder, in order to make their own plays and programmes. Corin would always be a great director arriving in a helicopter, for which he made the sound effects. Vanessa was a poetess doing imitations of Edith Sitwell, making up her own verse, one I recall being:

> They crossed the land, they crossed the sea,
> They crossed the land by tarns,
> They came upon a willow tree,
> And mouldy was the barns.

Lynn, being younger, would make her own versions of 'Listen with Mother'.

One day a BBC director was visiting us. Vanessa and Corin played him the tape, and he was so impressed that he said, 'Nobody would believe this if they heard it. They would think it was a real BBC recording.' He then offered Vanessa and Corin some work on children's programmes, from which they earned some useful pocket money. I think this was the beginning of their future careers.

*

On our return to London and Bedford House I was offered the role of Maman in *The Happy Time* with George Devine, Peter Finch, young Andrew Ray and Geneviève Page, a pretty but then not very good French actress. Poor Andrew Ray, the son of Ted Ray the comedian, had a rather dominating mother, who never stopped dragging him off to restaurants. In between the matinée and the evening performance she would make such a row in his dressing-room singing 'Knees up Mother Brown', supposedly to amuse Andrew, that none of the cast could have a rest between the shows, which they needed. Andrew became so tired he only just managed to stay the course.

Peter Finch had been brought over from Australia by Laurence Olivier to play opposite Edith Evans in *Daphne Laureola* at Wyndham's Theatre in 1949, in which he had a great success, Olivier directing. The play made a small fortune for his management company, which he lost on other ventures such as *Venus Observed* and *Top of the Ladder*. You couldn't help liking Peter. He was very goodlooking, humorous, and an excellent actor. He often invited a few of us back to his flat, where he entertained us with stories of Australia and the outback. I got to know him better when he played Trigorin in *The Seagull* with Vanessa as Nina, George Devine as the Doctor, Peggy Ashcroft as Arcadina and myself as Polina, directed by Tony Richardson, Vanessa's then husband, for the English Stage Company.

My dear friend Vivien Leigh came to see me at Bedford House. She told me she was in love with Peter. Rightly or wrongly I lent them our studio where they could be together. I must admit to feeling guilty about this because of the friendship of the two families, but she was joyful, and as she had given me a great deal of friendship I felt I must return her kindness. Many people were worried about the situation. In fact Vivien's maid became do distressed that she had a complete nervous breakdown as a result of the tensions of life with the Oliviers.

*

In 1953, we returned to Stratford for the start of the new season, and this time I was a member of the company. Michael played King Lear and I played Regan, in the production directed by George Devine. Yvonne Mitchell was a lovely Cordelia. Michael and Peggy Ashcroft played Antony and Cleopatra, with Marius Goring as Octavius Caesar, and I played Octavia, understudying Peggy's Cleopatra, which I eventually played in a matinée performance, Peggy having run off stage in the dark the night before and broken a rib against a piece of scenery. Not having ever thought I would play the part, I felt I was a bit behind on the words. That evening, Michael and I went through the lines until about three in the morning. Fortunately I seemed to be word-perfect. I was terrified beforehand, but as I gained confidence I realised that it was a thrilling role. Luckily Peggy was strapped up for the evening performance, because after the show I felt completely exhausted. The main difficulty in understudying a major role is that you feel that the audience would probably rather have their money back than watch you, but the applause was warm. Nevertheless I was pleased to get back to my small part of Octavia in the evening.

The third play of the season was *The Merchant of Venice* in which Michael played Shylock, brilliantly. Peggy was Portia and Yvonne Mitchell Nerissa.

*

Although it was good to be working with Michael again, our personal relationship, although not unhappy, was not totally fulfilling for either of us. And so it was that I met again a member of the company who was to change my life for many years. I shall call him Tom. I realised that this was the beginning of a very serious relationship, unlike any I had previously known, and he felt the same way.

Tom was married with a family and neither of us wanted to hurt our relatives, and so we were extremely careful about our intermittent meetings. If we were not playing in the theatre we went for long drives or walks in the country. If we were able to meet at my flat we would talk into the early hours of the morning about the problems of our situation, which seemed insoluble. It was agonising and exhausting. Both Michael and Tom's wife knew of the situation. Michael, being tolerant in these matters, was understanding and in a sense relieved. Tom's wife, Anne, loved him so much that she would put up with anything he did, as I had with Michael. Up to a point it was a parallel situation. Later Anne and I became great friends. We had in fact known each other since the early days of my marriage with Michael when I was pregnant for the first time.

When Vanessa was about two and a half Anne invited us to tea. She insisted we bring Vanessa with us, as they still had a high chair. Our nanny came too and stayed for tea. Then Michael and I were asked to stay for supper. The son, who was about twelve, lay on the floor by the fire. He wore grey shorts and a snake-buckled belt. He was reading *Little Folks*. His sister was about seven, and when Tom and Anne said she could stay up for supper she danced for joy. I remember Tom carving the cold beef that evening. It reminded me of supper at home on a Sunday night when my father always carved. It was a very happy evening.

We met again at a Buckingham Palace garden party. It was a sunny day, and Mike and Tom looked very smart in morning dress with grey toppers. Anne was small and pretty. I wore a white sleeveless dress with white hat, gloves and shoes. Tom told me years later that he had thought I looked very beautiful, and that he had been very attracted to me. I didn't know it at the time.

Our paths had crossed happily over many years, but it was not till we were at Stratford together in 1953 that we became aware of our true feelings for each other. We knew of course that we would never be able to marry because of our commitments. This realisation was extremely painful.

*

In 1954, I joined the cast of *Hedda Gabler* at the Lyric, Hammersmith. Peggy Ashcroft was superb as Hedda. George Devine played Mr Tesman; Michael MacLiamoir, Judge Brack; Alan Badel, Eilert Lövborg. I was Thea Elvsted. After our stay at the Lyric we went on tour. Peggy and George were worried about the production, which we all felt had been unsatisfactorily directed, so they sent for Glen Byam Shaw to give us notes and put the production to rights, which he did.

We travelled with *Hedda Gabler* to Holland, Denmark and Norway. The tour was great fun, with Michael MacLiamoir making us all laugh hilariously. He wore a toupé and full make-up day and night. We used to creep into his room in the morning to see if we could find out how the toupé was joined on – it turned out to be by a Kirbygrip.

The management, Jan de Bleik, our exceedingly nice Dutch impresario, arranged for four of us to have a car to drive to the various theatres. They were mostly one-night stands. Peggy, George and I drove in turns, having lunch at various restaurants along the way. One day we stopped for tea at a seaside hotel. Michael MacLiamoir said, 'Oh, Dotis (his pet nickname for us) you English are all mad about the sea. I find it very dreary – a lot of grey stones, white mist, and bashing grey sea.'

On the way to Norway we stayed at the Marienlist Hotel, crossing the narrow divide between Denmark and Norway, which was frozen on the Norwegian side. We went by train to Oslo, about an eight-hour journey. We had enormous fun, and at one point I was able to sit in the driver's seat. We arrived in Oslo fairly late, and everyone drank schnapps or aquavit, both very warming.

During our stay in Oslo Peggy was decorated by King Haakon for her performance as Hedda. He told her he had known Ibsen, whom he described as 'nutty'! We met some Norwegian friends of Peggy's, the Vigerts – Mr Vigert was a leading actor of the Norwegian National Theatre – who gave us a delightful evening at their beautiful house. We met a second cousin of Ibsen there, who said that in his view our production was far better than any of their own productions in Ibsen's time. We saw a Norwegian production which wasn't very good. It was gloomy and lacking in comedy. There are moments of laughter, after all, in *Hedda Gabler*.

Chapter Twenty-Two

Father's Death

At this time my parents were living in Bywater Street in Chelsea and visited us frequently. My father loved Bedford House, and got on extremely well with Michael and the children. He was a good gardener, and if he could come for a weekend he arrived at lunch time on Saturday and he and I dug and weeded all afternoon while Michael mowed. As dusk fell we would all go in and have crumpets, hot buttered toast and tea by the fire in the drawing-room.

My father loved these weekends as much as we did. Usually Doctors Mary and Tom Nelson invited us in for drinks before dinner. Father got on extremely well with Tom who, like him, was a good craftsman. He was so happy with us that even when he had arrived on a Saturday he would start to say, 'Oh dear, I have to leave on Monday.' He attended Chiswick Parish Church on Sunday mornings. Michael and I did not accompany him, not being regular churchgoers. My father would say, 'Never mind, I'll get down on my marrow bones and pray for you. It will do just as well. I don't think that the Almighty will mind as long as somebody prays.'

It was about this time that I began to notice that Father looked terribly tired. I used to say, 'Would you like me to drive you back?', but he always said, 'No, I'll catch a 49 bus. It will do me good.' I hated him going home on his own. At home he would stay in his bedroom and write. Sometimes he wrote letters, but he was also writing his autobiography privately for me.

One weekend he was invited back to Dartmouth for a reunion dinner with all his old friends. In the old days it had been called the Headmaster's night out. On his return, he arrived at Bedford House one afternoon. As I put my arms around him and gave him a hug, he said, 'Darling, it's been such a long time.' To me it sounded like 'It's going to be a long time', and I had a strange fear and premonition. He played with the children in the garden, and then went back to Bywater Street.

Aunt Norah Mellon was in London at the time and had invited Mother and Father out to dinner. I heard later that he had been feeling terribly unwell, but was so fond of Aunt Norah that he had insisted on going. That night the telephone rang, and before I answered I knew what it was going to be. It was Dr Mary's partner, who said that Father had had a bad coronary heart attack and been taken into the Middlesex Hospital in Mortimer Street. She said I could visit him the next day.

The first time I went by myself. The ward was airy and bright, but Father was lying in bed looking deathly pale. As I went up to his bed, he said, 'I knew you'd come, I knew you would.' I sat by him for some time, and he said, 'I have invented a delicious new drink, tea with lime juice.'

Before I left I was able to talk to the doctor, who said, 'It's very serious, but if you can get him over the first two days there may be some hope. You can ring whenever you like – there are no hours for patients on the danger list. You can bring your mother and your husband. Indeed if he is very bad, we can give you a room where you can stay the night.'

I was extremely agitated, and I went back to Bywater Street to tell Mother the news. The next day Michael, Mother and I went to visit him at the Middlesex. This time they said we should stay the night, and they would let us have a room. During the night they called us and we went up to the ward. A heart specialist and nurses were standing round giving him an injection. I am sure he was unconscious. He lived through the night.

Next day when I saw him he said, 'I think I'm feeling a little better.'

He had oxygen by his side, and gave himself a little. As he did so the connection between the cylinder and the mask broke.

'Curse the bloody thing,' he said. 'I'll fix it together myself.' Then he said, 'I'm sure I would get better if I could come and stay with you at Bedford House.'

I promised him that this would be possible, and he should have a bed in one of the rooms on the ground floor.

Later that day he said, 'You know, I think I've had enough. I'm not sure that I really want to go on.' He added: 'Your mother has been wonderful. I think we have got through to each other at last.' And then with his old humour: 'Better late than never.'

That night – we were still staying in the hospital – we were summoned again in the early hours of the morning, and the sister told us that there was no hope. Father was wheeled into a side ward, and they allowed me to help with the oxygen. He looked so ill by then that, with all my love, I didn't want him to go on. At the last moment he died with a sigh. He looked almost like a carved image of a saint, lying back so peacefully.

We left, taking mother with us to Bedford House. I was so upset that I said, 'I really don't want to go on living.'

Thoughts of my father, and all he had meant to me through my life crowded into my mind. I arranged the funeral with the Vicar of Chiswick, a charming and comforting man. The coffin remained all night in the church. Next day the Vicar told me that a number of small children stood round the coffin until quite a late hour, and that the atmosphere in the church was wonderfully peaceful.

The funeral was well attended by many of Father's naval friends and colleagues from Dartmouth, and our Cousin Lucy came up from Herefordshire and stayed the night. I arranged lunch at Bedford House for everybody. It was a cheerful affair because everybody had such happy memories of him.

Mother was very good on the day, but it was difficult for her later when she had to return to her house in Bywater Street. I arranged for someone to look after her. While she was with us she was very quiet, and sat in the garden of Bedford House. I ought to have kept her longer, but with the children, the house full, it wasn't easy.

One evening I walked to the graveyard with the children. When we arrived at Father's graveside, Lynn said, 'Where is Grandfather? Is he sitting on a cloud, kicking his heels?'

'It probably is just what he is doing,' I replied. 'He always said he was going to, and was perfectly cheerful about it.'

Being religious, my father always looked at life in a humorous way.

Chapter Twenty-Three

The Royal Court & Wilks Water

In 1956, just as I had been invited by George Devine to join the English Stage Company at the Royal Court Theatre, a devastating event took place. I was sitting in the drawing-room at Bedford House after dinner when Cecil Tennant, Michael's agent, arrived, saying, 'I have some very worrying news for you. As you know, you and Michael have been served a writ for bankruptcy. You will have to sell this house as soon as possible.'

I was horrified.

Cecil said, 'Well, my dear girl, there is nothing for it, unless you want to go bankrupt.'

Michael's affairs had been mismanaged for some considerable time, by the accountants. Also, the seasons at Stratford, though marvellous for his career, were not well enough paid, and certainly could not support the film-star life style that we had acquired.

Michael was in New York, directing *A Month in the Country* and starring in and directing *The Sleeping Prince*, so it was left to me, Nanny and Joan Hirst to organise the move. I went flat hunting, and I found a perfectly adequate place at Hans Crescent, behind Harrods. Michael flew over to have a look at it, and thought it would do very well for us all. We sold Bedford House, with great sadness, back to the previous owners. The children were very unhappy about the move, but I explained that it was inevitable. It was hard for them to imagine life away from the river and the large garden.

*

We packed up and moved on a Saturday and settled in on the Sunday. I had to start rehearsing at the Royal Court on the Monday morning. I didn't feel exactly fresh for a new start. At the same time I was very much looking forward to the work. It was a daring new venture funded with very little money. The designer was Jocelyn Herbert. Tony Richardson was George Devine's assistant director. Other members of the company were John Osborne, John Welch, Kenneth

Haigh, Mary Ure, Joan Plowright, Nigel Davenport, Rosalie Crutchley, Agnes Lauchlan, Michael Gwynn, Alan Bates, Gwen Ffrangçon Davies, and many more. George's plan was to introduce fresh talent, and most of the plays were by new authors. The company was to be run in repertoire, with the plays alternating every week. The first season was for a year.

I felt that I was part of something important, and although we rehearsed every day, and played at night, which was hard work, it was very stimulating. George was a wonderful director, helpful and sympathetic to the company. Jocelyn Herbert and he worked brilliantly together. She even helped decorate the theatre, and had a room in the basement where she made her own props. I was very impressed by the talents of Alan Bates, Mary Ure, Kenneth Haigh and John Osborne. None of us knew that Osborne was writing *Look Back in Anger* in his spare time, which was to be the Royal Court's greatest success.

The first play I appeared in was *The Mulberry Bush*, a light comedy by Angus Wilson, in which I played Cora Fellowes. I also played Goody Putnam in *The Crucible*, a rather grim play by Arthur Miller. In *Cards of Identity* I was a very old woman with an ear trumpet, Miss Black-Panorbis, whom I modelled on a great-aunt of mine. In *The Good Woman of Setzuan* I was Mrs Mi Tzu, and had to smoke a cigar, which made me feel sick.

I was due to play in *The Country Wife* when it was discovered that I had an ulcer. George gave me a few days to decide whether I could carry on or not, but the doctor said it was impossible. I had been to him thinking I had eye trouble, because the pavements seemed to come up into my face when I was walking. He looked into my eyes and said that there was nothing wrong with them but that I was suffering from overstrain. I took a weekend off and went to the country, but when I returned to London I felt no better. I regretfully realised that it was time to leave the English Stage Company. I was not the only one who felt the strain. Others in the company also suffered from exhaustion.

*

During my time at the Royal Court, John Fowler had bought an enchanting hunting lodge in the woods near Odiham in Hampshire. Legend had it that Henry VIII as a boy and his elder brother Prince Arthur stayed at the Palace of Dogmersfield which belonged to the Bishop of Bath and Wells. While boar-hunting in the woods, Henry VII, Prince Arthur and Prince Henry would use the hunting lodge as a place to picnic in and relax.

John told me that the cottage near his lodge, which he had bought as an annexe for guests, was up for sale. He took me to see it, and I decided there and then that I would like to buy it. He said that considering its state of disrepair he would let me have it for £1,250. Cousin Lucy, who wanted me to have a place for myself where I could get away from London, lent me the money and promised me more later to do it up. Mother also helped.

The cottage had brick floors, a copper for the washing, a stinking scullery with hooks for curing bacon and windows that had been bricked up at the time of window tax. It was reached by a cinder track through the woods. The hedges were completely overgrown, and old zinc baths, shoes and bicycle chains were buried in the garden. These had belonged to old Granny Porter, who had lived there for sixty years, going to the village once a week, pushing an old pram for her shopping. However, it clearly had great possibilities. It was very pretty with its old pinkish bricks, and John and I realised we could make a lake out of the swamp at the foot of the garden.

Old Granny Porter had come to the cottage as a bride of twenty and had helped in the fields digging potatoes. Charley and Gilbert, her son and grandson, had lived with her to keep her company, sleeping on an iron bedstead under a bulging ceiling, with an iron hook on the wall to hang their clothes on. When she was dying, John visited her with food and soup, and when she died the family spent a great deal of money on a satin-lined coffin. With great pride, they asked John to come down to see her, which he did. Granny Porter had rented the cottage from John, who had acquired it when he bought the hunting lodge. When she died he was able to sell it.

John decided that we must start work on the garden immediately. He found a young man to help, who did nothing at all except stick his pocket-knife into trees. One day a man appeared in the garden and said to me, 'You don't need my son – 'e's no good – you need me. I'll show you 'ow to set about it. You starts from the porch door and works outwards.'

Will Richardson, as he was called, was a local man of gypsy extraction who had a wonderful knowledge of gardening. He stayed for the next twenty-seven years.

When Michael first saw the cottage he loved it, but I think he was a bit worried that he might be dragged into the clearing-out process. Although he enjoyed moving and clearing out ants' nests by means of boiling water, he didn't really like the basic tasks involved in garden clearing. John came down with secateurs and helped with the pruning and digging. He brought me samples of Colefax and Fowler beautiful chintzes, and choices of paints. We engaged local builders to knock down walls to make one long sitting-room, and to connect us to the electricity supply. The wires had to be brought on posts through the wood.

*

One weekend, when we were in deep in disarray, I invited Ann Todd for the weekend, and she arrived with a large amount of luggage and many gold bracelets, obviously expecting a smart country house. During the evening there was a power cut. I lit candles and was able to boil a kettle on our oil heaters. Ann got into a great state, rang the electricity board and said, 'I've got a patient here who is very ill and we must have electricity immediately.' They were not too concerned, since the cut was regional. However, we sat by a nice log fire, the electricity eventually coming on, and Ann was able to have a bath in the morning before making a hasty departure back to civilisation.

Another visitor was Rosalie Crutchley, who worked hard clearing the stream, getting bitten by mosquitoes which thrived in the swamp. One evening we went for a long walk. After a while we found that we were totally lost.

'Look,' said Rosalie, 'there is a cottage. I wonder who lives there?'

'Let's go and find out,' I replied. We walked towards the flickering light, only to find out that it was mine!

I had first met Rosalie Crutchley in 1944, in the Oxford Repertory Company, where I had played before in the old rep where the clothes were soaking wet. Rosalie and I became friends immediately. She is a very forthright person. I always called her by her nickname, 'Bun', because she was the one who made the teas and the coffees and produced the buns! She is an enormously positive woman, strong and healthy. She comes from a naval background, and although she has the looks of a Spanish peasant woman, with dark eyes, a fine-boned face, which has earned her many parts, she is in fact extremely English. She likes the theatre, but now works in films and television. She once said to me, 'I'm not dedicated to acting. I just do it for the living. What I like to do is to relax and read or listen to music.' Of course she does work very hard. I find her extremely amusing, and she has been a good friend to me for many years.

Dorothy Tutin was also a great help. We dug up a mound of earth to put round the lilac tree at the back door. Dottie kept digging up worms and exclaiming, 'Ugh, I can't bear them.'

Dorothy Tutin and I had met at Stratford when she was playing Juliet; Richard Johnson was Romeo and I was Lady Capulet. I remember it in particular because the production was directed by Glen Byam Shaw, who made a speech on the opening night party in which he kindly said, 'If Rachel Kempson played Juliet here in 1932, she must have been in her pram.' Dorothy and I became great friends. She was ill at the time, and constantly sick, but forbade me to tell anybody because, she said, 'I have to get through this season'. She was a pretty, lovely creature – very sensitive, extremely attractive and graceful in her movements like a swallow. I have always greatly admired her acting, and she was one of the very best Peter Pans I have ever seen. When Michael decided to act in *The Importance of Being Ernest*, directed by Anthony Asquith, I suggested that Dorothy play Cecily, and she was quite delicate and enchanting in the part. I always enjoyed having her to stay at Wilks Water. We used to go for walks and she used to love picking wild flowers. She felt that every single one was special, and preferred wild to cultivated flowers. She was sweet and amusing in her own original way, a loving companion.

*

The whole place was beginning to get quite civilised. The stream was flowing through the garden, and the lake was about to be dredged. An old boy came to see me and said he would do the entire job for £1500.

'Oi'll make a lake for you,' he said. 'And oi'll make a little island where woild fowl will nest, and you'll be as 'appy as the day is long.' He added: 'When oi was a boy, many's the bunk up oi had with a girl, lying in these woods with 'er.'

It took about a month, with carts going to and fro carrying the clay, and dumping it on farmers' fields, where it acted as a fertilizer. John and I brought trays of tea and coffee for the workman. He was as interested as I was, because the lake benefited both of us.

The children came down every Friday night: Lynn from Queen's Gate, Corin from Westminster and Vanessa from Central School, where she was now a drama student. They were thrilled with the cottage and the lake, loving the idea of once more having a garden. They could punt, and swim in the lake, and in the winter they skated.

Lynn was given a chestnut pony of fifteen hands, which she named Gay Rosalinda. The stable was refurbished. We got in bales of hay, and her saddle and bridle hung up in the small harness-room adjoining the stable. Lynn was an excellent rider, and at that time, having no thoughts of going into the theatre, had set her heart on becoming a showjumper. She met Pat Smythe, who told her, 'It is inadvisable to enter showjumping unless you can get to the absolute top. You would have to start as a groom.'

Nanny, Lynn and I took enormous pride in her being well-dressed to go hunting with the Hampshire Hounds. She wore a velvet jockey cap, a black riding-jacket and white stock, fawn breeches and black boots. She looked extremely smart as she set off at nine o'clock in the morning. She enjoyed the hunting, was very good at the jumps and met some very nice girls of her own age, with whom she made friends. Nanny and I would go into the neighbouring villages to the meets.

Lynn and I used to ride for miles together round the countryside, with me on a borrowed horse; but Michael, Vanessa and Corin were not very keen on riding and did not join us. Corin was happier being driven by Lynn up and down the drive with him sitting on top shooting rabbits.

Eventually we built on a new kitchen. I bought a pretty pine dresser for a few pounds and installed it in the kitchen. We had a large pine table and an Aga cooker, and the kitchen quickly became the centre of the house. The small dining-room was used occasionally.

In any case, from its humble origins, Wilks Water Cottage was eventually featured in *House and Garden*! In autumn and winter I enjoyed sitting by the fire, looking through seed and bulb catalogues and choosing plants and flowers for the following spring. With Richardson's help I planted a circular tapestry hedge of yew and holly, a cream-coloured ornamental cherry which hung over the front gate, and damsons and plums, which I made into jam. From the side of the lake we took marsh marigolds and planted them along the edges of the stream and by the statue of Neptune which stood over the water. Over the front door we grew a white climbing rose called Madame Alfred Carrière. We also planted japonica, clematis and, facing south, a vine which covered the south side of the entire cottage and eventually yielded grapes: I gave some of them to friends, who made them into wine, not quite the best. There was a large orchard with old-fashioned roses planted down the side of the stream. In it were twelve new apple trees and one pear, which all bore fruit. I used to cook the pears in red wine for a delicious pudding. Outside the kitchen door I started a vegetable garden in which I grew herbs – parsley, rosemary, chives, bay – and I tried my hand not so successfully at beans, peas and new potatoes. After a while it really seemed cheaper to buy vegetables than to spend the labour and time on growing them.

Working in the garden, always one of my great joys, was a great help and therapy when I was recovering from the ulcer brought on by the hard work at the Royal Court.

Chapter Twenty-Four

Mother's Death

I have talked a great deal about my father in this book, and it seems that I have neglected to talk about my mother. Our relationship was not always an easy one, as is often the case with mothers and daughters.

Mother once asked me to accompany her to Switzerland as she was not feeling well and thought that the mountain air would do her good: she loved flowers and fields. She had never flown before but, as it turned out, she thoroughly enjoyed the flight.

Barboleusaz, our final destination, turned out to be a pretty village in the mountains. Each bedroom had its own balcony, and every morning we had breakfast of coffee and croissants overlooking the large valley. Mother loved the sight and sound of the cows with their swinging bells.

The fields were full of marvellous wild flowers, and we went for tremendous walks in the mountains. We would walk part of the way and then take a mountain railway up to a village with a hotel overlooking a lake where you could have lunch. Mother was a strong walker, but I noticed that she tired easily. She had developed a short dry cough. At the time I didn't know what it was, but it worried me. During the long walks we talked a great deal and began to get to know each other better. She bought me little presents at the local shop.

We returned to England, and after her holiday she seemed much better. A year later she wanted to go again, but I wasn't able to, and she went with an elderly friend. But this time she wasn't really happy.

She used to come and stay at Wilks Water, and I noticed that the cough was much worse. One year, as we were giving our usual firework party, she was in too much much pain to go outside but watched from the window. We returned to London, she to her flat in Chelsea, which she had moved to after Father's death. One morning, when I went to see her, her nice daily told me that she was very ill and shouldn't be continually on her own. At that point I decided to get a day and a night nurse. A doctor said she must have an X-ray for her chest. They found old scars and explained that TB had lain dormant ever since she was a child. I couldn't understand this, but they told me it was perfectly possible to have a recession of the illness.

Now I went to see her every day. I would cook a meal for the day nurse and Mother, and something for the night nurse in the evening. They were very sweet to her, and she asked them to pack up her various special treasures. Finally the doctor said she must go into hospital. She was very worried. The nurse went with her in the ambulance and I followed in my car. I saw her settled into a nice private room, but it was terribly hot. She asked for a window to be opened. I gave her lots of books and papers, but she was too ill to read.

To my great regret I did miss a day, and then they sent for me. I missed it because I had a cold, but I think this was an excuse on my part: I did dread going. I felt very guilty about it. When I got to the hospital they told me that she was terribly weak, but was so fastidious that she wouldn't use a bedpan, but with help insisted on getting out of bed.

The ward sister said that despite her weakness, her hair was always beautifully done and she used nice scent. One night she said to me, 'I don't know how it is possible to feel so ill, and go on living.' They said I should stay and that she ought to have oxygen. She hated the idea of the mask because she felt she would suffocate.

I sat by her for a long time, and put a little brandy into the water in her feeding cup. But she was almost too weak even to drink that. Finally, I stayed in a nearby room, going in and out during the night. Each time I went in she looked at me and just said 'Nice, nice', which showed that she realised I was there.

It was Christmas time and carol singers were going round the wards. The hospital vicar wanted to visit her, but I persuaded him not to. She was too weak and tired. On the last morning, when they put the oxygen mask over her face, she was almost unconscious and so didn't realise anything. One of the doctors said to me, 'Would you like me to use resuscitation?' I asked if this meant that Mother would return to normal health. The doctor replied that this was extremely unlikely, but it was a medical rule that the closest relative must be asked. I said that although I didn't want Mother to die I didn't want her to go on living in that state. She finally died quite peacefully on the night before her 80th birthday.

They said I should have a short rest, and when I went to look at her, there wasn't a line on her face. She looked like a small child.

I sent for Nicky, who was in the country, and he arrived immediately. He felt sad too, because latterly they had had a good relationship. Even if she couldn't go out to dinner, she would give him money to go to her favourite restaurant, The Queen's in Sloane

Square, a place where she and I had gone many times together.

We arranged the funeral to be held at St Nicholas' Church, Chiswick, as she had said that she wished to be buried in the same grave as Father. It was a small congregation, as most of her friends had died. Being winter, and a cold day, it was naturally a rather gloomy tramp up the churchyard. I found it deeply depressing. In their way Mother and Father had done their best to make a go of an unsuitable marriage. My knowledge that at the very end they felt they had got together was a help to me in alleviating sadness.

As I was not working at the time, I was able to spend a long stretch at Wilks Water. Tom, who had been very fond of my mother, came and stayed as often as his work allowed and was a great comfort. Once again, gardening was a therapy. I remember a lady journalist once ringing me up for an interview over the phone.

'What time of year is your favourite?' she asked.

I said, 'I love the winter. I love log fires, making bonfires, the bare trees and the sunsets, and looking through garden catalogues, planning my garden for the following year.'

The journalist seemed quite shocked. 'Oh really, Lady Redgrave,' she said, 'how strange. I thought you'd want to talk about the summer.'

It seemed to me that winters are more predictable. It will snow, rain and blow, whereas, though one hopes for a fine summer, one is often disappointed. In winter in the country you can have the most beautiful frosty days. Even when John Fowler and I got snowed in, we enjoyed ourselves huddling round the log fire. I remember a kingfisher diving into our stream. Its plumage, brilliant gold and blue, was shown up by the white snow.

When the various grandchildren came to stay, they loved making snowmen and throwing snowballs and then having tea round the fire, toasting crumpets.

Snow in the country is extremely beautiful, like a white carpet, unlike snow in the city which is merely grey slush.

Chapter Twenty-Five

Russia

In 1958, Michael and I were once more engaged for the season. My parts were to be Lady Capulet in *Romeo and Juliet*, directed by Glen Byam Shaw, with Dorothy Tutin and Richard Johnson starring; Dionyza in *Pericles*, directed by Tony Richardson; and Ursula in *Much Ado About Nothing*. Michael's parts were Hamlet, the second time he had played it, and Benedic in *Much Ado* with Googie Withers as Beatrice.

I moderately enjoyed playing Lady Capulet, Juliet having been one of my favourite roles. I enjoyed Dionyza, a very wicked character, who is thought to be a study for Lady Macbeth. On the first day of rehearsal, when the director gives a talk, Tony Richardson was munching an apple and held a knife in his hand which he kept stabbing into the table in front of him.

'Now, my darlings,' he said, 'this play is terribly, terribly sexy, and you mustn't forget it.'

Of course he was right. The production was astonishing. The stage was filled with masts, tarpaulins, ropes and rope ladders, to represent a rather threatening sea shore. Richard Johnson played Pericles, Zoe Caldwell the 'Green One'.

I am unused to playing wicked women, so I found it difficult and used to dry up out of fright at her evil character. Donald Eccles, who played my husband, was extremely helpful, suggesting that I go and see his doctor brother, who treated me by using a form of mild hypnosis. He instructed me to sit in a chair and concentrate on a ring. While I was concentrating, he would quietly talk, saying, 'Don't try to listen. Close your eyes and think of the ring.' He would continue, still quietly, 'Now raise your arm', and I would find that when I opened my eyes my arm had raised itself without my being aware of it. The result was very helpful and I became confident of my memory once again.

Michael's Hamlet proved to be one of the great Hamlets of our generation, second only to John Gielgud's. Ophelia was played by Dorothy Tutin.

*

At the end of the season the entire Company was invited to Russia. Michael's agent, Cecil Tennant, said he oughtn't to go because the money wasn't good enough. Glen Byam Shaw, the director of the theatre, was worried and sent for me, and begged me to have a talk with Michael. Of course I was excited at the prospect of visiting Russia, and so was Michael, but the previous experience of near bankruptcy had alarmed him. Finally, after a certain amount of prevarication, and much worry on the side of the management, he agreed to go.

Paddy Donnell, the Company manager, gave us a long talk about the sort of food we would get, the allowance we would be given in roubles and the kind of clothes we would need to buy for the extreme cold of Russia in the winter.

We flew to Moscow in the winter of 1958, going by British Air, who fêted us with champagne all the way and a special menu entitled 'Shakespeare Memorial Theater'. Paddy had gone ahead to make the arrangements, and the scenery and costumes had been sent by sea.

On arrival at Moscow Airport the temperature was 30 degrees below zero. We gasped as we got out of the plane, and poor Angela Baddeley had a bad attack of asthma. We were all, as instructed, wearing fur-lined coats, boots, hats and gloves. Sitting in the arrivals hall waiting to go through Customs, we noticed the Russians staring at us as if we had arrived from another planet. Eventually cars picked us all up and took us to the Hotel Metropole. My first impression of Russia as we drove through the streets was that everything looked grey and depressing. At the hotel we were served with an inadequate meal, and then caught the night train to Leningrad.

We all had cubicles to sleep in, and between each carriage sat a Russian peasant woman who made Russian lemon tea on a samovar. I don't think anybody slept. We were all too excited, and talked all night, running to and fro to the samovar. At the end of the twelve-hour journey we arrived at eight in the morning at Leningrad, which was snowbound. We were taken by car to a very nice hotel in St Isaac's Square opposite St Isaac's Cathedral. My impression, through the car window, was of a much brighter and more beautiful city than Moscow.

Breakfast consisted of cold boiled eggs and yoghurt – hardly appetising. We went up to unpack and discovered that the bedrooms were quite attractive. You collected your bedroom key from a nice elderly man who reminded us of Firs in Chekhov's *Cherry Orchard*. The hotel lounge was very pretty with white linen covers over sofas and chairs.

We were taken on a tour of the city by a Russian guide who spoke perfect English. His main interest seemed to be Peter the Great, of whom he talked continually. Poor Michael was frozen and shaking. We got out at an enormous snow-covered stadium and wandered around rather desolately. What struck me most was the absence of cars on the streets, except for those of the Commissars, and that the shoppers were mostly Commissars' housekeepers, ballet dancers and actors, they being the only ones who could afford the high prices.

That night we attended the Kirov Ballet and sat in the one-time Royal box of the old St Petersburg Opera House. It was very luxurious and beautifully maintained. We were photographed in the box for both *Pravda* and the London press.

The ballerinas were exquisite. We noticed that the wigs for the men were very bad, rather woolly-looking, but the male dancers were very, very masculine, and danced with more male authority than their counterparts in Europe. During our two weeks in Leningrad, apart from our own performances, those of us who had evenings off went to many other ballet theatres. During the intervals, the people from the audience walked in a circular procession round and round the foyer. Beer, the only refreshment available, was very cheap.

At some of the lesser ballet theatres we attended the audience smelt horribly of B.O. There were rows of fat men and women wearing thick coats in a very hot theatre. Of course ballet in Russia is the great joy of the workers, second only to the museums, which they pile into at lunch time.

The next day we were all taken to our theatre for rehearsal and discovered to our horror that much of the scenery had been damaged en route. We rehearsed as best we could to the sound of hammering. The Russian stage staff were willing and excellent, and our own chief carpenter talked to them with the help of an interpreter. Everything was finally ready for the first night, which was *Romeo and Juliet*. The response was superb. They gave us the slow handclap, which in England means audience disapproval but in Russia is the highest accolade.

*

Michael and I were introduced to Leningrad's Chief Architect, Michel Kraminsky, to whom we had been given an introduction by his brother and sister-in-law in London. He had been given the task of redecorating all the domes and spires of the many cathedrals with gold leaf. The golden spires and domes were very beautiful in the bright sunlight. Many of the eighteenth-century buildings were painted pale pink or turquoise blue.

Michel Kraminsky was married to a doctor. Being Chief Architect, he was given a State apartment, which he shared with his son and daughter-in-law and their small child. His doctor wife, who was unwell, had her bed behind a screen in the sitting-room. We took one of our interpreters with us, although Michel could speak French, as educated Russians often did. The apartment was not luxurious, but it was pleasant and light with lots of books and pretty antique furniture. We were served a reasonable meal in their small dining-room and drank vodka, with much toasting. Even by our Western standards it was not uncomfortable. During lunch Michel told us about the siege of Leningrad, at which time he was serving in the Russian Army. To keep warm they would chop up furniture, anything they could lay their hands on, and many even ate glue. One of his brothers finally died of starvation. They were saved in the end, because of course all armies have been defeated by the terrible Russian winter when they have tried to cross that vast country.

We also met the director of the Children's Theatre who invited us to a matinée performance of a Russian fairy tale. There was the wicked witch, and a scene when two children, the equivalent of Hansel and Gretel, appeared to be hiding under the water, their upturned faces looking up through the reeds and swirling water weed. I was sitting by a little girl in her black dress and white pinafore, the regulation school wear of the time. At the moment when the old witch was being defeated by the children who had come up through the water and their parents who had joined them, the little girl shrieked and flung herself across my knees because she was so excited. The play ended with shouts of joy from the large children's audience, and we were taken round to meet the cast.

It seemed to be a great pleasure to them, and we told the director how much we admired the work and wished that we had an equivalent Children's Theatre in London. The director told us that for the older children they would perform Shakespeare, Chekhov and many others. The Russians, from childhood onwards, have a great love of the performing arts.

We visited the Theatre of Comedy, and saw *The Government Inspector*, by Gogol. It was a permanent repertory company. We were invited round afterwards to discuss the pros and cons of a permanent company with the director and cast. The director said, through the interpreter, that it was all very well but he couldn't get rid of his old actors and actresses. Indeed they remained with him until they were too old to go on and had to retire. He added, 'Often middle-aged parts have to be played by elderly actors and actresses.'

We saw the truth of this for ourselves when we went to see a production of *Anna Karenina* with a middle-aged Anna. Afterwards we met the actress who had played Karenin's mother, a beautiful woman in her late seventies who spoke perfect French, which enabled us to speak unreservedly with her. She had worked in the time of the old regime. She was obviously not unhappy: she had work and this was her life.

Television was in its infancy in Russia, but they televised Michael's *Hamlet* in black and white. I watched the recording on a little monitor without sound by the side of the stage.

In the intervals of the various plays, actors, actresses, and ballet dancers of all sorts would come round to visit our casts and compare notes about plays and performances.

After a crowded two weeks, we all departed on the night train, and this time we all slept soundly. Back in Moscow we returned to the Metropole with its strange Victorian bedrooms, very ornate with a lot of red plush, hermetically-sealed double windows and white lace bedspreads.

*

Michael had been at Cambridge with Guy Burgess, who now lived in Moscow, having defected from the West. On the first night of *Hamlet* Guy turned up to see Michael after the performance in his dressing-room. He had been crying. He would ring me in the hotel bedroom every morning and talk for about a quarter of an hour, saying how wonderful it was to hear an English voice. Many years later when I acted with Alec Guinness in *The Old Country* by Alan Bennett, playing the wife of an English spy who defects to Russia, I understood much more clearly the isolation and loneliness that he must have felt. When he walked into Michael's dressing-room he was immediately sick in the basin – a result of too much vodka. He was with his boyfriend, whom the State had thoughtfully provided. He told Michael how much he missed England, and that he was not guilty of espionage: if he returned to England, he said, the Government would be unable to pin anything on him. He had made the decision to live in Russia in order to promote understanding on both sides. He had thought that in Russia he would be given a good job, being a Cambridge scholar, but in fact all he got was a few translations. This failed to keep him occupied, and left him too much time for drink. He invited Michael to lunch at his flat, where he had a cook-housekeeper. The main dish for lunch was a sucking pig, in which the gall-bladder had burst, making it so bitter it was uneatable. His apartment was quite pleasant in one of the modern blocks of Moscow. The last time Michael saw him was after their lunch together. Guy got out of the taxi and walked away without even looking back.

*

Angela Baddeley and I decided to take a shopping trip to Gum, the famous Moscow store which stretched the whole length of Red Square. It was on four floors, each floor containing a gallery surrounded by iron railings, and had the forbidding air of a prison. The fur hats, fur coats and boots were not terribly expensive, but rough and unstylish. We watched people stopping at a little kiosk, and went to take a look. You pressed a button and got a squirt of scent, which was called Stalin's Breath and smelt disgusting. Angela and I bought postcards to send home. These of course, we later found, were censored.

On Christmas Day, the British Ambassador and his wife, the Reillys, invited the entire Company for dinner. The large dining-room had soft lighting, and was filled with round tables. Michael sat on Lady Reilly's right, with Glen Byam Shaw on her left, and the rest of us were evenly distributed. It was quite wonderful for us to have English food again, and we enjoyed the traditional turkey and Christmas pudding. The servants were all Russian, and we were told by Lady Reilly that every table was bugged. One topic of conversation to be avoided was Guy Burgess, because naturally he was taboo at the British Embassy. As to the bugging, it didn't really matter to us since we were only talking of the ballets we had seen and our families at home whom we all missed.

The food in Leningrad was just passable, but in Moscow it was really very bad. There was a distinct lack of fresh vegetables; salads were unheard of; the meat was a grey stew – we decided it must be goat; the bread was heavy and black, which we were unused to; and we never even glimpsed the famous caviar. As a result most of the cast succumbed to the dreaded 'Moscow tummy', which we were told was picked up from a bug in the water supply.

I woke one morning feeling ill and completely exhausted. Fortunately I was only in one of the three plays. The Embassy was contacted and they sent their doctor, who said I should drink lots of tea. Finally, since there didn't seem anything I could eat, the American army attaché and his wife invited me to stay with them during the day because their official position entitled them to better food. In the evening the attaché drove me back to our hotel. He told me to look in the mirror and I would see a car following. On arrival at the hotel three members of the KGB went to the desk to enquire who I was. They left, satisfied, and I was able to go to my room in peace.

After three days there was a performance of *Romeo and Juliet* and I was able to go to the theatre to play, fortunately not having missed a performance.

Dorothy Tutin, who was in all three plays, had been ill before the tour. Crates of Guinness were brought out and that is what she lived on. She got through all the performances.

We had noticed that it was large women who swept the Russian streets, clearing the snow and shovelling it up into enormous carts, wrapped in thick black anoraks, trousers and boots. The stodgy food was necessary to them to keep out the cold.

*

Night after night the Russians gave parties and receptions for the Company. At every one of these Glen Byam Shaw had to make a speech, which terrified him. We could see that the backs of his trouser legs were quivering as he talked. One of the rather grand Lady Commissars fell madly in love with him and insisted on sitting next to him at every reception. This was extremely useful to everybody. It allowed us many perks: free seats for the ballet and cars whenever we wanted them. I don't think the arrangement suited Glen as well as it did us. In fact he became ill and had to go home!

One of the American Embassy staff knew a charming American woman married to a Russian living well and comfortably in one of the old wooden houses in Moscow. She very kindly had sent to my hotel large thermoses of chicken soup and other delicacies. I visited her and her husband at their home. It was really an entrancing Chekhovian house, and contrasted greatly with the modern apartments we were used to. I felt that under those conditions it would not be so bad to live in Moscow.

The highlight of our visit was an evening at the Bolshoi Ballet, where we saw Ulanova dance Giselle exquisitely. The theatre was beautiful, with its facade of great white pillars and white stone steps. It was vast inside and extremely elegantly decorated. Being the Prima Ballerina of Moscow, Ulanova must have been one of its wealthiest citizens and would have had a good apartment in Moscow and a dacha in the country for weekends. We were taken backstage. She must have been about forty, and was very slender, fair-haired and attractive. She seemed pretty cross and was probably tired and didn't want to see anybody. Michael asked her if she would honour him by giving him one of her ballet shoes. She autographed it and I have it in a glass case to this day.

After a month in Russia we were all excited to be going back to England. The Reillys and the Embassy staff came to the airport to see us off. They all said, 'Oh, if only we could come with you.' They may have been getting to the end of their term and longing for a change. Most of them had their families with them and life was not too bad, but the work was difficult under the constant surveillance.

When we finally arrived at Heathrow an enormous champagne party was awaiting us, with press everywhere. I do remember that we were all slightly hysterical and talked too much, so delighted were we to get back. There was much toasting and speech-making, and then we drove off to our various homes. On reflection, it was an intensely interesting experience. We had seen so much and learned both the good and the bad side of life in Soviet Russia. We had all liked the Russians very much. Each night, after our performances, a group of men and women waited outside the stage door. One man gave Michael a fur cap, and many said most warmly, 'Come back if ever you can.' We were given many presents, such as painted cigarette boxes and trays. I was even given a record of Russian music by one of the interpreters. All our interpreters wore elegant clothes, which were unavailable to the rest of the population.

It was a great relief to be back at Hans Crescent. We were greeted by Vanessa, Corin, Lynn and Nanny. I had brought back embroidered linen shirts for the children and an ornament for Nanny. These were of such good quality that they have lasted perfectly to this day.

Chapter Twenty-Six

Milady, Vanessa, Corin & Lynn

A letter arrived one morning in the spring, offering Michael a knighthood. He came into my bedroom before breakfast, shouting 'It's come, it's come'. He was almost weeping with excitement. The letter was composed in such a way that the Queen would not be offended if he refused it. Nothing could have been further from his thoughts. He was absolutely delighted, and so was I. In many ways it was due to Glen Byam Shaw's persuading him to go to Russia.

One morning in May, Michael in a grey morning suit and topper, Corin in a smart lounge suit, Lynn in a pretty new dress and hat, and myself wearing a navy silk dress with a tight waist and bouffant skirt and wide navy blue hat, set off for the Palace. We were shown to our gilt chairs in the Throne Room. It was going to be quite a long wait. A military band in the gallery, played 'Bitter Sweet' and 'Tea for Two' and such songs of earlier days. The recipients of honours queued in an ante-room.

The Queen being away, the Queen Mother did the bestowing. She appeared wearing her usual chiffon dress and a blue hat with ostrich feathers, smiling as charmingly as ever. She stood on a dais. Gradually the recipients filed before her. In front of Michael was the painter Stanley Spencer, who was so small that when he knelt down he disappeared from sight.

It took me a long time to get used to being called 'Lady Redgrave'. In fact when somebody first called me 'Milady', I felt very peculiar. Even the villagers near our country cottage were excited. One of them said to John Fowler, 'Oh, Mr Fowler, what a great day for Odiham.'

*

In 1956, while Vanessa was still at Central School, Russia had invaded Hungary and she had begged to be allowed to go and help the refugees. As she was only seventeen, Michael refused, but said that she could take a collecting box round London, which she did. After leaving drama school, where she won the Sybil Thorndike Prize, she joined the Frinton

Repertory Company and first appeared on stage in 1957, playing Clarissa in *The Reluctant Debutante*.

She also played Alison in *Look Back in Anger*, which I saw. She was excellent. From there she went to the Arts Theatre, Cambridge, where she was very funny in *Come On Jeeves*. Her first West End appearance was in *A Touch of the Sun* in 1958, with Michael and Diana Wynyard. It was her first big success. She also began to take an active part in politics, becoming a founder member of CND and the Committee of 100, with Bertrand Russell, Canon Collins and Michael Foot. I used to watch in terror at the thought of her being arrested on demonstrations; and once she was, with Pat Arrowsmith, and they had to spend the night in prison, though they were freed the next day.

Both Michael and I supported Vanessa's stance on nuclear weapons. After all, what is the point in having them, when, if you use them, there is no world left to survive in? I took part in a CND play on the steps of St Paul's Cathedral with Mary Morris and others, which showed the horrors of nuclear war.

*

1961 was the year that assured Vanessa future stardom. She was offered a season at Stratford. Her Rosalind in *As You Like It*, directed by Michael Elliott, was exquisitely beautiful, and she received reviews of almost unprecedented acclaim. Tony Richardson was later to say that it was during Katerina's final speech in *The Taming of the Shrew*, in which she promises obedience to her husband, that he fell in love with her.

One night Vanessa and I went to the Aldwych Theatre. I don't remember what the play was, but in the interval Tony Richardson came into the bar. He and Vanessa looked at each other, and I had the feeling that it was love at first sight. He later came to a party we gave at Hans Crescent.

He said to me, 'I'm so much in love with Vanessa, what shall I do?'

I said, 'Ask her to marry you, if that's what you want. Or even live with each other until you make up your minds.'

Later, after they were married, Michael said to me in passing, 'How long do you give them?'

I said, 'Five years at a guess', and I was right almost to the day.

Difficulties started between them because Vanessa was still heavily committed to Stratford and Tony was in Dorset directing his great success *Tom Jones*, in which Lynn and I had parts. Vanessa would come down at weekends, and instead of giving her a restful weekend Tony would arrange an enormous party. She would go back to

Stratford on the Monday morning exhausted after staying up late with Tony, Albert Finney and the cast of *Tom Jones*.

Eventually they bought a beautiful house with a lovely garden in St Peter's Square, Chiswick, which I had found for them with the help of John Fowler. It was large enough to accommodate the family which they were looking forward to starting.

Vanessa's first child, Natasha, was born in 1963. I remember Vanessa's staying with me at Wilks Water during her pregnancy. She was wonderfully happy. One morning when we woke up she said her contractions had begun.

'Mum,' she said, 'I want to go and walk around the lake.'

It was the most beautiful May morning, and she went to the farthest edge. As she walked back with her billowing dressing-gown floating about her in the sunlight, it brought to my mind Oberon's speech in *A Midsummer Night's Dream*:

When we have laughed to see the sails conceive,
And grow big-bellied with the wanton wind;
Which she, with pretty and with swimming gait
Following, her womb then rich with my young squire,
Would imitate and sail upon the land.

I immediately rang Tony in Ireland, who said he would leave at once. He asked me to tell his chauffeur to take Vanessa to the London Clinic, where they had booked a room. I followed in my car and went to Hans Crescent until Tony rang me just after lunch. We sat by her in her room in the Clinic. She didn't seem in any way distressed, and was doing her gentle breathing, using the Natural Childbirth exercises she had been taught.

I left, and later in the evening Tony rang me saying, 'It's wonderful. We've got a girl. Can you come round? I was with her all the time, and at the moment of birth it was like a flower opening. It's the most beautiful experience of my life.'

Vanessa returned with Natasha to St Peter's Square, having engaged a nanny. Although she was determined to breast-feed, and to look after Natasha as much as possible herself, she needed also to spend time with Tony, whose work took him away a lot.

*

In the meantime Corin had left Westminster, having won a scholarship in Classics at King's College, Cambridge, where he was now living. I remember visiting him and thinking how dark and cold his rooms were, and I used to bring him extra blankets. He worked a lot in a theatre group with Ian McKellen, Clive Swift, Margaret Drabble and Derek Jacobi, writing, directing and also acting in various productions, most of which I saw. One was a send-up of *Love's Labour's Lost* which they tried out for a week at the Lyric Hammersmith. I began to think that Corin might decide on a career in the theatre, though in what capacity I was not exactly sure. While at Westminster he had played Portia and Lady Macbeth, following in his father's footsteps. He also played the lead in a couple of Greek plays, which only Greek scholars understood, and which we watched sitting under awnings in the rain.

Having achieved his degree, Corin started work at the Royal Court as Tony Richardson's assistant director, where he was deputed to hear Rex Harrison's lines for a Russian play *Platanov*. Rex, as always, had great difficulty with his lines. He later said that Corin had been of the greatest help to him, patient and understanding.

In 1962, Tony Richardson offered Corin the part of Lysander in his production of *A Midsummer Night's Dream*. It was not very well reviewed, but it contained a young cast of great potential: Rita Tushingham, Nicol Williamson, David Warner, Alfred Lynch, Samantha Eggar and Lynn Redgrave. For their one-night production of *Twelfth Night* they were joined by Albert Finney. This Sunday night production was due to George Devine, who felt that they had all worked so hard and deserved a reward after the disappointment of their reception. Nicol Williamson was one of the funniest Malvolios I have ever seen. George Devine always gave wonderful opportunities to young actors, who in later years, had he lived to see it, became great names in the theatre.

It was during the run of *A Midsummer Night's Dream* that Corin met his future wife, Deirdre Hamilton-Hill. They married in 1962, during the run of Corin's second play, *Chips with Everything* (brilliantly directed by John Dexter). Michael and I were a little worried, as they seemed very young to take such a step, but Corin was determined. Deirdre had been brought up in Malta, and when we met her parents we all got on very well, thanks partly to our common naval background.

One night, Corin had brought Deirdre back to Hans Crescent, planning to propose to her. As they stood on the balcony in the moonlight sipping champagne, Michael appeared, furious at being woken up, and even more furious to see that Corin had been at his wine rack. He so startled Deirdre that she dropped her glass on the head of a passer-by. The magic moment was lost. Next day Corin left a sharp note for Michael, requesting him in future not to interrupt his proposals.

They were married on a Sunday in the 'actors' church', St Paul's Covent Garden. As I walked out of the church on the arm of Deirdre's very handsome father Edward, I said to him, 'Edward, I suppose this is the last time I shall ever take your arm.' I felt I would like to do so again!

*

When Lynn left Queen's Gate – much to our surprise since she had always said that she did not want to act – she decided to go to the Central School in Swiss Cottage. I saw her in many productions, usually in the character role, and she showed great promise. In 1962 she decided to leave a little early, having been offered the part of Helena in Tony's *A Midsummer Night's Dream*. Some of the staff were annoyed, because the full course was three years. But Michael and I felt that a chance was a chance and you should take it. Lynn was a marvellous Helena. Bernard Levin wrote that this 'extraordinary child', despite youthful coltishness, showed much promise.

As a result she was cast as Sarah Elliott, the young lead in *The Tulip Tree* at the Haymarket, directed by Glen Byam Shaw and co-starring Celia Johnson. Celia told Glen that she could see, by every move that Lynn made, the complete truth of her acting. There was a scene where Celia, playing her mother, had to correct her, and Lynn stomped out of the room shrugging her shoulders exactly as a daughter would when irritated by her mother. It was a great success for Lynn.

Always having been the youngest child, she was now coming into her own and gaining more confidence. She decided to leave Hans Crescent and move to a flat of her own in Eccleston Square. She made her own curtains, and I helped her with the move, giving her odd bits of furniture that we didn't need, but which were useful to her. It was a bit of a wrench for me. All my three children had now left home and were leading independent lives. Lynny told me that because I had let her have her freedom, we should be closer than ever. Over the years, this proved to be true.

After the run of *The Tulip Tree*, Lynn was invited by Sir Laurence Olivier to join the National Theatre Company. She was excited at the prospect, but she found herself in a bad production of *Hamlet*. The movement of the scenery kept going wrong, the curtain constantly stuck, and the whole production was beset with difficulties. Michael himself was very unhappy as Claudius, in a suffocating costume in which he could hardly breath. All this added to Lynn's anxiety.

In the same season she played a court lady in *Saint Joan*, Rose in *The Recruiting Officer* and Barblin in *Andorra*. During this production, Sybil

Thorndike wrote to Michael that Lynn had proved herself as a comedienne but would in time show that she had far more depth and be able to play tragedy as well as comedy. Lynn told me that there is a scene in *Andorra* where she had to be raped by Tom Courtenay, who was so enthusiastic about his task that she was black and blue every night.

Much to Lynn's delight she was invited to stay on at the National for the 1964 season, this time playing larger roles, such as Jackie Coryton in *Hay Fever*, which was directed by Noel Coward himself. She and Noel got on wonderfully well and she nicknamed him 'Dad': after that season he went to all of her first nights.

All did not go so well with Edith Evans, however. She was cast because of her name, but in fact was too old to play Judith Bliss. In her latter years she disliked young girls and made it plain. This disconcerted Lynn. One day during rehearsals, Edith called out to Noel, who was in the stalls, 'What is that young girl doing waving her fan? I find it very irritating.' But the production was a great success. The rest of the cast – which included Maggie Smith, Anthony Nicholls and Robert Stephens – were all superb. Lynn also played Kattrin in Brecht's *Mother Courage*.

*

I was very happy that all the children were flourishing in their own lives, and it gave me the opportunity to think about my own. I began to spend a lot of time at Wilks Water. Michael didn't come down often, partly because he didn't enjoy the country as much as I did and partly because he was still busy at the National. In various ways I was extremely lucky. I had my career, at a time that some women find so trying, and many of the family joined me at weekends.

It also gave me more opportunity to see Tom. Our relationship had remained strong and was a great support to both of us. He would come for the occasional weekend at Wilks Water, where we were able to be completely alone, which was rare for us. He got on very well with John Fowler and the three of us often had dinner together. In the past, when I was still living at Bedford House, John had lent us his Hunting Lodge in summer and winter. He had been wonderfully generous. He never took sides, and while he had been my confidant for many years he was equally fond of Michael, understanding perfectly every kind of relationship. Except for his house and his garden, he had so little, but he gave endlessly of himself to his friends. He was a great romantic, and encouraged lovers and friendships of every sort.

Chapter Twenty-Seven

More Family

In 1964 I was asked to join the cast of *The Seagull* at the Queen's Theatre, which was directed by Tony Richardson and designed by Jocelyn Herbert. Vanessa was to play Nina, Peggy Ashcroft, Arkardina; Peter Finch, Trigorin; George Devine, Dr Dorn; Peter McEnery, Constantin; Mark Dignam, Shamrayev; and Ann Beach, Masha, while I played Polina Andreyevna. We were so happy in the production that we looked forward to every performance, which we found more enjoyable than our own home lives. The season was limited to eight weeks, and we played to packed houses. It was the first time I had acted with any of my children. Vanessa and I had adjoining dressing-rooms, and it was after a performance one evening that Vanessa joyfully told me that she was pregnant again.

After *The Seagull* had ended, Vanessa and I started to rehearse for Brecht's *St Joan of the Stockyards*, also directed by Tony. It was an enormous cast, and her part as St Joan was very demanding. I worried about her, as she was obviously getting very tired. We rehearsed all day every day, and ten days after the beginning of rehearsals she told me she thought she was starting a miscarriage. I immediately called a doctor, who said that if Vanessa was to save the child she would have to leave the cast immediately. She was reluctant, but a car was called and she went home to bed. Tony was told, and he and the whole cast were very worried about what to do.

Finally it was decided that the production must continue. Siobhan McKenna was asked to come over from Ireland, which she did at a moment's notice. I spent a lot of time hearing her lines. She had played it before, but it was short notice for such an important part. Without Vanessa my heart had gone out of the production. Siobhan was not the delicate actress Vanessa was, though she was a good trouper.

By staying in bed Vanessa saved her baby, but she resented having to give up the part, and her pregnancy was therefore not as happy as it would have been in different circumstances.

Deirdre was also pregnant, for the first time, and her baby was due on the same date as Vanessa's. Corin was thrilled at the prospect of becoming a father. He rang me excitedly one morning saying that Deirdre had started her labour, but he was worried because he had both a matinée and an evening performance to get through, and he asked if I would sit with her until he arrived at the hospital at round midnight. This I did. Deirdre and I played cards, and when the contractions came I held her hand. Her mother was abroad at the time. It was the most extraordinary day. There was a thunderstorm raging around Queen Charlotte's and a roaring gale that made all the shutters and windows bang, reminiscent of *Wuthering Heights*. It added a dramatic flair to the situation.

Next morning Deirdre gave birth to a daughter, Jemima Rebecca. Vanessa had also given birth to her second daughter, Joely Kim. Both mothers were breast-feeding their children, and they spent a lot of time together playing with their babies.

*

In June the same year, Michael directed the opening season of the Yvonne Arnaud Theatre at Guildford. The plays were to be *Samson Agonistes* in which he played Samson, while I was in the chorus; the musical *Lionel and Clarissa* in which I played Lady Mary; and *A Month in the Country* in which he played Rakitin opposite Ingrid Bergman as Natalia Petrovna.

Samson, which was too difficult a play for a provincial audience, was not a great success. Michael, however, was particularly fond of it, having produced it and played in it when he was teaching at Cranleigh. *Lionel and Clarissa*, however, which starred Max Adrian and John Quentin, who played my son, was more successful. I was a snobbish old woman with pretensions to grandeur. I had to sing a song in French, and as I knew French reasonably well I enjoyed it a lot.

The crowning success was *A Month in the Country*. Apart from Michael and Ingrid, the cast included Emlyn Williams as Ignaty Illyich, Max Adrian as Ignaty Illyich Shpiegelsky and Fay Compton as Anna. She had a wonderful line replying to her son, who tells her to shut up. 'I shall turn into an oyster. I shall not speak a word!'

It was the first time we had met Ingrid, though we had seen many of her films. I thought her very beautiful. She found it hard speaking English without an accent and needed extra coaching. She told me that it was difficult working with Michael. He would sometimes disappear to London leaving the cast feeling unrehearsed, which worried her. She also complained that he never praised her, and that to gain confidence she needed encouragement. I told her that I knew that Michael was always very critical when he was directing.

The play was a huge success and eventually transferred to the West End, at the Cambridge Theatre. Jeremy Brett joined the cast as Beliave, the tutor, with whom Natalia Petrovna falls in love. It could have had a much longer run if Ingrid had not had to leave.

*

All three children were now beginning to make names for themselves in films. Lynn achieved enormous success in *The Girl with Green Eyes* and *Georgy Girl,* a classic of the sixties. Vanessa had become a big star from *Morgan, a Suitable Case for Treatment* and Corin had a good part in *A Man for All Seasons.*

As a result of *Morgan,* Vanessa was hailed as the new screen beauty and photographed by David Bailey and Norman Parkinson. But although she had never looked more beautiful, her private life was becoming increasingly difficult, with Tony away all the time. They went on a holiday to Rome with Tony's parents. Jocelyn Rickards, the costume designer on *Morgan,* had made some mischief between them, and Tony hardly spoke to Vanessa, which was extremely tricky for her when both his parents were there. She arrived back very unhappy, with the premonition that all was over. She tried her best to patch things up, but Tony moved out of St Peter's Square.

I understood something of Tony's point of view. He had wanted to engage a cook-housekeeper, but Vanessa adamantly refused, saying she could manage everything herself. Of course coping with the children, her work and the household left her exhausted, which irritated Tony because he could easily afford the help necessary to make the house run smoothly. Instead of which he had to get the children up in the morning himself and give them their breakfast. Fond as he was of them, this kind of life did not suit him.

After the split Vanessa and the children came to stay with me at Wilks Water. Tony came to visit the children and, as he left, Vanessa, watching from the front door as he walked to his car, said, 'Oh, the if-onlys. If only I had gone about things in a different way.' Most people in break-ups feel the same.

In April 1967, Deirdre and Corin had a son, whom they named Luke Jordan Michael. He was our first grandson. Michael would come and visit her in the hospital, and hardly saying a word to her would sit gazing at the first grandson who would carry on the family name.

Lynn, meanwhile, had gone to New York to act in *Black Comedy* by Peter Schaffer, with Peter Bull and Geraldine Page. While there, she met for the second time a young actor, John Clark, who as a child had played Just William on tour and in a radio series. He had later made a career for himself in Canada, and was now playing in a send-up of *Macbeth*, called *Macbird*. I had said to Lynn before she left for the States that I felt she was going to meet the right man in New York, which of course she didn't believe. Shortly after she left I received a letter from her saying, 'Mum, it's happened. I have met the man, and we are going to be married.'

Michael and I and John's mother, Greta, flew to New York. Michael and I stayed at the Algonquin Hotel and Greta at a friend's apartment nearby. We all assembled for tea in our suite at the Algonquin and met John for the first time. We liked him enormously. The wedding was planned for the following Sunday at Sidney Lumet's house: Sidney's wife Gail had decorated a mirror over the fireplace with greenery and white camellias. Lynn wore a short white dress, with a camellia in her hair from which fell flowing white ribbons.

After the wedding we stayed for four or five days, seeing *Black Comedy* and returning to Hans Crescent after a very happy week.

When John and Lynn returned from America they settled in Merthyr Terrace, Barnes, a dear little house overlooking allotments. Their son Benjamin was supposed to have been born at home, but there was a slight difficulty, and John drove her to Queen Charlotte's hospital where he stayed with her for the night.

The next day I went to see them. When I arrived, Benjamin was pressed to her face and sucking at her cheek.

They returned to Merthyr Terrace and engaged a nanny. Lynn, like Vanessa, was a loving and tender mother, determined to breast-feed and spend as much time with her baby as her work would allow.

I loved having all the various grandchildren to stay at Wilks Water, but when they crawled around on the grass on summer days there was never a moment's peace, as they always seemed to head straight for the lake or the stream. I remember that Luke, when he was about four, used to love walking in the woods, but the noise of snapping twigs frightened him, so he would say firmly: 'Granny, I want you to come into the woods with me, but stay out of sight so that I can pretend I'm on my own.'

*

After Vanessa's enormous success in *Morgan* she was for the first time wooed by Hollywood to play the lead in the musical of *Camelot* with Richard Harris, Franco Nero and David Hemmings. She decided to accept the offer and was entertained as befitted a new star. I went out to join her and watched a lot of the filming. The sets and costumes were superb: huge halls with Arras curtains and large mastiffs lying about. There was a scene where Lancelot, Franco Nero, rides into the great hall on his prancing horse wearing armour, looking absolutely magnificent, and I felt there was a great possibility that Vanessa might fall in love with him.

It was a sad romantic film, with wonderful music. Vanessa sang her own part, as did Richard Harris. Years later Vanessa hired a cinema and showed the film on Natasha's birthday. The scene in which Guenevere is burned at the stake so upset the children that a sobbing Natasha, Joely, Jemima and Luke had to be taken out, though they could see Vanessa sitting next to them, large as life.

Vanessa and Franco duly fell in love. But it was not without its problems. Vanessa is an extremely independent and strong-minded woman, who was used to making her own decisions, while Franco wanted her to be like his wonderful mother, a regular housewife. He was in love with 'Guenevere' and wanted to change her into an Italian wife. This caused much friction. He would come round to see me saying, 'I want to marry her, I want to marry her. She is my wooman, she is my wooman.' I, not knowing what to say next, replied, 'Shut up, Franco, and have a whisky.'

In Italy I stayed with Vanessa and Franco at a lovely farmhouse between Venice and Vicenza. It had a huge flag-stoned kitchen where Franco's mother cooked wonderful pasta for us all. It was a happy time for them because Franco had Vanessa to himself, away from her other obligations. They were both filming *A Quiet Place in the Country*. I would go to join them for lunch on location, and we bicycled all over the countryside in the evening. It was quite beautiful. The farm had a dovecot like the one in *Romeo and Juliet*. It was a very happy time. I remember Vanessa saying to me, 'Oh Mama, darling, the smell of your scent was still in your bedroom after you had left.'

At Vicenza we saw the balcony which is thought to have inspired the balcony scene in *Romeo and Juliet*. There was a wonderful old theatre there, with old-fashioned scenery, but we did not see a production.

Much to Franco's disappointment, Vanessa decided against marrying him but wanted to continue the relationship. Their son Carlo was born in 1969, at home in St Peter's Square. Franco, being Italian, dreaded the child's being a girl, and Vanessa too was anxious to have a son; so Carlo's birth was a joyous occasion. The moment I heard the news I went to St Peter's Square wondering what they would call the child. 'Charles' came to my mind, but then I realised that as he was Italian it should be 'Carlo'. They seemed to like the name, and Carlo he remained. Vanessa was lying back on the pillows with an expression of total fulfilment. Franco was simply gazing at his first-born. After all the turmoil of their relationship, it was a very happy moment.

*

The same year Lynn and John's second child, Kelly, was born. They had moved to a large house on Barnes Common to make room for the new arrival. I now had seven grandchildren, and I saw as much of all of them as I could. Vanessa would bring Carlo over to Lynn's and we all sat on the bed admiring the two dark-haired bundles. I went to Lynn's a great deal and in the summer we would sit in the garden while the children played. Benjamin was a strong, brave little boy. I remember once he burnt his foot quite badly but complained hardly at all.

Lynn, John, Benjamin, Kelly and the nanny all came to stay with me at Wilks Water, where they had a bad attack of flu. Benjamin slept in my bed and his body felt like a little furnace. He would keep saying, 'Stroke me, Granny. Stroke me, Granny. Keep on stroking', which I did. The next day we called the doctor, but such are the recuperative powers of children that his temperature had gone almost back to normal, unlike the other poor adults.

Sadly for me, Lynn and John decided to move to Ireland, as their house had become too much of a liability. The repairs were endless, and they had built an enormous underground garage, which had cost too much.

They found a delightful house overlooking Balscadden Bay, just outside Dublin in Howth. It was an enchanting place. All the woodwork was honey-coloured pine. A bow window in the sitting-room overlooked the bay, and from the window seat you could see straight down into the water. There was a small garden, with a steep cliff-walk down to a rock pool, where you could swim. Some days we would go down to the port and buy fresh fish straight out of the sea. At other times we would visit a castle in the woods, which were full of rhododendrons and azaleas.

During one of my visits, Michael came to join me. We decided to stay at a small hotel on the cliffs two miles from the house. Michael seemed far from well and was weak and shaky. I didn't realise then that it was the beginning of Parkinson's disease.

Lynn and John had a dalmatian bitch called Waldo. The last time they had stayed at Wilks Water, Waldo and Barney, our golden labrador, had rushed into the woods, with the result that Waldo was pregnant when they left for Ireland. She had a litter of twelve puppies, white with large brown spots and brown noses. Lynn wanted to keep them all, but had to get rid of them as she was leaving.

Sadly for me, Lynn and John decided to move even further away than Ireland, because of work, and went to live in America. This proved to be a very successful choice for them, and Lynn has worked there steadily in films, theatre and TV.

*

Before the birth of Carlo, in 1968, Vanessa starred in the film *Isadora*, the life story of Isadora Duncan, with Jason Robards and James Fox as co-stars. She had to have special dancing lessons from Litz Pisc.

I thought it was one of the most moving and brilliant of films, and in my opinion Vanessa's greatest screen performance to date. Her ability to play the elderly Isadora as an imperious and yet tragic woman was quite extraordinary. Isadora, being very unconventional, was a character she would well understand.

All the Russian scenes were shot in Yugoslavia, and the horrific scene at the end, when Isadora gets into the Bugatti of her new lover, and is strangled by her scarf catching in the spokes of the car wheel, was shot on a Yugoslavian sea-front.

Chapter Twenty-Eight

No Sense of Detachment

In 1972, Corin appeared at Stratford with the RSC for the first time, playing Octavius in *Antony and Cleopatra* and Antiphilus of Ephesus in *The Comedy of Errors*. He had taken a nice flat outside Alveston, but Deirdre and the children did not join him, partly because she was working in London, but also because Corin had become part of a group called the Socialist Labour League, which was causing difficulties in their relationship since Deirdre was left alone a great deal. She and the children often came to stay with me at Wilks Water at weekends, but Corin could only ever stay for a few hours. Deirdre thought for a time of joining the Group, but her heart was not in it. I was able to sympathise, having spent so much time alone myself when Michael had joined the People's Convention which, thankfully, he left.

*

In 1972 I had been asked to play 'the older lady' in a play by John Osborne called *A Sense of Detachment* at the Royal Court. I didn't like the play very much, but I wanted to get back into the theatre and it seemed a good opportunity. It was directed by Frank Dunlop, and the cast included Nigel Hawthorne, Denise Coffey, John Standing and Michael Relph.

When I first read the script I misunderstood the effect that my character would have on the audience. I played a woman in her eighties who gets pornography pushed through her letter box and reads it aloud to the audience, clearly not understanding a word of it. Of course the audience understood only too well and, helped by Mr Osborne's device of using plants in the audience to help what he called 'audience participation', my lines were greeted with 'Say it again, Rachel, say it again'. I found this horribly disconcerting. On many nights vegetables and boots were thrown on to the stage, only just missing me. One day I sent a note to John Osborne, because I was so upset. His reply was, 'Never mind. You're very good officer material', whatever he meant by that.

Towards the end of the play there was a love scene between John Standing and Denise Coffey, which seemed perfectly innocent. There were yells and shouts, particularly from two young men in the front row of the stalls.

One shouted, 'Christ-all-bloody-mighty, what's all this rubbish about?'

At this moment I got so angry that I saw red sparks in front of my eyes. I jumped off the stage, grabbed one of the young men by his hair, saying, 'Either shut up or get out.'

The company were startled and said, 'For God's sake come back quickly.'

I jumped back in time for the curtain. Meanwhile many of the audience chased the young man up the aisle and out into Sloane Square, where somebody knocked his tooth out.

When I heard this I was horrified. Nigel Hawthorne gave me an address to write to. I tried to explain that a play isn't television, actors can hear, and I was sorry this had happened but the audience were as angry as the actors. After this, security men were in the theatre every night on guard, and every evening when I was going to the theatre they were outside our flat to see that I got away safely.

Michael was never able to come to the Osborne play, which I thought was probably just as well, because he was starring in *A Voyage round my Father* at the Haymarket Theatre, by John Mortimer. He had taken over from Alec Guinness. Jane Baxter played his wife, Amanda Murray his daughter. It was a lovely production and went very well. By now Michael had to wear a hearing aid in order to receive his prompts, which was irritating to him because sometimes it buzzed in his ear; but he would rather have any discomfort than give up the theatre he loved, especially this play.

*

We had moved from our flat in Hans Crescent, which had become too large for us now that the children had left home. One day I saw an advertisement for a property, 35 Lower Belgrave Street, described as part of an old coaching inn, with stable and stable yard. We went straight to see it, and it was totally original.

You entered through a hidden doorway into a large sitting hall on the ground floor, and beyond the hall was a door to a large studio suitable for a housekeeper. There was a pretty dining-room with french windows onto a large balcony where we could sit out in deckchairs in summer. There was an adequate kitchen, for which I bought Casa Pupo tiles. The drawing-room was very elegant, with a lattice window looking onto the balcony, and there was room for pictures and our nicest chairs and sofas. Upstairs was a bathroom and two adjoining bedrooms for me and Michael. Both were airy and looked down on the balcony and adjoining gardens.

Though we couldn't really afford it, we decided it was for us and made an offer, which was accepted, so we moved yet again. Unfortunately we were only able to stay there for about four years: once again accountants had miscalculated our financial affairs and, as with Bedford House, we were obliged to sell.

*

In 1973 I was cast as Lady Childress in a play called *Gomes*, with Roy Dotrice. It was a disaster and lasted one week at the Queen's Theatre. The reviews were quite appalling. As it was the first time I had had my name in lights, more's the pity.

I then went to the Old Vic in the National Theatre Company to play Nancy in *Freeway* by Michael Frayn, directed by Jonathan Miller. The cast included Paul Rogers, Graham Crowden, who played my husband, Irene Handl and Joan Hickson. Nobody was happy. The play was about an enormous pile-up on a freeway. There was a bus on the stage and a great many cars all hooting. I played an old woman with an enormous amount of padding. At the end of the play Graham and I had to get into what looked like a chair on a ski-lift, and we were winched up into the flies. We then had to look down and wave to the other characters. It was terrifying and I got vertigo.

I told Jonathan that I didn't think I would be able to go on.

He was very sympathetic. He said, 'Well, it's coming off anyway, so why should you upset yourself for one more week? The understudy can take over.'

I felt bad about leaving my first opportunity as a National Theatre Player.

Corin and Vanessa, though still working hard, were intensely involved in politics. Corin's involvement had finally led to a break-up in his marriage to Deirdre, an event which they both felt sad about. Vanessa's involvement with Franco Nero had also ended. I understood many of the causes which Vanessa and Corin were fighting for, and I have helped them by appearing at one fund-raising occasion, which Deirdre also attended. It is naturally upsetting to me that they have so many critics. I feel proud that they have the courage to fight, however uncomfortable it may be, for their convictions. They are not doing it for personal gain.

*

In 1975 Alec Guinness asked if I would play Blanche in *A Family and a Fortune* by Ivy Compton Burnett. I was a little apprehensive, having had a flop in *Gomes*, but Alec was reassuring.

'We shall have a short tour first,' he said, 'so there will be plenty of time to run the play in, and to feel safe by the time we get to London.'

The cast was Alec, Margaret Leighton, Nicola Pagett, Jill Balcon and Anthony Nicholls. I died at the end of the first half. Blanche was a gentle and loving character. I was very happy in the production.

Margaret Leighton, whom I had known for many years, was suffering from multiple sclerosis but fortunately was playing my slightly crippled sister. In the part she used a stick and was able to sit for a good deal of the performance. For the final curtain Alec used to take her by both hands and lead her down to the footlights. She was always joking and full of fun, and when her husband, Michael Wilding, came backstage at the end of the performance she always gave him a big hug and said, 'Oh, my little darling, you're so clever.' He looked after her with loving care. She would always arrive by car, and the chauffeur would help her out. In spite of all her difficulties, she remained immaculate and beautiful.

I thoroughly enjoyed the tour, which opened at the Theatre Royal, Bath, where it was well reviewed. In London we opened at the Apollo to excellent reviews. It was an enjoyable run for about seven months

I was living in a tiny cottage in Ebury Mews off Elizabeth Street, which served as a London pied-à-terre, while Wilks Water had become our main home. Michael lived there, doing the preliminary work for his autobiography, and I would join him at weekends; but it was becoming difficult to have a large number of the family to stay, because Michael's illness was developing and the scampering of children tired him. On fine days he would sit in the garden reading, as I did the gardening, and on cold days by the fire, and I entertained friends from round about for dinner. We both knew that the disease was progressive, and he faced his future with great courage. There was a drug which controlled the shaking but at the same time caused drowsiness. It was hard for me to see Michael, a man who loved life and had lived it to the full, feeling so depressed and isolated.

*

After the success of *A Family and a Fortune*, Alec again offered me a part, that of his wife in Alan Bennett's *The Old Country*. It was the story of an

English intellectual who had defected to Russia, having been a spy, and was settled in the countryside with his wife, spending his time listening to English music and bird-watching.

It had a sparkling script, both witty and tragic: the story of a man trapped by his principles in a country he did not really care for. It provided a marvellous part for me as the slightly homesick wife who, though not really happy with her husband, remains loyal to him. It was certainly one of the best West End roles I have ever had. Alec left the company after seven months to be replaced by Anthony Quayle, and I stayed on for a year.

Alec, with his generosity, endlessly entertained Faith Brook and myself, sometimes with his wife Merula. We would dine in the nearby Soho restaurants and sometimes at the Connaught. I once tried to take him out for lunch. I booked a table at La Popote and arranged with the head waiter to give me the bill and not let Alec know anything about it. When it came to paying, Alec was rather annoyed: he liked to be the giver.

Alec always liked Faith or me to sit in his dressing-room for about a quarter of an hour before the performance while he finished off his make-up. I think that talking a little before the performance relaxed him. His dressing-room was extremely elegant: everything was in perfect order, reflecting him. Alec was a reserved man, but years before when we were living at Bedford House he would say, 'You and Michael come to St Peter's Square to have a drink with Merula and me. We'll all have a glass of champagne.' After which he became wonderfully tranquil and amusing.

He had many funny stories to tell of his young life and the various influences on it. Merula had given up her career as an actress to look after their son Matthew, but being a fine painter concentrated on that. She and Alec moved to the country to a house near Petersfield, where they kept goats and dogs, and she had a studio for her painting. She always painted their Christmas cards. I don't think she missed the theatre at all.

*

One of my favourite television parts was as Kate, in *Kate the Good Neighbour*. Kate is a spinster of about 60 living in a small house in Brook Green, where she spends a lot of time writing her diary. One day she is knocked down by a group of ruffians on roller skates and becomes crippled. She is taken back to the house, walking with a stick. The landlady, who is worried about her, wants to help her and do her shopping, but Kate is too proud and too independent. She is obsessed with managing on her own. Various people come into the house and try to help her, but she stubbornly refuses. The story goes into flashback and shows the young Kate in love, and how she could have happiness. She becomes pregnant and tries to procure an abortion on herself, taking castor oil and having boiling hot baths. She has talked to a waitress in a café, but doesn't get a great deal of help. Eventually, however, the abortion works. From the abortion scene it switches to the older Kate who we know has had an accident, and she gets into a bath to ease her limbs, making a visual parallel. A young man from Welfare comes in and finds the bathroom door locked. He bashes down the door and, seeing what a state she is in, he picks her up, wrapped in a blanket, and lays her on her bed. He is exceedingly kind for a young man from the Welfare. He persuades her, against her will, to go into a 'sheltered home' because, he says, she will meet other people and not be so lonely and in her present state she can't live alone. She arrives at the home, meets a lot of people, has tea in the communal sitting-room, meets an elderly man who knew her before, who says, 'It isn't bad here at all, you will find.' She goes into the large sitting-room, and the Welfare officer tells her to look out into the garden. The object she sees is a little chestnut plant gradually sprouting, symbolic of hope for the future.

Chapter Twenty-Nine

The Redgrave Theatre

The first time I had realised that something was seriously wrong with Michael's health was when I went to see him at the Mermaid Theatre, in 1971, in William Trevor's play *The Old Boys*. At one point he had to walk across the stage holding a glass of sherry, which he handed to Sylvia Coleridge. As he walked I noticed his hand shaking badly. I thought it was more than nerves, but I decided not to mention it to him, especially with a first night coming up.

We used to go for walks together in Pimlico, looking in the various antique shops. We would go arm in arm and I noticed that he stumbled a little: his foot movements seemed uncertain. As we stopped at the window of one shop, I saw that his eyes appeared to be staring as if he couldn't quite focus on what he was looking at. We would walk on together, and sit in Ranelagh Gardens. He didn't actually complain of anything, but he did seem preoccupied.

When we got home I said, 'I think you ought to go and see a doctor,' and he agreed.

The first specialist he went to advised him to cut down on drink. I knew he drank a certain amount but it was clear to me that there was much more to it than that. After all, I had lived with him for many years and knew how he behaved when drinking, but this was completely different.

Finally he was recommended to the Hospital for Nervous Diseases in Queen's Square. He saw Dr Kocin, who said he would take him in for three or four days and do every kind of test. I sat every day in Michael's room with him, trying to lessen his apprehension. But I must admit that I was very fearful too.

When Dr Kocin diagnosed Parkinson's, our first reaction was one of shock, but we had both realised that something was very wrong and we felt that now, diagnosed, it could be helped. Dr Kocin prescribed sinemet, a derivative of L-Dopa. Michael was surprised how cheerful he felt. He put it down to his contented nature, and then found that it was an effect of the drug. But the drug also made him drowsy and, at first, nauseated.

Lynn and John with the help of an American friend, Dr. Rizzo, arranged for Michael to go to New York to be treated at St. Barnabas Hospital, where Drs Irving Cooper and Joe Waltz had performed a number of operations on Parkinsonian patients with some success. Various tests and observations were made. Michael was so impressed with the efficiency of the hospital and the wonders of modern medicine that he said he was ready for an operation the next day.

To be told that it wasn't necessary was an unexpected reward for bravery. 'Fine,' he said, 'but what next?'

Dr Waltz said he must go home, rest a certain amount and be sure that his drug intake was monitored. This was extremely important, since an overdose would create too much drowsiness and an underdose would not help his shaking.

*

Michael returned to England, feeling disappointed in one way because he had thought that the operation might be a miracle cure. But such things did not exist.

His memory for parts he had played remained unimpaired, but he was nervous of breaking new ground. He was delighted therefore when, in July 1973, came an unexpected bonus: would he care to accompany Peggy Ashcroft and others to Central City, Colorado, to appear at its festival in *The Hollow Crown*? This was an anthology devised by John Barton for the Royal Shakespeare Company about the kings and queens of England. An excellent dresser was provided, and he felt secure in the company of a friend, Mavis Walker, and Peggy Ashcroft.

The production, which started in Colorado, was to tour the world for the next two years, in 126 theatres in 115 towns across four continents. This would have been a daunting prospect for the most healthy person, but Michael was thrilled to be able to carry on working, which he had not expected to be able to do. The final production was at the Redgrave Theatre, in Farnham. He said it was a marvellous homecoming.

The original theatre in Farnham had been the Old Castle Theatre, which had been made out of a barn. In the 1960s a new theatre was planned and Michael was asked by the Trustees if it could be named 'The Michael Redgrave Theatre'. Michael, though flattered, realised that Vanessa and other members of the family were now as famous as he was and therefore asked that it be called simply 'The Redgrave Theatre'.

*

There were many fund-raising events – garden parties, readings and performances, one of which I attended with Noel Coward. Princess Margaret and Lord Snowdon graced the occasion.

After the performance, Noel and I had been invited to Rules Restaurant to join them, but Noel, who was feeling very weak, said to me, 'I don't feel up to it. Would you mind coming back with me to the Savoy?'

'Quite truthfully,' I said, 'I would rather be with you.'

We had a light supper in a corner of the grill-room and afterwards went upstairs to his suite, where we reminisced for hours.

Noel was a fascinating raconteur, and we laughed and gossiped till about three in the morning. He had had an extraordinary life, starting as a boy actor. He wrote *Private Lives* in two weeks. What he liked was a well-constructed play with a beginning, a middle and an end: he wasn't very keen on 'the new wave'. About Stanislavsky he said: 'They had a little company, they went away for three months, and then they never opened.' Noel liked everybody to know their lines before they started rehearsing, which wasn't always easy. He felt that a lot of discussion beforehand about the 'how, why and motivation' was a waste of time. Once you knew your lines you could mark out positions, and from there you had a good basis to get on with the play.

There was a great deal of truth in this. I have known discussions go on for an hour about why someone lifts a teacup, how they lift it. I think lifting a teacup is lifting a teacup: moving is moving. If you have a good director who places the moves well and takes half a day for an act you are well on the way. In most plays you have at least four weeks rehearsal and then previews. If you spent two weeks of that time discussing motivation, you would have wasted half your rehearsal time. The Stanislavsky method was excellent for the Russian actors because they could go away for three months and rehearse and talk. In spite of what Noel said, they would have been ready to open. Michael fell somewhere between the two schools of thought. Like Noel, he was practical and strict, but he also read with great interest about alternative methods of work. Like Noel, he had been associated with the theatre since childhood, and therefore had practical experience.

Our lives had crossed with Noel's over many years. Michael had never appeared in any of Noel's plays, but he and his partner, Fred Sadoff, produced *Waiting in the Wings*. This led to a series of rows with Noel who felt that Fred was asking too high a percentage of the takings. Michael was upset. He admired and liked Noel a good deal, but felt loyalty to his partner. He hated rows of any sort, and this sort of situation was anathema to him.

That evening Noel said to me: 'I have loved Michael, but he is very difficult, and you must have had your difficulties.'

I told him that in fact he, Noel, had upset me greatly one night at the beginning of the war. It was the last night before Michael went to Plymouth to join up. I had wanted to spend the evening with Michael but he had spent it instead with Noel.

Noel said that he hadn't wished to hurt me, and that it was no use having regrets about what you had done but he had found Michael so irresistibly charming.

I couldn't but agree with him.

Noel's nickname for Michael was 'dear China'. This comes from Wycherly's *The Country Wife*, where Lady Fidget, looking through the keyhole at Mr. Horner making love, says, 'Nay, nay, wait for me. I'll have some China too.'

During the war Noel had wanted me to be in *In Which We Serve*. I would have loved to be, because it would have meant being directed by him and spending time in his company. But Noel thought that, as Michael was going to be an ordinary seaman earning very little, it would be better for our financial situation if I went on a five-month tour in *Blithe Spirit*, earning a reasonable salary. I went on the tour and first played the very boring part of Mrs Bradman. However, I understudied Irene Browne as the wife. Irene had a lover who, she said, was going to the 'white man's grave'. Noel said, 'Rubbish! White man's grave, my foot. He's going to enjoy himself, and get away from Irene!' Because Irene wept and sobbed so much about the lover who was going to the white man's grave (and I did sympathise with her), Binkie Beaumont gave her ten days off and I played the part. This was great fun, because it was opposite Ronnie Squire, who was thankful for her absence. He always said, 'Bloody woman. We can hardly get into a hotel without her fussing and demanding the best room. We'll have a bit of peace for a week.'

Binkie Beaumont told me years later that he had invited Noel to see his production of *Showboat*. He was worried that it was too long and asked Noel whether it should be cut.

'In my opinion,' said Noel, 'you should cut the entire second act – and the child's throat!' He was always funny, and never really meant to be cruel.

I loved Noel. He was always charming and, despite his strange looks, I found him attractive. It was marvellous to be with somebody who was so witty.

*

For the laying of the foundation stone for the Redgrave Theatre, Michael, Peggy and I travelled to Farnham. We paraded round the town in a horse-drawn coach. The Chairman, William Douglas-Home, who had written many plays himself, welcomed us to the ceremony. This consisted of Michael burying a stone under the foundations, and he had to knock out a brick, which fell on Peggy's ankle: a doctor had to be called. The building was to be in the beautiful grounds of Brightwell House, which provided a lovely space for people to have drinks before a performance.

The theatre was very comfortable, and they had thoughtfully provided a great deal of leg-room. The only drawback was that there wasn't a fly tower, but as they had very simple sets this was not a problem. There were excellent lighting facilities and good dressing-rooms. The project was financed by the town council. There was a club membership from which they raised a great deal of money, as they also did from local firms who sponsored it. They did their best to have a permanent company, but had guests for certain plays. A production of Noel Coward's *Cavalcade* used many members of the Farnham population: in its simple way, it was almost as good as the original.

Princess Margaret was at the opening performance, *Romeo and Juliet*. There was a much-too-young Juliet and a not-very-good Romeo. They only had two weeks' rehearsal, which for that play is impossible. The first director was David Horlock, who had done a brilliant production of *Julius Caesar* in the limited Old Castle Theatre, one of the best productions of *Julius Caesar* (a difficult play) that I have ever seen. I think it was the first time I really understood the play.

We went to many productions at the theatre, which we greatly enjoyed. They were always delighted to see Michael, although his illness was progressing. They always welcomed him, and the various actors talked to him afterwards. They honoured him with a bronze bust in the foyer.

*

On Michael's return from America with the Hollow Crown Company I went to Heathrow Airport to pick him up. He was wearing a cowboy hat and carrying his own hand luggage. He looked brown and well.

He felt justly pleased with himself at having got through such a gruelling tour. He didn't complain about feeling tired. On the contrary, he was elated by the whole experience and the success they had all enjoyed; his courage had been quite extraordinary, as he travelled endless miles by bus, ship and air. He was desperately ill but never missed a single performance. It was that old curer, Dr Theatre.

Michael settled down back at Wilks Water once again. Although he needed the rest, it was depressing for him to be stuck in the country, which he didn't much enjoy.

We exchanged visits with Bryan Forbes, who was writing a biography of Edith Evans and wanted to talk to Michael about his relationship with her. He also asked me what I felt, in order to be tactful about it. I was perfectly happy with what he had written. It was moving and accurate, and a remarkable account of Edith's life.

I have written a good deal in this book about Edith Evans – that great actress and unusual and remarkable woman. She and I became good friends in time. When filming in *Tom Jones*, she was not happy because the way of working was not hers. Hugh Griffith, the squire who played her brother, was drunk from lunchtime onwards. He was marvellously 'Fielding' in character, but upset Edith. I used to sit with her in her caravan at lunchtime. I remember her saying to me: 'Good girl. With all the difficulties, you've stuck it.' I stayed at her Gate House in Sussex after she had visited Michael and me at Chichester. She had seen him as Vanya, a superb performance. Somehow, in her own home, she seemed to shrink in size. She sat by a log fire, and we watched television. I helped her get the supper. She had a wonderful chauffeur, Albert, who remained devoted to the end.

*

Although I hated leaving Michael for long lengths of time, I made sure that he had a housekeeper and a cleaner to look after him when I went to stay with Lynn and John, who were now settled in California. They had rented a house in Beverley Hills with a swimming pool.

Benjamin and Kelly were at a local school. One afternoon there was a school party. Kelly was very excited running round with cakes and tea, and we were shown examples of their work, especially painting and drawing, at which Kelly showed great promise. It was always lovely to be able to see Lynny wherever she was living, but there were such long gaps in between

Lynn was then starring in the TV series *House Calls*. She had not yet had Annabel Lucy, whose birth in July 1981 was surrounded by controversy. Universal fired Lynn, saying she couldn't bring Annabel onto the lot, so that she could breast-feed her during work hours.

I used to go and have lunch with Lynny near the studios. One day the writers of the series asked me if I would like to work for them. Naturally I said I would love to if they had a suitable part for me to play. I didn't get it, but very much enjoyed my three weeks' stay.

John suggested that as Lynn and I had had so little time on our own, we should have a few days' holiday together. We flew to Colorado, where Michael and the Company of the Hollow Crown had performed. Lynn hired a car outside the airport and we drove on to Denver, where we took rooms in a skiing hotel. As it was out of season, the apartment was let at a very reasonable price, complete with a cleaner.

There was a big log fireplace with a grill, and the first evening Lynn charcoal-grilled wonderfully tender steaks and baked potatoes in the coals. The next day we went out and wandered round little souvenir shops, stopping for coffee.

In the afternoon we drove up the hairpin bends of the mountain to the Great Divide. The top was snow-covered. We tried walking a few yards, but the high altitude made us breathless. We drove on down to Aspen, famous for the aspen trees which lined the streets. It was reminiscent of early America, with wooden houses and sawdust-strewn floors in the saloons.

We had lunch in a small restaurant in the village. After lunch we started the long drive back, crossing the Great Divide where this time we didn't stop because it was getting late.

We arrived at Denver at about half past seven, and again Lynny cooked a lovely meal for the two of us. The house was large, with great big windows with window seats looking out over the skiing slopes. Lynny had a room in a gallery over the main sitting-room. There were two bedrooms with a bathroom in between.

We had a delightful last evening. Next day, we looked at the theatre in Colorado. It was an old mining village, with little chalet houses for visitors. We went for long walks, and eventually took the plane back to Los Angeles, where I stayed a few more nights.

I always hated these partings. Lynn and John gave one such a wonderfully happy time. At the airport, when we said goodbye at the barrier, I didn't cry, but my throat ached, and I always told them to leave quickly.

*

When I got back to Wilks Water I found Michael in reasonable health.

He was asked to be in *Close of Play* at the National Theatre, written by Simon Gray and directed by Harold Pinter, co-starring Peggy and Annie Leon. It was possible for him to do this because throughout the play he sat in a chair. During the run he stayed at a hotel in London. Although he only had one line at the end of the play, the cast all said that his total concentration, and the expression in his eyes, was a great help to them.

Michael was so happy to be back in the theatre that he wouldn't have minded how long it ran for. But this was to be, sadly, his last performance in the West End.

Chapter Thirty

Jewel in the Crown

Through my agent, Anne, I heard that I had been offered a part in a long television series, *The Jewel in the Crown*, directed by Christopher Morahan. It was to be fourteen episodes, and I was to be in four. It was a tremendous cast: Peggy, Art Malik, Charles Dance, Judy Parfitt, Geraldine James, Eric Porter, Fabia Drake, Saeed Jaffrey, Susan Wooldridge and many others. My part was Lady Manners. I was told that many of my scenes would be shot on location in India.

The entire company was at the first reading, and we read the whole script through, which took all day. We rehearsed for a time in London, and then flew to Bombay as our first stop and went on by car to Simla.

At Simla Peggy, Fabia and I stayed at Rose Cottage as guests of General Gurbash and his wife Cuckoo. Although it was cold, there was brilliant sunshine and blossom all over the garden. The cottage was perched on the top of a steep hill and the luggage was carried up by the house servants. The garden had lovely green grass and cherry trees in full blossom, and the view from the paved terrace of the house looked right across a beautiful valley to the Himalayas.

The General and his wife took us to our rooms, which were divided from each other by a passage and two bathrooms. It was so cold that Peggy came along to my room, where there was a small electric fire. We got under the covers to get warm, and Nandhi, their servant, with his long white coat and feathered turban, brought tea to our room. We couldn't help wondering what on earth he thought of us. However, with his perfect manners, he showed no sign of surprise, and indeed, as the days went on, was like our personal servant. Nothing was too much trouble for him.

Hot bottles were put in our beds for the night, because although it was spring it was still very cold. Where we were, high up in the mountains, the water and electricity supply had to be carefully rationed. Nandhi would go to the well and bring cans of water to the cottage, and he would heat it, and we then could bathe in a tub.

Two of the married servants had a small boy, whom we called the little prince. He walked about the gardens and terraces with his hands

215

behind his back, looking like Royalty. We enquired about the servants' quarters, out of interest. The General said that he wanted to build on extra rooms for the staff, but they refused, saying they had always been used to their small quarters and preferred them the way they were. Everything was beautifully clean. Bedrooms were scoured and swept early in the morning before anybody got up.

The next morning work started, and members of cast involved in the first scene arrived, walking up the hill. As I wasn't involved in the first scenes, Cuckoo would take me into Simla to see the sights and help with the household shopping. We went to the markets where barefoot boys would carry great baskets of fruit, vegetables and whatever was needed for the household on their heads and eventually load them into the car. In Simla town there were wide open spaces where you could sit in the cool after you had done the shopping. Goods were cheap. You could buy lovely scarves and saris for very little in the stalls on the edge of the market. I did one scene in the market-place, getting in and out of a car, and was much stared at by the local inhabitants.

*

After three weeks the Company moved to Srinagar, where we stayed at the grand Oberoi Hotel, which belonged to the millionairess, Madam Oberoi, who owned chains of hotels all over India. It had a lovely garden overlooking the lake. The bedrooms were very pleasant, and Peggy and I were next door to each other.

From the hotel we walked down to the ferry for the day's shooting, and were taken by boat across the lake to the opposite side where the houseboats were moored in readiness. The crew put up huge marquees with trestle tables and chairs ready for the midday lunch. It was an attractive place with grassy slopes, so most of us sat outside. The English crew had English food transported in vast canisters wherever they went: it was part of the contract that the English crew must have good English food! The sausages and mash didn't seem to me appropriate in the heat of India. The location was pretty, like a small orchard, and there were white ropes to keep out the Indian boys and girls who were curious to watch the filming. The left-overs of the English lunch were very welcome to the poor children.

*

My first scene was in the houseboat, and I was reading a letter that Daphne Manners had sent to me, partly apologising for any trouble she had caused over having the baby and asking me, if she died, to take care of her child. This Lady Manners agreed to do, causing great trouble with the other English families, in particular the Layton family, who were horrified that Lady Manners would take care of what they thought of as an Indian bastard. After Daphne's death there was a scene by her grave. The little place was under some trees in a shaded part of the woods, quite a long way back from the location overlooking the lake. The ayah was there, and myself, in a black hat and veil, and I threw a small bunch of flowers onto the grave. It was a terribly sad scene, as I looked at the resting-place of the niece to whom I had been devoted. Daphne's death meant a great deal to Lady Manners, because she had been entrusted with the little Indian baby and was devoted to them all but equally did not know what the future would hold for the child.

There was a scene where Geraldine James, playing Sarah Layton, came to visit Lady Manners on her boat and asked to see the baby. Lady Manners showed her the little girl, who was called Pavati. Sarah thanked Lady Manners for allowing her to see the child, having thought she might refuse because of her parents' disapproval. In that respect Lady Manners was unconventional. She had loved her niece Daphne and had made up her mind to do anything for her that she possibly could.

Later there was a scene where Lady Manners was in a small boat, with the ayah and the baby. The boat passed the Laytons' houseboat, and the family averted their eyes from the shocking sight. I liked the character of Lady Manners, because I shared so many of her views.

It was enjoyable sitting on the water with an awning to protect one from the hot sun, the lapping water and always a cool breeze. On days off you could hire a boat, and I took one of the designers with me on a journey round the islands and beautiful water gardens in the lake. The peasants who lived on the islands had their own chickens and ducks and fruit, and also their own boat. They seemed happy with their lot. I spent a lovely day. We took a picnic and a bottle of wine, which we trailed in the water by a string to keep it cool. As various boats passed, they would approach us to sell souvenirs. I was told that one must be fairly strict, because although we had an allowance of spending money it wasn't unlimited and the peasants were insistent.

For the beginning of the prison scene Nicholas le Prevost and I set off in an old Rolls for a vast fortress in which we were to film. We drove down a bumpy, dusty track and were stopped endlessly by goats, chickens and cows wandering into our path. Finally we arrived at the white stone fortress. This particular scene was the one going into the prison where Hari Kumar was to be tried for rape, which he had not committed because he was truly in love with Daphne Manners. The scene preceded the trial in the prison, which was done later. The shooting lasted a whole day, because of interruptions of animals, the dust and the speed of the car. It was tiring because of the heat, and because the windows of the car had to be closed to avoid the dust.

We went back to the hotel, changed out of costume and make-up, got into cool clothes and sat out on the lawn where the servants handed round drinks. After dinner, when the hotel residents went to their bedrooms, we were visited by a small group of bedroom servants holding out their hands for money, which we gave them. They were appallingly badly paid. The dining-room staff weren't so badly off, because they received tips and at least had food from the kitchens.

*

Finally the time came to leave India and head back to Delhi airport. Fabia, Peggy and I shared a car. The heat was excruciating. About half way through the day one of the wheels punctured, and we had to sit and wait by the roadside for about an hour, while the driver got the wheel repaired at a small shack on the other side of the road, helped or hindered by the locals. The three of us managed to get a bottle of tonic water to quench our thirst.

Eventually we arrived at Delhi on a hot dusty evening. We went to the airport where there had been a muddle about the tickets and the flights. It was useful to have Fabia, because she was capable of insisting that we got on the flight on which we had been booked, since we wouldn't have had enough money to stay another night in Delhi.

At the airport we went through the usual frisking by Indian ladies, but finally got on our flight back to Heathrow. I then had to depart for Manchester, to complete the prison scene.

They had built a very realistic prison there in the studios. Art Malik as Hari Kumar was in the lower part, Nicholas le Prevost and I in a gallery upstairs. It was a very painful scene. Art played it with complete truth. He is an actor who, in my view, will go far.

Although *The Jewel in the Crown* was fiction, it was based on the truth of the relationship between the upper-class well-educated Indians and the snobbish English middle class. They were mostly living in India because their husbands held positions in the Army. They were not used to dealing with servants, and therefore did not know how to treat them.

Chapter Thirty-One

Out of Africa

I flew to Nairobi in early January 1985 to film in *Out of Africa*. My first view of Africa was of high-rise blocks and derelict areas – not at all as I had expected it to be. After lunch we were taken to a large shack for costume fittings, but the heat was so great that it was difficult to get our delicate Edwardian clothes on and off. The location, one and a half hours outside Nairobi, was beautiful in the misty early mornings. The actors had canvas tents to dress in, a camp bed for a rest during breaks and a table for lunch, while we ate alone in our tents.

The location was surrounded by miles and miles of grassland and eucalyptus trees. The natives, who lived nearby in shacks, were very friendly, but of course they stared at us a great deal and wandered round the tents. The make-up was done in an enormous marquee, and there was a vast team to cope with the great number of actors and extras. It was difficult to keep one's make-up fresh in the great heat, and a lovely girl called Norma had a wash leather wrung out in eau de cologne, with which she dabbed our foreheads and necks between shots.

The first day's shooting was the important wedding scene in which Karen Blixen, played by Meryl Streep, marries Bror, played by Klaus-Maria Brandauer – whom I thought very goodlooking. At one point in the scene where Klaus has to kiss Meryl, the director, Sydney Pollack, kept stopping them saying, 'No, *you* must kiss *her*, not let *her* kiss *you*, Klaus.' I think perhaps Klaus was a little nervous. I would have thought it must have been marvellous to kiss such a beautiful woman.

I was introduced to Meryl Streep just before a scene we had together. She was very beautiful and, considering the heat, looked cool and collected. I found her charming, gentle and smiling, and she asked after Vanessa; she had had a small part in *Julia* and was a great admirer of Vanessa's. Her make-up man had been Lynn's when Lynn starred with Ruth Gordon in *Mrs Warren's Profession* in New York. He kindly dabbed my forehead and neck as well as Meryl's.

During the wedding scene we all drank mock champagne. One day

219

Meryl had the real thing, hidden away, and she said, 'Come on, let's have a real swig.' The real champagne was a treat. Meryl's husband and son, aged about four, had rented a house, and every day the little boy and his nanny would join her for lunch in her tent. She was a devoted mother, and said how she was longing to finish the work and return home to be with her family.

*

My first visit to Africa lasted a week. During my stay Corin had rung to say that Michael's condition had worsened and that he was to go into hospital, so I was glad to be able to return so promptly, knowing that I would have to go back soon to finish my role.

During the six weeks I was in England Michael died. I will talk about this in a future chapter.

I returned to Nairobi in the company of Corin and Deirdre's twenty-year-old daughter Jemma. Jemma and I have always been particularly close, and therefore it was a great comfort to me to have her with me. Fortunately this fitted in to her drama-school holidays; she was studying at LAMDA. We arrived in a monsoon, and we stood in the rain outside the airport for twenty minutes awaiting our car – not a happy introduction to Africa for Jemma, who was expecting blazing sunshine. She was given a little part in the film and looked stunning in her period costume.

Jemma and I were entertained a good deal, and went to a cocktail party on board a British naval ship. We were taken to a restaurant miles and miles away, set between a lake and the sea, where we sat outside under an awning in the most beautiful surroundings. On our return to the hotel young naval officers kept ringing Jemma asking for dates. When young officers are ashore naturally they long to meet beautiful girls.

On days when I wasn't working we swam and sunbathed by the pool. We had been warned against the sun's rays, but Jemma did get quite badly burned. One day we were taken by car to see the animals in the Safari Park.

The Park was wild, the landscape on the whole dry and dusty. We stopped at one waterhole, where we were able to alight, as there was a guard with a gun, and we could look down into the deep water at a rhinoceros blowing. As we went back we saw ostriches, giraffes and lions. I wanted to get out and pat the lions, who looked so docile, but the driver warned us that this might not be a wise thing to do.

We returned to the hotel somewhat exhausted. My impression was that it was less exciting than I had imagined it might be. Perhaps one has seen too many films of wild life for it to be a really novel experience. However, we did journey one day high into some hills to a lodge where there was a really spectacular view of the great circles of pink flamingoes on a lake.

Neither Jemma, who had been longing to meet him, nor I, had the chance of speaking to Robert Redford. I watched him dancing with Meryl in the great ballroom scene, but as there were three hundred people drinking their mock champagne, throwing streamers and singing God Save the King and Auld Lang Syne, one did not get near him. Again the crowds and the heat were excruciating. We mostly danced waltzes, which Jemma seemed to know well enough for her part in the scene. In between shots you had to go and sit in a mock bar, where you were absolutely aching for anything but ginger ale.

Jemma and I spent a day at the races. It was a beautiful race-course, in lush surroundings, where of course we lost all our money. We also went riding right into the country. One of the local women who had had a part in the film owned racing stables. We were not put on race horses, however, but rode with her and one of the grooms for miles round the farm. We ended up in her house, where we had tea with her and her daughter. Then we returned to the hotel by car.

Given the sadness we had experienced at home, Jemma's presence compensated a great deal. Our walks together in the market, buying scarves and local crafts, and the journeys we took together helped me. Something we found distressing were the masses of beggars down every street in and around the bazaar: one who was completely blind used to sit on a corner holding out a tin mug for alms. We gave what we could, but the problem seemed so great. Another aspect of the poverty was that if one left food on one's plate in the restaurant, or by the pool, the waiters were absolutely delighted and took it home to their wives and children.

*

Our stay lasted three weeks, and we were both sad to leave. I was pleased to see that, at the Oscars, this moving film won many awards, but was disappointed for Meryl, who was superb in the film from start to finish. Sydney Pollack said she took endless trouble with her lines and was always word-perfect when it came to shooting. She was deeply moving and completely truthful. Whatever one's opinion of the value of an Oscar, it is always nice in life to be rewarded for work well done.

The British première at the Empire Leicester Square was attended by the Prince and Princess of Wales. My brother Nicky came with me as my escort. Before the showing of the film, as many of the cast who could attend lined up in the foyer to meet the royal couple. We were introduced in turn. Princess Diana was wearing a slinky black dress with white at the throat, with no tiara, and looked incredibly beautiful and relaxed. Miraculously both the Prince and Princess seemed to know what our roles were in the film.

Princess Diana asked me if I had enjoyed it, and said, 'Do you think I'll recognise you?'

I replied, 'I don't think you will, Ma'am, because my part is so small.'

She said, 'I will, you know.' Then she said, 'What do you think is happening to us tonight? We've got to go to Hull', and propping one eye open with her fingers, she added, 'It's going to be matchstick time for us.'

We all took our seats. The film lasted three and a half hours with no interval. But it passed as if by magic to a silent audience. As the Prince and Princess came down from their seats, she was holding a handkerchief to her eyes. She was crying, as were many others.

Chapter Thirty-Two

Michael's Memorial

I arrived back in London to face the reality of Michael's death. I began to hate our large flat in Rosetti Garden Mansions, and I couldn't bear to go into his empty room, though occasionally I was obliged to do so. It may seem fanciful, but I began to sense his presence in the flat, which was disturbing. Sometimes I would put on a record of his, wanting to hear his beautiful singing voice, but then I would take it off just as quickly. It was too upsetting. I decided to move as soon as could be arranged, but this took a long time. Michael's absence seemed to create a vacuum. I would do anything to get out of the flat – walk by the river, sit on a bench. It seemed so empty and gloomy. I felt in limbo.

On the other hand I was relieved that Michael no longer suffered. I just couldn't work out what had really happened to him. What is death? I found the funeral deeply moving but the sight of Michael's coffin almost unbearable.

*

There were two memorials: one a religious memorial at the actors' church, St Paul's Covent Garden, and the other a celebration of his work at the Old Vic.

The service at Covent Garden was organised by Joan Hirst, Martin Tickner and my brother Nicholas. Yehudi Menuhin played exquisitely. Jane Baxter, John Mills, Googie Withers, Valerie Hobson, John Gielgud all read. So did my brother, who was extremely nervous in such exalted company but did very well. The church was packed. The choir sang from *The Beggar's Opera* and afterwards we all returned to the flat for lunch.

The second memorial was organised by Corin and Vanessa, helped by Thelma Holt. Again the place was packed. The performance opened with Corin and his new wife Kika playing Michael's parents, Roy Redgrave and Margaret Scudamore, reading from their letters. Others included the clown Popov and the Georgian actor Ramaz Tchkhikvadze, who played a scene from *Richard III* in Russian quite brilliantly. Peggy Ashcroft played Lilian Baylis. Ian McKellen called people out of the audience to help him, and then told them that they must lie on the stage as the French dead in *Henry V* which was very funny. Peter Hall played the messenger to Ian McKellen and had to kneel to him, which made Ian comment, 'I have been waiting for this moment for years!' Peter Hall's wife, Maria Ewing, sang beautifully. Wendy Hiller, Vanessa and Christopher Reeve did a scene from *The Aspern Papers*, Natasha Richardson and Jonathan Pryce one from *The Seagull*, and Jemma and Guy Roberts Arnold another from *The Taming of the Shrew*. I, for light relief, recited Thomas Hardy's 'The Ruined Maid'. Julie Walters and Ian Charleson played a scene from *Car Trouble*. John Gielgud recited two speeches of Prospero, and Kika and David Tomlinson brought on Michael's youngest grandchild Arden in a scene from *Mary Poppins*.

It was a joyful evening. After the performance, we all went upstairs for refreshments. During the drinks my grandson Luke was introduced to the famous American musical comedy star Mary Martin. He displayed a total lack of interest in this honour until he discovered that she was J.R.'s mother!

*

All these events helped me to get a perspective on Michael's death. I have since moved from Rosetti Garden Mansions and am working and starting a new life, but I still don't like passing the old flat. Perhaps, if one day I could visit it, it might lay the ghost. Perhaps one day I will.

I couldn't help becoming aware of the curious fact that when somebody is very ill, people tend to be nervous of seeing them. Michael had few visitors, and yet after his death there were weeks of telephone calls, many people turned up at the memorials and his films were constantly shown on television: something he would have been delighted to see when he still lived.

Chapter Thirty-Three

Reflections

Reflecting on my life I can recognise various recurring themes. First, fear of not succeeding. Why? And does it matter? It matters to me mainly because I want to go on working. I enjoy working, and it is my living. It is important that I earn money so that I am not a burden, and so that I can continue to employ those who need their share; also so that I can give some to any grandchild in need, and indeed not get into debt.

My father worked hard for all of us. We loved him devotedly. He had a hard life, but at the end in spite of all difficulties he said he counted himself happy on the whole. My brothers and I got on well together. I was bad about education and I hated school. Was this just a desire for enjoyment? My chief education has been through Shakespeare. Some of the happiest times of my life have been working at the Shakespeare Theatre in Stratford-on-Avon. I am an incurable romantic. Shakespeare and Stratford are romantic to me.

My family have been a joy. Wilks Water during twenty-seven years was a lovely place for all of us and many others. It had to go when Mike died of the awful slow Parkinson's disease, which he had borne so patiently. His end was peaceful. A few days before he died he saw Natasha, our grand-daughter, play Ophelia in *Hamlet* at the Young Vic. According to the matron of the hospital, he talked and talked of her with great pride.

I loved my holidays with Michael: Venice six times, Florence, Rome – in a way I was spoiled to be taken about in luxury. I never had to bother about the tickets, or reservations. He saw to it all, as long as he was well and able. His work paid for everything. Now I am on my own. I have work and friends, and so much that Michael left me. I miss him, but he is in my heart. Everyone has difficulties, but finally one remembers the good times.

*

I would like before I die to have a small country cottage and a car.

That is probably a pipe-dream, and will depend on health and work. In many ways I seem to be getting more work in my older age. If some catastrophe strikes, it will strike us all. I have noticed that catastrophes, such as war, bring people together. In good times we seem to become complacent. I am talking of the Second World War when people all talked to each other in tubes and buses and shelters. My family and I had wonderfully happy times when the children were evacuated to Cousin Lucy Wedgwood Kempson, who was endlessly generous to us. But one can only hope there won't be another war, because in the atomic age such a war might be the end of everyone on this planet.

Progress has achieved a lot, especially in medicine, but the marvels of science often appear to result in the expense of millions of pounds and dollars in an effort to get away from the planet as fast as possible Perhaps in years to come life will be discovered on other planets and there will be day trips to Mars and so on. Not, one hopes, to the moon, which is so dead and cold. As a child I was fascinated by the moon and the stars, and I still am.

My father believed in an after-life. He once said to me, 'If you can believe in the marvels of science, why can't you believe in something much simpler?' I don't know. I wish I could. Perhaps it is good that the future is unknown. If one knew, it might be despair-time. We don't know, so it's hope-for-the-best-time.

I know people who really 'do good'. I don't think I do. I just carry on to the best of my ability. It's too late to nurse and go among the sick and diseased. So, because I am trained for it, I go on in the business of entertainment, so-called. I think my daughter Vanessa and my son Corin do a lot of good. Their extreme socialism harms no one, and they don't pursue it for gain. The fact that I am not politically oriented, is, I fear, negative. I only hope I don't do harm. To my mind the salt of the earth are working people – ordinary people with their kind warm-heartedness. Perhaps one shouldn't generalise, but I do believe this.

I admire people who live alone and require little. I fear living alone. I think I put upon others. My brother cooks very well. He is a wonderful friend to me and many. I used to cook. I'm sure I could again, but since working fairly continually I've lost the art. Perhaps in time I'll pick it up again. I'm a bad 'getter upper' in the morning. Someone brings me tea. Is it selfish? Yes? No? I don't know.

My mother used to describe a feeling she had of being a 'parcel' in life, and I have the same. It comes partly from 'doing what you have to do'. Much of it is enjoyable. But in fact there doesn't seem to be a choice. It's a feeling of not being in control of one's life: a lack of autonomy. Other people do without help, live alone, do their own shopping, have almost no help. I see very old ladies on sticks in supermarkets being battered around and having to bear up. I don't have to do my own shopping. I am more fortunate. But this brings its own problems. Back to the 'parcel' syndrome. The fact that I still work gives me less time for domestic chores. Having many things done for one is nice but makes one feel a bit useless. It removes one from reality and makes one feel guilty.

My main regret is that I was not sufficiently sympathetic, first to my mother, and secondly to Michael. I loved my mother very much, but she was not an easy person. Who is? I used to get impatient and angry with Michael, not of course when he was ill, but earlier in our marriage. He was often demanding, and I would lose my temper. One day he threw a vase at me, and I jumped up and down shouting, 'Missed, missed', as I flung another one back, also missing him. These rows ended in laughter or tears or both. Michael and I had agreed that we would 'never let the sun go down on a row', and we tried very hard to stick to this. I do regret the times I did go to bed without having made up. I tended to give way in these rows, which resulted in my spoiling Michael a little. Rows are quite healthy, and the trouble was that I was so fearful of them that I was apt to give way too easily and leave the problem unresolved. I even had the feeling that our homes were really his, not mine (with the exception of Wilks Water), and felt embarrassed to have my parents to stay when I would have wished, in case it put upon Michael, whereas his mother could come whenever she wanted to.

*

I have always believed myself that it difficult for husband and wife to act together. The Lunts were the great exception. Acting together was their life. But this is not true of most couples. The Oliviers often did, though Laurence sometimes felt that he drove Vivien too hard. He had remarkable success, however. Her illness had nothing to do with her work. He told me that he admired Vivien as an actress. He admired her courage and energy. She would rehearse day and night to get things right.

I went to Stratford to see them in the first night of *Macbeth*. Like many others, I felt that Larry had to some degree thrown the part away, whereas Vivien was electrifying. Her voice (always her main problem, and the critics' gripe) had deepened for the role. I was convinced that next morning the notices would be hers, and wondered how Olivier would take it. To my horror they were in fact superb for him and damaging to Vivien. The worst notice was that of the dreaded Ken Tynan, who had said he was determined to break the partnership. Vivien had worked so hard to achieve her magnificent results and, with her fragile and sensitive nature, she was deeply depressed. She was already ill, and this unfair criticism was a terrible blow. Glen Byam Shaw, their director, felt exactly as I did. I often wonder whether it was her fabulous beauty and huge success as a film star that counted against her in the eyes of theatre critics.

When I was young I wanted to act with Michael, but I always found it difficult, partly because he was already a big star and very critical of his fellow actors. Michael was a perfectionist. This put a strain on the less secure members of the cast, especially the wife! However, as soon as he was in performance he was generous to others. He once said that one of the great arts of acting is listening. I have found this to be true. If you really listen to what the other person is saying, you will find your response is more realistic.

I never felt competitive with Michael, or resentful of his great success. I did envy, if that is the right word, his talent. I think, however, that it is difficult being married to an extremely handsome leading man. With the magic of the footlights, many of the female audience feel themselves to be in love, and in Michael's case they threw themselves at him in droves, whether he appreciated it or not. Michael, who of course was flattered, treated it with humour.

Michael was magnificent as King Lear, magical as Prospero, tragically moving in *The Browning Version* and reputedly the definitive Uncle Vanya of his time; but if I had to choose, my favourite would be his Hamlet. Although the most obvious element of Hamlet's character is his indecisiveness, I could not say that Michael was himself an indecisive man. But he understood vulnerability only too well. All his major acting achievements were based on this theme. Even my mother, who was not a great admirer of Michael, was in floods of tears at the end of his Hamlet and said she had never been so moved. In his performance he allowed the audience to glimpse the real insecurities and confusions that had followed him since his lonely childhood. It was his great courage in allowing his audience to glimpse his personal frailty that distinguished him from the many great actors of his generation, each of whom contributed in a different way.

I have always found it easier to act with people who are not close personal friends. It is most difficult to identify someone with whom you have had dinner the previous night with their character on stage. Corin, Vanessa and I were all in *The Charge of the Light Brigade*, and many of the English scenes were shot in my country cottage at Odiham. I had acted previously with Vanessa in *The Seagull* but it was the first time that Corin and I had been on the same set. Vanessa had been unwell during the run of *The Seagull*, which distracted me, and Corin during our filming of *The Charge*, which naturally was a worry. I therefore prefer not to be emotionally involved with other members of the company. One can be concerned about one's fellow actors, but not in such an intense way.

The actors and actresses I have most admired are, in their different ways, John Gielgud, Laurence Olivier, Alec Guinness, Ralph Richardson, Anthony Quayle, Peggy Ashcroft, Beatrix Lehmann, Diana Wynyard, Vanessa, Marlon Brando, Margaret Leighton, Ian Holm, John Hurt, Peter O'Toole and Maggie Smith. But the list goes on.

I have found acting in Shakespeare to be the most satisfying, partly because most of the women's parts are written in blank verse, and the rhythm is a great help. In television one learns a day at a time. In the theatre, apart from knowing your words as well as possible beforehand, they become established in your mind over the month's rehearsal period and tryout week or previews. Six weeks' rehearsals would be ideal, as we had in the Michel St Denis production of *The Three Sisters*, but in these days of cut-backs, four weeks' rehearsal and a week in a provincial town is considered adequate.

Being an actress, enjoyable as it may be, is actually hard work. The old idea that we all drink champagne out of slippers is unfortunately far removed from the truth. For the majority work is hard to come by. It is an overcrowded profession, and as you get older anxiety about learning lines increases. Stratford is out of the question; Shakespeare wrote few parts for older women and Edith Evans cornered the Nurse!

*

In general I have never felt quite at home in any particular society of group. Although I liked the people I met at Dartmouth, I never felt quite part of that life, as other young girls seemed to. I have a few close friends, but have never felt part of a gang. Even in theatrical circles, Michael was always the raconteur and would criticise my lack of social acumen — what he called 'keeping the ball rolling'. I am not good at small talk. It's not that I don't enjoy meeting people, it's just that they all seem to have their own particular circle, and I don't.

I don't see very much of my children and grandchildren, with the exception of Jemma and Luke, Corin's and Deirdre's two children. With Lynn, this is because she lives in America, and when I visit her I am completely at ease. Both Lynn and I are very sympathetic to each other, and neither of us is political. My relationship with Vanessa is less close. People say that a difficult birth can result in a lack of communication in later life. She is very loving when I see her. She is away a great deal, working hard, and I suppose this puts a small barrier between us. When people are preoccupied, it is difficult to make close contact. My meetings with Corin are more frequent, and although he also is preoccupied we are quite happy when we are together, the mother/son relationship being easier than the mother/daughter.

I have ten grandchildren. The eldest is Natasha Richardson, aged 22. Then come Joely Richardson, 21, Jemma Redgrave, 21, Luke Redgrave, 19, Benjamin Clark, 18, Kelly Clark, 16, Carlo Nero, 16, Annabel Clark, 6, Harvey Redgrave, 5, and Arden Redgrave, 2.

Natasha is an excellent actress – lively, brown-eyed, a mixture of Tony and Vanessa. Joely is very like Vanessa – beautiful, grey/blue-eyed, fair-haired. She is doing extremely well, having played the young Vanessa in *Wetherby* and Beauty in *Beauty and the Beast* at the Old Vic, and she is just starting out at the Royal Shakespeare Company.

Jemma is the grandchild whom I have got to know best. She has left LAMDA where I saw her play Vittoria Corombola in Webster's *White Devil*. I thought she was moving, beautiful and brilliant; the whole production was superb and quite remarkable for a student company. The standard at LAMDA is astonishing. They are fortunate enough to have a well-equipped theatre; the lighting is excellent and the standard almost professional.

Luke is training to be a film cameraman. He has already worked at the BFI as production assistant in *A Zed with Two Noughts*. *Screen International* recently said of him that he was so goodlooking that he should be training on the other side of the camera.

Benjamin, who is at university in Colorado, is not considering the theatre as a profession. Kelly is still at school, but she is doing a drama course and wants to go into the theatre. Carlo, the son of Vanessa and Franco Nero, wants to go to drama school. He is very handsome, a fine-looking boy. Annabel loves ballet and already dances well. Arden and Harvey are too young to know. Personally, I would hope that at least two of the young Redgraves would choose a more stable career!

The nice thing about being a grandparent is that you can enjoy children without having the constant responsibility. I don't think I am what I would think of as an ideal grandmother. I love them all when I see them.

When I still had Wilks Water it was much easier to see a lot of them, and so I feel that the eldest ones had a better deal. We would picnic in the woods, make a fire to boil a kettle and toast marshmallows, bake potatoes in the cinders and punt on our lake. Sometimes the children would bring a wigwam, which would be erected on the lawn, and they would insist on sleeping in it. But at about midnight they would come shaking into the house, having heard an owl hoot and trees sighing in the wind, to find refuge from the ghost in the cottage!

*

My grandchildren have to make their way in the world and I will support them in any way I can, but I also have to get on with my life. I get happiness from simple things. At the hairdressers, for instance, the girls are fun and enjoy their work; it's pleasant seeing them together. I love flowers in the park; reading in bed at night; learning lines for a forthcoming play, in bed at night and in the morning; seeing a good play well acted, or a good film. If I see good acting, I believe I can act. It gives one a feeling of security in work. Michael agreed with me in this. Then there are small things like a letter, a walk, a day in the country in the longed-for spring; a meal in pleasant company; a day spent with Deirdre and friends having a delicious Sunday lunch cooked by her – she's a beautiful cook; seeing programmes of the wonderful Queen and Royal Family; a letter from beloved Lynn – staying with Lynn and her family in California, even if only once a year, is something to look forward to.

*

As I watched the Queen's 60th birthday celebrations the other day on television and saw the Queen Mother standing beside the Queen, my thoughts went back to an evening many years ago when I had been invited to the private house of the American Embassy in Regent's Park in honour of the Queen Mother. I had known it would be evening dress, but stupidly I hadn't realised it should be long evening dress and I wore a gold lamé dress of medium length. I stood slightly in the background when the Queen Mother came into the drawing room. The women were presented and curtseyed, and the men bowed. The dining-room was laid out with round tables for twelve, which made it more intimate. I found myself on the right of Lord Drogheda. The Queen Mother was on his left. She looked beautiful in a white dress and wearing a red rose. The conversation was easy.

I dared to say, 'Ma'am, may I say how sorry I am to have been stupid enough not to wear a long dress?'

She said most charmingly, 'But your dress is beautiful, don't worry.'

Lord Drogheda made rather tactless remarks about the New Wave in the Theatre. The Queen Mother said, 'I don't mind. There is room for every kind of theatre.' I realised what a genius she has for putting people at their ease.

David Bruce, the American ambassador, was my aunt Nora Mellon's son-in-law, having married Ailsa, Nora and Andrew Mellon's daughter. At the time of this party he was happily married to his second wife, the beautiful Evangeline. Poor Ailsa had been an unhappy, difficult girl. Aunt Nora said she had never fathomed the trouble. Possibly it was to do with her divorce from Andrew Mellon, twenty years her senior. The evening was delightful. It was made by the Bruces and the lovely Queen Mother.

Years ago when Michael and I sometimes met the Queen Mother, and occasionally the Queen and the Duke of Edinburgh, it was always very enjoyable. Since Michael died, and time has gone on, I am naturally not invited to those functions. Much as I would love to meet them again, I realise that there are so many new people for them to meet. The miracle is that they manage to meet as many as they do.

Michael and I had met the Queen Mother once or twice before, at the house of Maureen Dufferin and Ava and her husband John Maude in Hans Crescent. John was the son of Cyril Maude, who had been instrumental in getting me to drama school. The Queen Mother was fun as always, talking to me about Dartmouth when she and George VI had visited in my father's time, bringing with them the young princesses, Elizabeth and Margaret. They were sent off with a young cadet to play croquet in the Captain's garden.

My feelings for the Royal Family are strong and have nothing to do with politics. They bring colour and pageantry to millions, and give of themselves unsparingly all over the world. The idea of a President in Buckingham Palace is to me unthinkable. Our Royal Family are the envy of many countries. I noticed that even in Russia, the official guides talked of Peter the Great, and adored their Tsarist treasures.

Michael and I once went to a private cocktail party at Buckingham Palace given for people in the arts. It was a very wet night, and while I was talking to the Queen I remarked upon it.

'I know,' she said. 'My Mum wasn't able to get here, which is very disappointing.'

We also attended a private tea party at Buckingham Palace. Princess Marina, Duchess of Kent, whom I had met many times before, was disappointed that Lynn had not come with us.

'I so wanted to meet Lynn,' she said.

'I'm afraid she was too shy to come,' I explained.

'What a pity,' she said. 'She needn't have been.'

It was a delightful occasion, informal and friendly. People are nervous of meeting the Royal Family. But when you do they always put everyone at their ease.

*

If I had been born into another age, I think I would like it to have been in the First Elizabethan Age. It was a time of exquisite music, dancing, poetry, painting and, of course, of Shakespeare: a time of beautiful gardens everywhere. One would have wanted to be among the privileged, but that goes for any age, though if you were an aristocrat, you were liable to be put in the Tower. I played Kate Ashley, Elizabeth I's chief lady-in-waiting, in the film *Elizabeth R.*, Glenda Jackson playing the Queen. We arrived early one morning by boat at Traitors' Gate. We were drenched by rain, and walked side by side up the slimy steps to be ushered into the Tower with our hands folded, reciting the Magnificat. The feeling of going back in time was eerie and frightening. It made me wonder whether I really would like to have lived in that age with all its cruelty. Certainly not if one had been close to the court. The ideal would have been to be a nobleman's wife, living in the country with dogs and horses.

My favourite writers are Shakespeare, the Brontës, Jane Austen, Henry James, Dickens, Edith Sitwell and Rosamond Lehmann, and I enjoy the autobiographies of my contemporaries. About three times a year I reread *Wuthering Heights, The Turn of the Screw* and *Jane Eyre*. I also admire Somerset Maugham, whom I met once at Sybil Colefax's during the war, at one of her weekly lunch parties, which was attended also by H.G. Wells. I had expected to find him intimidating, but he wasn't at all. He had a bad stammer, but was extremely friendly. He was small and dark, with a rather saturnine face. He was married then to Syrie, a designer and friend of Sybil's. Years later Michael went to his 80th birthday party at the Garrick. In making his speech, Maugham had stammered so badly that it contained the longest pauses Michael had ever known in an after-dinner speech.

I had often been to the Garrick with Michael, and we used to take guests on Sundays when women were allowed. I loved the atmosphere and the paintings. We once took Bette Davis there when Michael and she were making a film called *Connecting Rooms*. She stipulated that we shouldn't bring either Vanessa or Lynn as she hated being in the presence of beautiful young women. She was by now in her sixties but looked older. She had huge bags under her eyes and was quite large. Unfortunately there was no sign of the famed Davis wit: she just seemed a thoroughly unhappy, embittered woman. It was very difficult to talk to her. Both Michael and I had admired her early films, but were thankful when the evening was over, though Michael was as charming as possible because he had to finish the film with her.

We met H.G. Wells several times, and I became very friendly with his ex-mistress, Moura Budburg, who often entertained us at her home in the Cromwell Road. She was also a great friend of Vivien Leigh. Moura translated from Russian into English for Alexander Korda, notably *Anna Karenina*. Wells was a largish man, with a slightly high-pitched voice. He was very amusing and we talked a lot about his books, one of which, *Kipps*, Michael had made a film of, directed by Carol Reed. He had great charm. He was a visionary, but to me he came across as a large cuddly man one wanted to hug.

Stephen Spender, an excellent poet, was not an entirely good influence on Michael. They liked and admired each other, but Stephen introduced Michael to some undesirable friends, notably 'Tommy Hindeman', who was always asking for loans of money, which were never repaid. Stephen himself was a fine man who had fought in the Spanish Civil War. At this time he took Michael off on poetry-reading weekends, which he enjoyed. I was left on my own a good deal at 102 Clifton Hill. Much later, when I got to know Natasha, Stephen's wife, I visited their home in St John's Wood, where I met many interesting people, including Robert Graves, Cyril Connolly and many more. I found their intellectual talk almost impossible to understand.

Later I went on a poetry-reading tour for the Arts Council with Natasha and Robert Speaight. We went to various places in the Potteries and visited the Wedgwood factory, where we had lunch with young Josiah and where I was helped to make a black basalt vase on the original Josiah's potter's wheel. It was very interesting. Young Josiah, a delightful man, stayed at Whitegate during the war when Corin and Vanessa were there. Lucy was his second cousin. Her mother, Louisa Wedgwood, who became blind, had married my grandfather's brother, Alfred Kempson, who died young.

*

I have written in my book about the happy times, and the sad ones. I have never even considered suicide. The thought of my family, and the memory of my father's words, 'Darling, you can go so far down that automatically you have to come up again', has always prevented me thinking seriously of it. Also, Lynny once said to me, 'If ever you get too depressed, please ring me up.' I couldn't bear it. In *Hedda Gabler* there is a wonderful line when Hedda shoots herself and Tesman walks over to her body and says, 'People don't do things like that.' The trouble is they sometimes do.

*

Some evenings I sit up late drinking coffee. Michael and Corin look down on me with loving troubled eyes – fanciful perhaps, but the two portraits are there; Michael's by Augustus John, and Corin's by Robert Buhler.

I saw beloved T. today. He looked low and ill, but he held my hand and said in a whisper, 'You look so pretty.'

Some mornings I wake up having had a bad dream. Fear? I am fearful of not being able to afford to have someone to stay with me overnight, so that when I am working, and wake with the usual boring headaches, someone will be here to get tea and breakfast, and for company.

Recently I dreamt that Michael was with me and appeared to be well. We went off together and bought an expensive car and drove to a place near a river with the intention of returning to Bedford House – the house that we and the children have loved most in all our lives. We got out beside the river. Michael jumped, missed his footing and plunged into the water. When he came out a man screamed, 'He's lost his sight. Oh God, he's lost his sight.' I screamed and woke up, pouring with sweat. It was four a.m. I went to the bathroom, drank some water and got back into bed. At first the dream was full of hope, but I realised as I thought about it that it referred back to a time many years before at Wilks Water when I had gone to bed late at night. I woke hearing shouts which, being half asleep, I thought were dogs barking. I went downstairs to see if all was well. I went out into the garden and saw Mike lying in the stream with the water gushing over him shouting for help. I dragged him with great difficulty out of the stream, across a stretch of grass, to his studio, and somehow got him into the bathroom and ran a good warm bath, because he was chattering with cold. Leaving him for a few minutes, I telephoned for the local doctor, who said he would call an ambulance. I sat with Michael, sponging hot water over him. Finally, the ambulance arrived and the men wrapped him up in thick, warm blankets and took him to the Odiham Cottage Hospital on a stretcher.

The doctor said to me, 'You'd better have a stiff whisky.'

He rang me up later and said I could go and see Michael. Michael was better but had cut his head and was mainly suffering from shock, and was able to return home in a day or two.

Another recent dream was that I was in the woods looking at Wilks

Water, which wasn't in its usual position. John Fowler was with me, and one or two others. He pointed out that three more cottages had been built within four or five hundred yards of each other. They were all extremely pretty and John said, 'I don't think you'll find them a nuisance. It may be rather enjoyable to have a few extra people around you.'

All this must be connected with longings for the country and past times. This was not an unhappy dream, but at the same time it shows my secret longing for somewhere in the country again. London, as far as I am concerned, is all right for seeing friends and family, for going to the theatre or the cinema, but not a place to walk about in.

I spent a weekend recently in the country with friends. They live in the most glorious countryside. The house has panelling, beams and great open fires, which they don't use. They have two acres of beautiful gardens full of daffodils, roses and shrubs, and the house faces a village green. With all this, they seem unhappy and discontented. This may be due to health, but I feel that if I lived there or somewhere similar it would be a delight. Maybe this is a romantic dream, but it is what I would like.

*

My future, like anybody's, is uncertain. Work is essential to my feeling of well-being and financial security. My family, although loving and kind, cannot provide for me my own sense of personal security. I must find it for myself. As yet, I don't have it. Why? Is it the still recurring theme of never belonging to a group? Bridges Adams said to my father, when I was a young girl, after a big success at Stratford as Juliet, that he doubted if I possessed the toughness which is necessary for the theatre. This is clearly not true. But I still do not believe in myself. I am apprehensive about much of the work I undertake. However well it goes, and however much acclaim I receive, I am still doubtful. I don't have confidence in myself.

Other people are extremely helpful to me, but I still flag and get tired. In the theatre it is no good getting tired. Nobody is interested. They want you to get on with the job, which I do, but not without difficulty. I often feel in the early morning, 'I can't, I can't carry on', but of course I do. And I shall continue to do so for as long as possible.

Michael carried on his life so bravely in the most extreme discomfort.

Then can I drown an eye, unused to flow,
For precious friends hid in death's dateless night,
And weep afresh love's long since cancelled woe,

And moan the expense of many a vanished sight;
Then can I grieve at grievances foregone,
And heavily from woe to woe tell o'er
The sad account of forebemoaned moan,
Which I now pay as if not paid before.
But if the while I think on thee, dear friend,
All losses are restored, and sorrows end.

Index

Natasha Richardson, 45, of British acting dynasty

Actress succumbs to injuries suffered in skiing accident

BY ADAM BERNSTEIN
The Washington Post

OBITUARY | 3.19.09

Natasha Richardson, a glamorous and talented member of a British acting dynasty and wife of actor Liam Neeson, died Wednesday in New York City from head injuries suffered while she was skiing. She was 45.

The death made international headlines and prompted expressions of shock and grief. She fell on a beginners slope near Montreal during a ski lesson Monday and initially appeared fine, but an hour later she complained of a headache. As her condition worsened, she was flown to Lenox Hill Hospital near her home in New York City, where her family gathered.

She was the daughter of Academy Award-winning actress and human-rights activist Vanessa Redgrave and the Oscar-winning director and producer Tony Richardson ("Tom Jones"). Her maternal grandparents were the actors Michael Redgrave and Rachel Kempson. Her aunt is actress Lynn Redgrave, with whom Natasha Richardson and her mother appeared in the 2005 Merchant-Ivory production "The White Countess."

Natasha Richardson was widely respected for the high

quality and versatility of her performances.

She won a Tony Award for a 1998 revival of the musical "Cabaret," in which she played the bohemian show-girl Sally Bowles, and starred in a variety of film, television and stage roles, ranging from Blanche DuBois in Tennessee Williams' "A Streetcar Named Desire" on Broadway to a Disney remake of "The Parent Trap" in Hollywood.

The actress's most recent film credits came in last year's "Wild Child" opposite Emma Roberts and 2007's "Evening" with Meryl Streep, Claire Danes and Redgrave. The "Evening" part was one of a number of recent roles Miss Richardson had had with her closest relatives. On

TINA FINEBERG / THE ASSOCIATED PRESS, 2005

Natasha Richardson is shown at her opening-night performance in the Broadway production of "A Streetcar Named Desire." The actress died Wednesday.

guest judge on the just-concluded season of the cooking show "Top Chef."

In films, in addition to "Patty Hearst," in which she played the title heiress-turned-terrorist, and the psychological thriller "The Comfort of Strangers" (1990), Miss Richardson starred in movie dramas including "A Month in the Country" with Colin Firth, "The Handmaid's Tale" with Robert Duvall and

"Widows' Peak" with Neeson.

She made some attempts to raise her income and public recognition, appearing in "The Parent Trap," with Lindsay Lohan, and "Maid in Manhattan" as a frosty socialite.

Film scholar David Kipen said of Miss Richardson: "As an heir to the Redgrave theatrical and film dynasty, she was the British Drew Barrymore, if Barrymore had better taste in roles and men. Richardson radiated intelligence in everything she did. She won raves for Shakespeare, Chekhov, O'Neill, Williams and Ibsen, and she could sing besides. If the movies never knew quite what to do with her, that strikes me more as the medium's fault than hers."

She made her acting debut at 4, directed by her father and playing her mother's bridesmaid in the movie "The Charge of the Light Brigade." The marriage ended around that time because of Tony Richardson's infidelities. He died of AIDS-related complications in 1991.

Besides Neeson, her survivors include their two sons, Micheal Richard Antonio, 13, and Daniel Jack, 12; and her mother; her sister, the actress Joely Richardson; and a half-sister, Katherine Grimond.

Material from The New York Times and Los Angeles Times is included in this report.

Actress died from blunt impact to head

The New York Times and The Washington Post

3-20-09

NEW YORK — An autopsy of actress Natasha Richardson on Thursday indicated she died of a brain hemorrhage caused by "blunt impact" to her head, the chief medical examiner for New York City said.

Richardson, 45, died Wednesday in a Manhattan hospital, two days after what appeared to be a minor fall on a beginner ski slope north of Montreal. She initially turned down medical treatment but an hour later complained of a severe headache and was taken by ambulance to a hospital.

The autopsy suggests the fall tore an artery in Richardson's head, resulting in bleeding in an area between the skull and the lining covering the brain, called the dura matter.

Richardson's death was ruled an accident, said Ellen Borakove, a spokeswoman for the medical examiner's office. She said the medical examiner's office would not comment on whether Richardson was an organ donor.

The official cause of death was an epidural hematoma. A hematoma is a collection of blood, and epidural in this case refers to the space between the skull and the dura. If surgery is performed quickly, it may be possible to save the patient's life, doctors said.

Although many details of Richardson's accident have not been made public, she apparently demonstrated a

Natasha Richardson was not wearing a helmet when she fell.

"lucid interval" often described with traumatic epidural hematomas, a period soon after the impact when the victim is alert and feels well that is followed rapidly by a decline into unconsciousness.

The Toronto Globe and Mail newspaper reported Thursday that an ambulance was sent to the Mont Tremblant ski resort in Quebec but "turned around" when paramedics were told they were no longer needed.

After her fall, Richardson reportedly went back to her hotel to rest. When her condition began to deteriorate, another ambulance was called.

The actress was reportedly taken to a nearby hospital, then to a hospital in Montreal and finally to Lenox Hill Hospital in New York, where she died.

A spokeswoman for Mont Tremblant, said Richardson — who had not been wearing a helmet — fell on soft snow, did not appear to have hit her head, did not lose consciousness and joked about falling.

After the medical examiner's office released the cause of Richardson's death Thursday, the spokeswoman said Mont Tremblant would not comment further out of respect for the family's privacy.

---

mayor could drive to work, according to interviews with plow drivers and street crews and thousands of department records analyzed by The Seattle Times.

"Mr. Jackson had no idea of what was going on," said Sione Kongaika, a plow driver who recently retired after 31 years with the Seattle Department of Transportation. Two or three days into the first major snowfall, "all he was doing is yelling, 'We have to get more plows downtown. The mayor can't get to the office.'"

West Seattle, home to the mayor and transportation chief an inordinate amount of attention right show. Ten employees spent a total of

See > SNOW, A8

COURTNEY BLETHEN / THE SEATTLE TIMES, 2008

Denny Way, going down toward Interstate 5, turned into a sledding street during the storms.

City tried to blame failure on Mother Nature > A9

TO FAMILIES | Report: